SONGS
AND
SOLOS

**CREATING
THE RIGHT
SOLO FOR
EVERY
SONG**

RIKKY ROOKSBY

'Guitar playing, in and of itself, does not mean a whole heck of a lot. But guitar playing within the context of great music and great songs **is** a big deal.'
BILLY CORGAN (THE SMASHING PUMPKINS), *GUITAR WORLD*, AUGUST 1995

'The more I'm into music and the more I'm into guitar playing, I realise it isn't about how great a guitar player you are, it's about writing songs and it's about fitting guitar and voice together.'
BRYAN ADAMS, *GUITAR*, NOVEMBER 1992

'Music expresses that which cannot be said and on which it is impossible to remain silent.'
VICTOR HUGO

SONGS AND SOLOS
CREATING THE RIGHT SOLO FOR EVERY SONG
RIKKY ROOKSBY

A BACKBEAT BOOK
First edition 2014
Published by Backbeat Books
An imprint of Hal Leonard Corporation
7777 West Bluemound Road,
Milwaukee, WI 53213
www.backbeatbooks.com

Devised and produced for Backbeat Books by
Outline Press Ltd
2A Union Court, 20–22 Union Road,
London SW4 6JP, England
www.jawbonepress.com

ISBN: 978-1-61713-103-5

A catalogue record for this book is available from the British Library.

EDITOR: John Morrish.
DESIGN: Paul Cooper Design.

Printed by Regent Publishing Services Limited, China.

14 15 16 17 18 5 4 3 2 1

CONTENTS

PREFACE

Many songs have a moment when the spotlight shifts away from vocals and lyrics to an instrumental solo. Very often this solo is played on guitar. *Songs And Solos* examines this neglected facet of songwriting. It is a unique manual of creativity for guitar-playing songwriters who want to make the best use of solos in their songs. For the songwriter who composes with a guitar, solos are a significant way a song can be intensified. Though lead guitar technique for its own sake has been widely discussed, this book takes a new approach, focusing instead on the relationship of the solo to the song.

Getting this right can make a big difference to a song's impact. Memorable solos are an integral part of great rock songs. Think of 'All Along The Watchtower' (The Jimi Hendrix Experience), 'Sultans of Swing' (Dire Straits), 'Paranoid Android' (Radiohead), 'Alabama' (Neil Young), 'More Than A Feeling' (Boston), 'Marquee Moon' (Television), or 'Enter Sandman' (Metallica). Each has a guitar solo that feels essential to the song.

Guitar solos have been part of popular music since the amplified electric guitar enabled guitarists to be heard as clearly as a jazz trumpeter. In the 1950s the guitar breaks in Bill Haley's 'Rock Around The Clock', Elvis Presley's 'Blue Suede Shoes', and Chuck Berry's 'Johnny B. Goode', were part of the amped-up excitement of rock'n'roll. In the 1960s a new generation that included Hank Marvin, George Harrison, Eric Clapton, Jimi Hendrix, Jeff Beck, Jimmy Page, Tony Iommi, Ritchie Blackmore, and Paul Kossoff emulated and surpassed their 1950s guitar heroes. During the 1960s and 1970s many chart hits and classic album tracks had solos, many played on guitar. In the 1980s bands as different as Van Halen and Dire Straits elevated the role of lead guitar to almost equal importance with the vocalist. Even the guitar excesses of the 1980s couldn't eclipse the appeal of the solo, which lives on in various guises to this day.

Songs And Solos takes a twin-track approach. It's a book for guitar-playing songwriters and guitarists who want a deeper understanding of lead guitar solos. Although the main aspects of soloing technique are covered, what's new about *Songs And Solos* is its broader, musical perspective. *Songs And Solos* focuses on how and why a given solo works in a particular song. It keeps the concerns of song creativity as the priority. It describes many ways a song can be enhanced with a well-crafted solo. It also demonstrates what great solos owe to their overall musical context.

Songs And Solos is a solid grounding in how to put a solo in a song, and surveys a wide range of types of solo, whether on guitar or other instruments. It comes with 42 solo examples, notated in Sections 8-11 and recorded on the CD. Each anticipates the question every player faces: given these chords, what can I play and which notes fit? These practical examples have a range of interpretative and stylistic features, and there's a backing track for each one so you can invent your own solos.

Songs And Solos will expand your sense of what a solo can do for a song.

Rikky Rooksby

HOW TO USE THIS BOOK

Songs And Solos has 12 sections. **Section One** relates a brief history of the solo since the mid-1950s, when the electric guitar changed the course of popular music. It narrates how, from the 1960s, the guitar became the most common soloing instrument, and how lead guitarists became potent musical and symbolic figures. Some of the roles and politics of the guitar solo are traced through musical genres popular in the 1970s, 1980s, and 1990s, including how attitudes to solos changed. **Section Two** is a practical look at basic concepts of soloing, and **Section Three** looks at how a solo is positioned and integrated. For the songwriter this section discusses what a solo can do for a song and where it might be placed for maximum effect.

Section Four surveys the use of other instruments than guitar to add solos to songs. This is important knowledge for a songwriter, because a guitar solo might not always be best for a given song. These other instruments include acoustic and electric piano, synths, saxophone, piano, trumpet, flute, recorder, and strings. All have been featured during solo breaks in songs.

Section Five looks at the implications for soloing of choosing one type of guitar over another, including nylon 'classical', steel-string acoustic, electric, six-string and 12-string. It also covers the way various guitar techniques and effects influence a solo, including harmonics, wah-wah, feedback, sustain, echo, vibrato, tremolo, phasing, and playing with the fingers rather than a pick. **Section Six** deals with the way scales and harmony relate. This has information about which scales are the most useful for solos and the chords they fit. **Section Seven** rounds up guitar techniques for soloing that are not based primarily on scales.

The next four sections illustrate this practical knowledge with short solos, designed to show a range of techniques, scales, and chord types, so by the end of the book you'll know which scales fit over the likeliest chords encountered in a song. These solos are written in standard notation and tab, and played on the CD. Each of the 42 audio tracks is repeated just as a backing track so you can use them to practise the example or improvise your own. **Section Eight** deals with scales and major key chord progressions, and **Section Nine** with minor key soloing. **Section Ten** looks at how to solo when a progression includes the common out-of-key chords used by songwriters – those labelled 'reverse polarity' and 'flat degree' chords in my other songwriting books. **Section 11** discusses how to solo over more complex harmony, including common altered chords and unrelated chords. **Section 12** has some interesting quotes about soloing from famous guitarists.

Note: *Songs And Solos* cites guitar solos in more than 800 songs by at least 600 artists. Features in these solos are mentioned and described for comparison, but there are no transcriptions of the solos in this book. *Songs And Solos* is about creating and playing your own solos.

Songs And Solos extends my multi-volume series on songwriting, published since 2000. To find out more on chord sequences, melody, guitar chords and guitar tunings, and writing songs on keyboards (especially if you're a guitarist), get *How To Write Songs On Guitar* (2000, revised edition 2009), *The Songwriting Sourcebook* (2003, revised edition 2011), *Chord Master* (2004), *Melody* (2005), *How To Write Songs On Keyboards* (2005), and *Lyrics* (2006). If you write riff-based songs, *Riffs* (2002, revised 2010) is the most encyclopaedic study ever published about them. To learn more about the elements that make a magic recording, 100 songs from 1960 to the present go under the microscope in *Inside Classic Rock Tracks* (2001). Tips on how to record your songs more effectively can be found in *Arranging Songs* (2007). There are more song ideas and inspiration in *How To Write Songs In Altered Guitar Tunings* (2010). Information about these titles is at www.Backbeatbooks.com and www.rikkyrooksby.com.

A BRIEF HISTORY OF GUITAR SOLOS AND SONGS

How the rock'n'roll rebel yell found exuberant expression in the guitar solo.

SECTION 1
A BRIEF HISTORY OF GUITAR SOLOS AND SONGS

The guitar solo originates in the rise of the electric guitar as the dominant instrument of popular music since 1956. In the early 1950s a number of musical genres had already laid the ground for the rise of the guitar solo as an important component of a hit song. Jazz players such as Django Reinhardt, Charlie Christian, and Wes Montgomery had helped promote the guitar's potential for being a lead instrument. In blues, similar attention was claimed by guitarists such as Hubert Sumlin (with Muddy Waters), B. B. King, and T-Bone Walker. Les Paul not only invented a solid-body electric on which so many classic guitar solos would be played, and the multi-tracking tape technology to capture them, he raised the profile of the guitar on hit records such as 'How High The Moon'.

1956-58: BIRTH OF THE ROCK'N'ROLL GUITAR SOLO

Around 1956 the birth of rock'n'roll created a shift in popular music that changed both the character of popular music and the groups that performed it. Rock'n'roll was harmonically simpler than the jazz-influenced songs of the Big Band era, and more repetitive, focused on bold rhythms emphasised by a drummer. Many rock'n'roll numbers were strophic (a repeated verse but no separate chorus or middle-eight) 12-bar songs with three primary chords. In them the solo had a new structural function: it removed the need for a middle-eight, whose music and lyrics would differ from the verse. The rock'n'roll solo was often ushered in by a mounting energy that culminated in a moment of hysteria expressed by a vocal scream, as coherent language gave way to sheer exuberance.

The vocal scream cued an instrumental solo most likely on guitar, saxophone, or piano. This device might be repeated after other vocal verses. It can be heard on one of the songs that sparked this revolution in popular music: Bill Haley's 'Rock Around The Clock'. Typical of the new concision of jukebox hits, 'Rock Around The Clock' is only 2:05 in length, and Danny Cedrone's solo arrives just two verses and 44 seconds into the song, complete with tremolo picking, effortful string-bending and a fast downward run, finished with an insouciant upward stroll. The song's second solo is chord-based and shared with saxophone.

The brass-driven arrangements of the bigger jazz bands were partly eclipsed by rock'n'roll recordings made by smaller groups of only four or five players. The rock'n'roll quartet preserved the rhythm section of bass and drums of the older ensembles, but often ditched everything else in favour of one or two guitars to supply harmony and solos. The guitar became necessary because, unlike in the jazz bands, there was no other instrument to play a solo. Amplification meant the guitar could now hold its own with other instruments, no longer constrained by the limited volume of its acoustic origins. This affected lead-playing even more than rhythm-playing, because shifting from strumming chords to playing a melody line comprising single notes greatly reduced the volume of the acoustic guitar.

In its brightly-coloured new guise, the electric guitar seemed an instrument for the space age and youth. The solid-body electrics mass-produced in the 1950s by companies such as Gibson and Fender had smaller bodies and were cheaper than the larger hollow-body guitars of the 1930s and 1940s favoured by jazz players. The solid-body electric was free of stuffy conservatoire associations and, unlike the piano, was portable. String-bending (albeit at first restricted by heavy-gauge strings), and the discovery of valve-amp distortion, took the guitar a small way toward imitating the rock'n'roll saxophone's rasping tones. A track like Link Wray's 'Rumble' (which inspired The Who's Pete Townshend and Jimmy Page) was one of the earliest to use distortion. Bo Diddley's rectangular electric guitar seemed an outrage merely because of its shape.

Scotty Moore (Elvis Presley), James Burton (Ricky Nelson), Carl Perkins, Cliff Gallup (Gene Vincent & The Blue Caps), and Chuck Berry all contributed guitar solos to songs. Of these the most important was probably Chuck Berry, whose witty 12-bar three-chord songs usually kicked off with a guitar solo, reprised and developed in a middle break. He popularised a vocabulary of blues-derived techniques specific to the guitar, such as unison bends, slides, slurs, and double-stops, that were replicated, with varying accuracy, by 1960s rock guitarists and went on to dominate rock into the 1970s. In late December 1957, a recording session at Chicago's Chess Studios produced three Berry classics: 'Reelin' And Rockin'', 'Sweet Little Sixteen' and 'Johnny B. Goode'. The latter helped mythologise the figure of the guitarist in popular music, making it likelier that young musicians would aspire to be in the spotlight (literal and figurative) for their solos.

These 1950s-style guitar breaks appeared in later decades in the music of bands like The Stray Cats (see 'Stray Cat Strut', 1981). Queen's 'Crazy Little Thing Called Love' has a solo that evokes the 1950s, in keeping with its Elvis pastiche, and the band's 'Now I'm Here' has two solos which reprise Chuck Berry's style over a hard rock backing.

1958-63: THE GUITAR SOLO POST-ELVIS AND PRE-BEATLES

By the late 1950s, the popularity of the sound of the electric guitar and its perceived modernity had overflowed the limits of the solo break. For about five years there were a number of chart hits that were guitar instrumentals: in the USA, records like Santo and Johnny's 'Sleepwalk' (later to influence Peter Green), and hits by Duane Eddy, including 'Rebel Rouser' and 'Peter Gunn'. Eddy's low-pitched electric guitar melodies established a defining twangy timbre that pre-dates the later valve-driven distortion that became the archetypal rock guitar tone. Eddy's twang gave birth to the so-called 'surf guitar' genre of Dick Dale and The Ventures, was reprised by Vic Flick on the soundtracks to the early James Bond films, and informed The Shadows' 'Dance On' and Them's 'Here Comes The Night'. Its use on film soundtracks marked the electric guitar's coronation as the king instrument of pop.

SECTION 1

The guitar's percussive ability to deliver a riff was caught on many of Eddie Cochran's hits, and on The Kingsmen's 'Louie Louie' (1:28-59), where the guitar solo circles around the same pentatonic minor ideas while the band play the riff. This directly influenced the solos on The Kinks' early records. The stripped-back production of the new guitar music was typified by Johnny Kidd & The Pirates' 'Shakin' All Over', a track dominated by Joe Moretti's pentatonic minor guitar riff and 14-bar solo. It showcased the different tones the guitar could provide, including heavy muted sounds, slides, etc. These could be heard clearly because there wasn't anything else on top of the arrangement. The guitar dominates The Routers' 12-bar derived 1963 hit 'Let's Go', where saxophone also takes a solo. Buddy Holly played a famous chord-based solo in 'Peggy Sue'. Pop singles like Bobby Vee's 'Rubber Ball' acknowledged the rise of the new kid on the instrumental block by including a guitar solo (albeit a polite one).

During 1960-63 the British charts were dominated by instrumental hits from The Shadows. It seemed that the glamour of the electric guitar meant a vocal was no longer needed for a hit. Some Shadows tracks also feature guitar solos that break away from the set melody, with Hank Marvin demonstrating an early grasp of twangy, echo-laden string bends, coloured further with tremolo-arm vibrato. This showed what might be done with an electric guitar solo. Marvin also enhanced the guitar's profile with short solos on Cliff Richard hits such as 'The Young Ones', and by smuggling a few 'blue' notes into 'Summer Holiday'. After the decline of The Shadows as a chart singles group, Marvin's solo style survived in the hands of other players, mostly in middle-of-the road music. One notable later hit that links back to Marvin is Jeff Beck's (mostly) instrumental 'Love Is Blue' (1968).

There probably hasn't been another period in popular music that featured so many chart single instrumentals, and I think this can mostly be attributed to the novelty of the electric guitar. In the week of November 4, 1960, there were no fewer than nine instrumental hits in the *New Musical Express* UK Top 30, including The Ventures' 'Walk Don't Run', The Shadows' 'Apache', Duane Eddy's 'Because They're Young', and Bert Weedon's 'Sorry Robbie'. In 1963 Jet Harris and Tony Meehan had the instrumental hits 'Diamonds' and 'Scarlet O'Hara' which are pure Duane Eddy/Shadows, and further instrumental hits came with The Tornadoes' 'Telstar', The Chantelles' 'Pipeline', and The Surfaris' 'Wipe Out'. Meanwhile hits such as Heinz's 'Just Like Eddie' (1963) had the guitar taking a melodic line, adding fills, and taking a standard Chuck Berry-style solo. Even songs like Billy J. Kramer's 'I'll Keep You Satisfied' and Ned Miller's country hit 'From A Jack To A King' (both 1963) had short guitar solos. All these hits confirmed the electric guitar's status as *the* desirable musical gadget of the era, frowned upon by older generations and despised by music teachers as 'not a proper instrument'.

1963-66: THE BEATLES AND GUITAR GROUPS

The rise of The Beatles during 1963, based on the three distinctive vocal personalities of John, Paul, and George, and their world-wide success from 1964, caused a decline in the popularity of guitar instrumentals. However, the guitar was an integral part of the Merseybeat sound. With two guitarists, The Beatles had the option that if George Harrison played a solo John Lennon on rhythm guitar would keep the sound full with chords. As fans of rock'n'roll, The Beatles often put short guitar solos in their own uptempo numbers. In 'Can't Buy Me Love', the guitar solo that fills a 12-bar break also toughens the sound by introducing blues-derived elements such as 'blue' notes. 'I Feel Fine' has a six-bar solo made up of a two-bar blues phrase repeated that runs straight into a reprise of the intro's eight-bar riff (1:07-15).

If Chuck Berry-style guitar solos were commonplace in early 1960s beat music, George Harrison's acquisition in February 1964 of the Rickenbacker electric 12-string suggested new avenues for the guitar solo. Initially used to play fuller chords and chiming arpeggios, the electric 12-string was a defining timbre of mid-1960s popular music. But the fact that its lower strings facilitated octave playing soon led to its use as a solo instrument. This possibility created the opening melodic motif of The Byrds' 'Mr Tambourine Man', and 'Turn, Turn, Turn', where the solo is picked over a verse and a chorus, partly developed from the melody. The Byrds took things further for the 12-string guitar solo proper on 'Eight Miles High', where Roger McGuinn consciously imitated the free jazz style of John Coltrane. This solo was an *avant garde* gesture for the time and is reinforced by its relation to the song structure. Almost the first 30 seconds of 'Eight Miles High' is taken up with the first solo, with a second at 1:45-2:20, and a third during the coda. There is also a chordal-based 12-string solo on The Who's first hit 'I Can't Explain' (1964).

By 1964 the brasher character of what would become rock music appeared within the confines of the single. The Kinks' 'You Really Got Me' was one of the rawest hits heard by that time, with a manic Chuck Berry-influenced solo notable for its addition of amp distortion. The British Blues Boom was another stimulus to the guitar solo, with the 12-bar form inviting easy improvisation and a more assertive instrumental tone than the clean Fender Stratocaster heard on The Shadows' records. During the recording of the John Mayall *Blues Breakers* album in 1966, Eric Clapton plugged a Gibson Les Paul into a Marshall 45-watt amp and turned it up, causing the valves to distort. Clapton's departure from The Yardbirds to join John Mayall resulted in a short-lived Yardbirds line-up in which Jimmy Page and Jeff Beck both played lead – a very early instance of the notion of twin lead lines. The Yardbirds experimented with the role of the guitar solo on tracks like 'Happenings Ten Years Time Ago'.

In mainstream pop in the mid-1960s, guitar solos were not that important. The guitar's main task was to supply harmony through rhythmic chording. Wayne Fontana & The Mindbenders' hit 'A Groovy Kind of Love' (1965) was not untypical in that the brief guitar solo simply uses the main vocal melody as a short hook (1:15-23 in a track lasting 1:58). However, competition in the music business meant that wacky new sounds could help make a record a hit by grabbing the attention of listeners and expressing a sense of modishness. This stimulated players to try special effects such as wah-wah, feedback, and fuzz, which coloured songs, riffs, and solos. The impact of the riff of The Rolling Stones' 'Satisfaction' owed much to Keith Richards plugging into a fuzzbox. The idea that the *sound* of the guitar could be as important as any notes it played in a solo encouraged breaks such as the 'op-art' feedback solo in The Who's 'Anyway, Anyhow, Anywhere'. For the solo in a song this was revolutionary; instead of melodic phrases, there was a burst of noise. It was also innovative that The

Who chose to have a bass guitar solo in 'My Generation' and a French horn break in 'I'm A Boy'.

1967-70: PSYCHEDELIA AND THE RISE OF ROCK GUITAR

From about 1967 a strand developed within popular music that self-consciously strove for artistic status. It mirrored the rise of the hippy counter-culture, with its desire for artistic leader-figures, and led to a division between pop and rock focused and legitimised by the rock press. Boundaries of self-expression were extending. Altered states of consciousness, whether induced by meditative means or chemicals, seemed to require new musical forms other than the short song with defined verses and choruses. The validity of the solo was enhanced, because what could not be put into words might be communicated by music alone. The impulse to be 'far-out' meant a solo could step into the unknown even if the rest of the song was more orthodox. Strange effects – like strong vibrato via a tremolo arm, bottleneck drenched in echo, backwards or bowed guitar – might conjure a 'freak-out'. The solo lead guitar on The Beatles' 'Tomorrow Never Knows' (1966) pointed the way as an early and apposite use of special effects in a break.

At this time rock music enthroned its first virtuosos, notably Eric Clapton (newly liberated in Cream) and Jimi Hendrix. That they were ever perceived as virtuosos had as much to do with the new musical culture in which they recorded as with technical command. Quasi-shamanic figures, Clapton, Hendrix, and Townshend *et al* mediated a new reality for the rock audience through the overwhelming sonic authority of extremely loud electric guitar. In rock, the role of the solo changed, and became more than a temporary distraction from the vocals. The late 1960s saw the guitar solo elevated to the moment in a song where a transcendent gesture was made. The solo, like the riff, came to rival the importance of the chorus in mainstream songs. Verses and choruses could now set the stage for the guitar virtuoso to 'speak' through a solo. The new aesthetic implied that the instrumental vision of a Clapton or Hendrix could not be contained by song structure. This contributed to the increasing antipathy of the rock audience toward 45rpm singles in the later 1960s, and the commercial rise of the 33rpm album (trends encapsulated in Led Zeppelin making it a point of honour never to release singles in the UK). There was more room for solos in long tracks, and long tracks didn't make singles.

Cream helped develop a hard rock based around loud, repeated guitar riffs, as their album *Disraeli Gears* (1967) demonstrates. Solos were more likely to occur in riff-based songs because the weight had already shifted from the vocals as the song's expressive centre. In 'Sunshine Of Your Love' Clapton starts the solo by using the jazz player's trick of improvising from a well-known melody, in this case 'Blue Moon', barely recognisable in this unfamiliar frame of 'woman-tone' guitar and Ginger Baker's sledgehammer drums. It is telling that the solo (after the second chorus at 2:01-51) takes up almost a quarter of the song's 4:00 duration. Clapton thickens the lead-line with double-stops, wide bends and vibrato, before switching scale from minor to major. His colourful solos significantly expanded the imaginative reach of riff-based songs like 'White Room' and the psychedelic Aegean fantasy of 'Tales of

Brave Ulysses'. His solo in the bridge section of 'Badge' (1:37-2:10 in a track of 2:40) has a searing intensity beyond what either lyric or vocal have spelt out. It is a fine example of how a lead solo can articulate feelings neither words nor vocal could. The later 'Bell-Bottom Blues' (recorded as Derek & The Dominos) demonstrated that the lead guitar break could also be tender and introverted, as Clapton coaxed 'pinch' harmonics from the strings.

Jimi Hendrix's profile as psychedelic priest (enhanced for the white rock audience by his African-American 'otherness') meant that his guitar solos were the part of the song where the greatest 'revelation' would occur. Hendrix's solos grabbed attention because of their timbre and phrasing, a fluidity of notes escaping the confines of bars and beats. The solo has a potent effect in Hendrix's early singles. In 'Hey Joe' it comes at the dramatic point where the lyric recounts the shooting of an erring lover; this was the guitar solo as stylised violence. The solo in 'Purple Haze' solo sounds like an outbreak of naked confusion as the singer asks for help. Hendrix used an octave splitter on this solo, and it returns in the coda. By contrast, the solo in 'The Wind Cries Mary' (which replaced any bridge) goes for a cleaner, sweeter sound with many high-pitched double-stops reinforcing the harmony. This solo is wryly lyrical, a consolation which suggests that maybe things aren't as bad as the lyric suggests, and there is a similar expressiveness on the gentle coda solo of 'Little Wing'.

Hendrix's celebrated cover of Bob Dylan's 'All Along The Watchtower' (*Electric Ladyland*, 1968) was perhaps his greatest single demonstration of the role of lead guitar in a song. Each of three verses is prefaced by a short lead solo. The central solo section has an extended solo terraced into three by contrasted timbre and musical approaches. Hendrix begins with an echoed slide melody, follows with a wah-wah blues-inflected solo, and finishes with a chordal soul break which climaxes in ascending high unison bends. In this song, and on the rock arrangement of 'Voodoo Chile' (a posthumous UK Number One single) the lead guitar had gone far beyond the confines of a set solo. The lead guitar was shown to be a potential equal partner to the voice, with the song shared when it came to which was the focus of attention. This can also be heard in Fleetwood Mac's 'Black Magic Woman' (1968), and on the Latin-influenced Santana's *Abraxas* (1970), and became common in hard rock.

Hendrixisms were revived occasionally for the next couple of decades, whether by Phil Manzanera on the freak-out coda solo of Roxy Music's 'In Every Dream Home A Heartache', which may have been influenced by the phased coda of Hendrix's 'Bold As Love', Ron Isley on The Isley Brothers' 'Who's That Lady', on Prince's 'Purple Rain', by Robin Trower, Steve Hillage (Gong), and Vernon Reid of Living Colour, who included Hendrix in an eclectic mix of blues-rock, jazz and funk styles.

The rebel gesture of the guitar solo also made itself felt in covers by rock bands of songs from genres where they were uncommon. Rock covers of Motown songs are examples, like Vanilla Fudge's 'You Keep Me Hanging On', as are some tracks recorded by Janis Joplin, such as her covers of Erma Franklin's 'Take Another Little

> *Hendrix's solos grabbed attention because of their timbre and phrasing, a fluidity of notes escaping the confines of bars and beats.*

SECTION 1

Piece of My Heart', and 'Little Girl Blue' with its continuous lead guitar counter-melody, and 'Summertime' with its outrageously counter-genre fuzz guitar solo.

Though dominant, the guitar didn't have the territory of the solo entirely to itself. In the late 1960s the range of instruments that might play a solo expanded as pop became artistically ambitious. The Beatles did much to make it acceptable for groups to enhance their recordings with non-rock instruments, such as the chamber strings on 'Eleanor Rigby' and the piccolo trumpet in 'Penny Lane'. Albums such as *Sgt. Pepper's Lonely Hearts Club Band* (1967) and The Beach Boys' *Pet Sounds* (1966) took this trend further. So, predictably, as rock aspired to be art it looked to traditional 'classical' music and its instruments, just as multi-track tape recording made it easier for rock groups to hire session musicians to add such parts. From the woodwind group, flute and recorder were not only associated with classical music but also lost green Arcadias at a time when the hippies dreamed of a return to rural innocence. A flute solo appears in The Moody Blues' hit 'Nights In White Satin' (1968), and in songs by The Mamas & The Papas. It becomes a lead instrument in bands such as Focus ('House Of The King') and Jethro Tull ('Living In The Past') in early 1970s progressive rock.

There was increased tolerance for musical eccentricity, especially in British pop, and this coloured which instruments might feature as soloists. David Bowie's 'Space Oddity' had a stylophone, Pink Floyd's 'See Emily Play' had (at 0:50-54) a harpsichord-like sound, while Thunderclap Newman's anthem for the packing up of revolutionary barricades, 'Something In The Air', had solos by honky-tonk piano and euphonium.

The boundary of the solo was also becoming porous. Greater freedom to improvise on stage, and an ideological resistance to planned form, meant that the lead guitar was licenced to thrill throughout a song, weaving in and out of the vocals. This was prevalent in West Coast bands such as Jefferson Airplane, on tracks like 'Somebody To Love' where the lead guitar also adds a spotlit solo to end the track, entering on a pre-bend at 2:25 and soloing to the end at 2:55. This looser approach can be heard on *Baron Von Tollbooth And The Chrome Nun* (a 1973 Jefferson Airplane spin-off project), Van Morrison's *Astral Weeks*, (the fills on 'Beside You' played by Jay Berliner), and on 'Long Time Gone' by Crosby, Stills & Nash. It was revived in the dense guitar textures of The Verve's album *Forth* (2008).

Some rock guitarists saw themselves as soloists on a par with the great names of jazz. Songs were extended to give an opportunity to show off this new status. Lead guitarists performed the music they played through body language. The guitar solo became a visual spectacle – a sequence where something expressive at the core of the song was physically squeezed out by the grimacing effort of bending strings and straining for notes high on the fretboard. On the more ironic, self-conscious periphery, not everyone went along with the elevation of the solo. The guitar playing on The Velvet Underground's albums was deliberately primitive, Lou Reed telling *Guitar World* in September 1998, 'We had a rule in the Velvet Underground: no blues licks.' Likewise, a band like The MC5 kept the 1950s rock'n'roll solo alive, in an amped-up garage style.

The rise of the guitar solo meant virtuosity could turn into egotistic display. Solos could become less integrated in the song as a whole, less of an organic expression of its concerns, perhaps only a showcase for the player. The British comedy act The

Bonzo Dog Doo-Dah Band recorded a song 'Canyons Of Your Mind' (1968) in which there is a parody of a wholly inept guitar solo. Frontman Viv Stanshall sometimes held a placard over soloing band members that said satirically "Wow I'm Really Expressing Myself". It was an early spoof of a phenomenon that had seen "Clapton Is God" graffiti on London walls.

In hard rock, songs were written around riffs and guitar solos by bands such as Led Zeppelin, Deep Purple, Black Sabbath, Free, Uriah Heep, The Groundhogs, Wishbone Ash, Grand Funk Railroad, Iron Butterfly, Vanilla Fudge, and Mountain. Both Deep Purple ('Strange Kind Of Woman', 'Black Night', 'Fireball') and Black Sabbath ('Paranoid') had hit singles with prominent guitar solos at the turn of the 1970s. A descending guitar scale started off 'Strange Kind of Woman', with the solo coming at 1:46-2:16 over the verse riff, and a second Ritchie Blackmore solo on the coda. Blackmore expanded the blue-rock vocabulary for solos by adding more chromatic passing notes and heavy vibrato from the tremolo arm on his Strat.

One of the classic rock guitar solos came from Paul Kossoff of Free on the band's Number One hit 'All Right Now' (*Fire And Water*, 1970). Patiently constructed from what seem unpromising initial phrases and only a couple of notes, it shifts to a repeated A pentatonic major phrase, and then higher still to a wailing A pentatonic minor scale at the 17th fret which shows off Kossoff's wonderful vibrato. Other Free hits such as 'Wishing Well', 'My Brother Jake', and 'Little Bit Of Love' are worth hearing for beautiful guitar fills; the latter with a four-bar solo (1:29-1:44) double-tracked imprecisely so the two parts can be distinguished, and climaxing with an expressive bend.

Even non-virtuosos could still make a guitar solo count, as with Neil Young's three-note solo on 'Cinnamon Girl' and solo on 'Southern Man'. Solos could also occupy a larger part of the song than before, as with the extended guitar/organ solo on The Doors' 'Light My Fire', and the sinister bow plus wah-wah break on Led Zeppelin's 'Dazed And Confused'. Their 1969 debut set new standards for heavy rock with blazing solos on 'Communication Breakdown', 'Good Times Bad Times' (with a Leslie speaker), the heavy blues of 'I Can't Quit You', and the use of reverse reverb on 'You Shook Me'.

Led Zeppelin II's 'Heartbreaker' has a set-piece unaccompanied solo, recorded in two or three takes in about 20 minutes on a different session and dropped into the song later (it is slightly out-of-tune with the rest of the track). Jimmy Page stated that it was an afterthought, and one of the first times he played a Les Paul through a Marshall amp. 'Heartbreaker' is a virtuoso display of multiple pull-offs, behind-the-nut bends, repeat licks, and fast tumbling runs (2:03-48). It is unquestionably a classic rock solo, a much-amplified update of the excitement of early rock'n'roll breaks. But its subject is guitar-playing. It does not enhance the imagined world of the song as do the Clapton and Hendrix examples cited above, or Page's later solos in 'Stairway To Heaven', 'No Quarter' or 'Achilles Last Stand'. The same applies to the second solo after the band's re-entry (3:07-38).

At the close of the 1960s the counter-culture faded, key groups such as The Beatles broke-up, and musicians such as Hendrix, Joplin, and Jim Morrison died, but the examples set for guitar solos in songs remained, and a younger generation were quick to run with them. These years often feature in polls and articles as the most popular era for best guitar solos.

SECTION 1

1970-75: GLAM ROCK AND PROGRESSIVE SOLOS

Looking at songs and solos in the first half of the 1970s, it is helpful to identify three main strands: hard-rock (described above), progressive rock, and glam rock. Hard rock continued the late 1960s style that had developed from the blues-rock of Cream and Hendrix. Progressive rock pushed toward art and experimentation, with longer songs and conceptual lyrics. Glam rock sought to recapture the primal energy of rock'n'roll for the age of the Apollo rockets. This accounts for the conspicuous revival of saxophone solos on records such as Wizzard's 'Ball Park Incident', and guitar solos that reference Chuck Berry.

Glam rock was singles-oriented, and glam solos had to be concise. T. Rex's first hit 'Ride A White Swan' has a short eight-bar guitar solo played without a pick. The band's second and biggest single, 'Hot Love', had a simple major-scale solo announced by a thrice-repeated G triad to grab the attention. 'Get It On' (as 'Bang A Gong' the band's only US hit) replaced any guitar solo with a saxophone break. On albums such as *T. Rex* (1970), *Electric Warrior* (1971), *The Slider* (1972), and *Tanx* (1973) Marc Bolan played melodic lead guitar solos. In the UK glam rock was also typified by Slade, David Bowie, Roxy Music, Bebop Deluxe, with Queen as a hard-rock version of glam.

A major glam guitarist was Mick Ronson, who played with David Bowie on classic albums such as *Hunky Dory* (1971), *Ziggy Stardust* (1972), and *Aladdin Sane* (1973). His solo on 'Life On Mars' was adept in its handling of a few telling phrases through some awkward chord changes. Ronson favoured a Les Paul Custom played with a wide vibrato and a wah-wah pedal acting as a tone filter. On tracks such as 'Hang On To Yourself' and 'The Jean Genie', he showed he could put a space-age slant on rock-blues lead by emphasising the colouristic potential of the guitar. He often achieved this by playing fewer notes and working more with sustain, as on the coda solo of 'Moonage Daydream', and the squall of toggle-switch feedback which ends 'John I'm Only Dancing'. Ian Hunter, lead singer with Mott The Hoople and later Ronson's musical partner, recalled how Ronson would get ideas for solos. "He'd stand in the middle of the room with the headphones on and he'd play back the track for a minimum of an hour before he'd even touch a guitar … You'd hear this horrible noise coming out and just when you thought it was time to go home, you'd start hearing something great. His whole idea was to write a song within a song. He had to listen to it until the song formed in his head, then he'd put it on guitar and learn how to play it." (*Guitar* USA, November 1994.)

Queen songs of the early to mid-1970s often featured innovative solos by Brian May, whose multi-layered guitar lead was a significant part of the Queen sound. He made effective use of echo on tracks like 'Brighton Rock'. 'Bohemian Rhapsody' is a rare example of a song where the guitar solo, after two verses, is not the peak of the song but actually out-shone by the mock-operatic vocal harmony extravanganza of the centre section. Another guitarist who played some memorable solos at this time in an art-glam rock band was Bill Nelson of Bebop Deluxe, as for instance in the flowing lines of 'Sister Seagull'.

In the mid-1970s, Thin Lizzy stood out for hard rock, with twin lead and some great solos within the context of a rock song. The blues-rock tradition was carried on by bands like The Rolling Stones, Bad Company, and AC/DC, who recorded *Back in Black* in 1980 and carried on their high-voltage veneration of Chuck Berry. But the most remembered guitar solos were still the ones that occurred in great songs.

In progressive rock a generation of more technical rock players emerged in the early 1970s with album-orientated groups. These included Robert Fripp (King Crimson), whose *avant garde* solo on '21st Century Schizoid Man' was outstanding, Steve Howe (Yes), Steve Hackett (Genesis), and John McLaughlin, whose Mahavishnu Orchestra's *The Inner Mounting Flame* (1971) was a jazz-rock album centred on guitar. On the band's *Birds Of Fire* (1973) McLaughlin played in a jazz style reminiscent of a saxophonist. These players tended to work outside the norms of short songs, and their lead-playing went beyond familiar blues-rock ideas.

One progressive band from the 1960s that reinvented itself was Pink Floyd. Guitarist David Gilmour recorded several acclaimed solos on some of the band's tracks, notably 'Money' from *Dark Side Of The Moon* (1973), 'Comfortably Numb', and 'Another Brick In The Wall'. Talking about 'Money' in *Guitar World* in October 1993, Gilmour described how "I really wanted to make a dramatic statement with each of the three solos. The first one is artificially double-tracked. And the third one is actually double-tracked. I think the first two solos were performed on a Fender Stratocaster, but the last one was done on a different guitar – a Lewis, which was made by some guy in Vancouver. It had a two-octave neck [ie, 24 frets], which meant I could get up to notes that I couldn't play on a Strat ... the effects consisted of a Fuzzface fuzz box and a Binson echo/delay."

For some players in the early 1970s, basing songs around lead guitar seemed an exhausted notion. It is instructive that, to get his career on track, Bruce Springsteen abandoned the guitar-hero ideal, ditching the long hair and Les Paul he sported with early bands like Steel Mill. Describing a permanent shift in priorities in Springsteen's music, E Street Band guitarist Miami Steve Van Zandt recalled, "By '72, pretty much everything had shifted to the songs ... everything that could be done with a guitar had been done, with the exception of Eddie Van Halen, who had yet to come. What were you gonna do that Clapton, Beck, Page, and Hendrix hadn't done? ... However good a guitar player you were at that point, you had now to work within the context of a song: our guitar playing was gonna come in handy and be useful, but not so much to just go off on long solos to impress somebody any more." As Springsteen put it: "When the guitar solos went on too long at the end of the 1960s, I lost interest and at some point I sort of opted out of the jam thing and got more into the solo being in the service of the song." (*Guitar World*, October 1995.)

1976-82: PUNK AND NEW WAVE

In the later 1970s the music scene in the UK diverged from that in the US, where arena bands toured, getting bigger and bigger with the support of US radio. These acts included Peter Frampton, The Eagles, Fleetwood Mac, Boston, Journey, Styx, Foreigner, and big tours by British acts such as Led Zeppelin, Bad Company, and The Who. Adult Oriented Rock to some degree returned to the principle of the guitar solo that enhanced the song. Take, for example, Lindsey Buckingham's delicate solo

SECTION 1

with a volume pedal on Fleetwood Mac's 'Dreams', or the double-stop solo in 'Over And Over' which takes that song somewhere beyond the vocal in a gradually intensifying coda. One of the finest examples at this time would be Tom Scholz's lyrical solo on Boston's 'More Than A Feeling' (1976).

In the UK around 1976-77 there was a musical revolution with great significance for the guitar solo. The spiky rhythm & blues chording of Dr Feelgood's Wilco Johnson on albums like *Stupidity* (1976) was an early warning of the coming change. Reacting against chart pop, glam, disco, and 'prog' in equal measure, punk rock stripped everything back to a minimal presentation with maximum energy. In punk rock, solos, if allowed at all, had to be short because the songs were short and basic, and often the players didn't have the technique to do much else even if they had wanted. The Sex Pistols' Steve Jones effectively recycled Chuck Berry lead guitar breaks, bringing to tracks like 'Holidays In The Sun' and 'God Save The Queen' a renewed ferocity. Some of Paul Weller's solos with The Jam have a similar edginess, as in 'Strange Town' and the Townshend-like noise solo of 'Eton Rifles'. There is an unexpectedly lengthy solo on The Only Ones' 'Another Girl, Another Planet' (1:44-2:20 in a duration of 2:59) which includes the E major scale, E pentatonic minor, some transposed phrases, and finishing with some high arpeggio pull-offs.

1980S: ROCK GUITAR: A TECHNICAL REVOLUTION

The next stage in the evolution of the guitar solo came from a handful of players in the US with a higher level of technique who changed its musical vocabulary. A generation now introduced into rock songs tapping, neo-classical scales, modes, sweep-picking, and big left-hand stretches. Eddie Van Halen popularised the tapping technique within the format of standard hard rock. The debut *Van Halen* (1978) album was probably the biggest game-change in rock guitar since Hendrix's *Are You Experienced* over a decade before. It marked a shift away from blues/pentatonic ideas, which for some years after in guitar-based hard rock consequently seemed *passé*. Two-handed tapping, extreme tremolo-arm scoops, and artificial harmonics were all delivered by Eddie Van Halen with a cheeky devil-may-care attitude. His showcase 'Eruption' was a solo that was its own track on the album. Its example meant many 1980s guitar solos would seem less about the song they were placed in and more about guitar-playing. He reached a wider audience when he added a solo to Michael Jackson's 'Thriller' in 1982.

Through the 1980s rock guitar solos got longer, flashier, and faster but the songs in which they were placed have not proved so memorable. The solo on Starship's 'Jane' (1980) shows the impact of technical virtuosity started by Van Halen. Gifted players such as Al Di Meola, Steve Morse (voted best overall guitarist in America's *Guitar Player* magazine five years running), Eric Johnson, and Randy Rhoads continued these technical developments, but are not remembered as songwriters. Rhoads's neo-classical contributions to Ozzy Osbourne tracks like 'Crazy Train' and 'Mr. Crowley' are often cited as stand-out solos. But perhaps none of this matched the unexpected raw elegance and poetry of the guitar-playing on Television's 'Marquee Moon' (1977), a song that contained a long solo which slowly built to an amazing climax without any rock/blues clichés.

1980-85: **THE GUITAR IS DEAD: LONG LIVE THE GUITAR?**

By the end of the Seventies punk had metamorphosed into the more interesting 'New Wave', which kept the punk ethos of the short, sharp single, but ditched its nihilistic amateurism, and was not ashamed to have a musical sensibility. It was dominated by groups organised around the guitar-keyboards-bass-drums line-up. Elvis Costello & The Attractions, The Police, Madness, Ian Dury & The Blockheads, Simple Minds, and Dire Straits all began as New Wave bands. The guitar solo appears from time to time in their song catalogues, usually with a fresh slant in terms of phrasing or timbre.

At the same time the New Romantic chart bands turned against the guitar and sought to define themselves as a new generation with the new technology of the drum machine and the synthesizer. By the mid-1980s some British music journalists were even predicting the "death of the guitar". In the US, classic rock maintained its grip on the airwaves. New wave British musicians in the US were horrified to find that tuning the radio to get away from 'Stairway To Heaven' (recorded 1971 and not often heard on UK radio after about 1975) they seemed only to find the same track at different points.

Although there was no rehabilitation of the guitar solo, there was a willingness to look for new avenues for the guitar. From several quarters the vocabulary of blues-rock guitar that had prevailed since the early 1960s was rejected. It was rejected by new wave groups, and to some degree by heavy metal groups. Out of new wave came players such as John McGeoch, who developed a heavily-modified guitar sound with Siouxsie & The Banshees, playing a memorable sonic nightmare of a solo on the epic 'Nightshift' (*Ju-Ju*, 1981). Mention should be made of the inventive guitar solos Neil Taylor played for Tears For Fears on tracks like 'Broken' (1:09-42) and 'Everybody Wants To Rule The World'

The Scottish band Big Country used guitar effects such as chorus, flanging, and delay to put a new slant on twin-lead and soloing elements in songs such as 'In A Big Country', 'Chance', and 'Wonderland'.

(3:35-fade). The Scottish band Big Country used guitar effects such as chorus, flanging, and delay to put a new slant on twin-lead and soloing elements in songs such as 'In A Big Country', 'Chance', and 'Wonderland'.

Three significantly successful rock bands in the 1980s – U2, The Police, and Dire Straits – each re-defined the sound of the guitar solo. In U2's case, The Edge did it by avoiding blues-rock ideas and riffs, keeping the guitar clean but using echo, either ambiently, or to create multi-repeat rhythms. It was an approach which, after the looser, experimental songs of the band's first two albums, had fully matured with U2's songs by the time of *The Joshua Tree* (1987).

With The Police, Andy Summers played almost no conventional solos, but worked with a subtle chorus/delay combination, also drawing on his knowledge of classical guitar and broader aesthetic strategies. This bore fruit in the left-field feedback solo on 'Bring On The Night'. Andy Summers told *Guitar* (US) in May 1996, "I used to be

SECTION 1

a really wailing blues guitarist. But I joined The Police during the punk era, and solos were sort of taboo back then. So we used to play really fast, short songs with almost no guitar breaks. The long solos disappeared and instead I spent my time using the guitar in different ways, like orchestrating the parts behind the vocals." Summers' guitar solos matured further on albums like *Ghost In The Machine* (1981) and *Synchronicity* (1983).

One of the biggest groups of the time, Dire Straits had elevated the role of lead guitar so that it was as if though the band had two singers. This was present on early songs such as 'Lady Writer' with its multiple solos, and 'Sultans Of Swing' where the guitar solos and fills are the voice of the character Guitar George mentioned in the lyric. The lead guitar becomes a matching voice to the vocal in songs like 'Brothers In Arms'.

Where traditional rock-blues went, it sometimes gained a new cache either from a supposed authenticity or by being placed in an unexpected context, as in the case of Stevie Ray Vaughan's post-modernist blues solo on David Bowie's 'Let's Dance' (1983). Vaughan found a highly personal take on the blues on albums like *Texas Flood* (1983), combining blues fluency with a muscular tone that bulldozed its way forward. His solo on 'Mary Had A Little Lamb' is a good example. Vaughan almost single-handedly revived the reputation of blues guitar in the 1980s.

New styles of heavy metal, including 'thrash', were played by bands like Metallica, Megadeth, Slayer, and Anthrax, who wrote riffs that were not only faster but based on different scales to earlier rock. They also favoured a new guitar tone: distorted and with the mid-frequencies scooped out. The popularity of tapping as a technique encouraged different types of scale or arpeggio figures that had nothing to do with blues-rock. Another group of players, partly inspired by Van Halen's 'Eruption', broke with 1970s rock guitar by taking a fiercely competitive and technical path.

Among these players were Joe Satriani, Steve Vai, Frank Gambale, Paul Gilbert, Nuno Bettencourt, and Yngwie Malmsteen. Each had his own style, but they were eclipsed by simpler players whose guitar-playing was subservient to songs. In fairness, they were not unconscious of these issues. Satriani sounded a belatedly cautionary note when he said, "The problem that faces me every day as a musician is, 'Am I going to write a really good song today or is it going to be a barren wasteland?' And it's true that people who spend a lot of time on technique don't have so much time to spend on songwriting." (*Guitar* UK December 1995.)

For those who wanted to emulate these players, magazine transcriptions became more detailed and helped make sense of extremely fast runs, pinch harmonics, and sweep-picking. The pursuit of guitar tone – particular combinations of effects that would unlock the tones of the famous – also increased. Luthiers responded by designing new guitars such as the 'Super-Strat' – characterised by a pointed headstock, a humbucking pickup at the bridge plus two single coils, a tremolo system and a locking nut that kept the guitar in tune whatever abuse it was subjected to. The febrile lunacy of the 1980s guitar hero ideal can be felt in the language of a 1988

> *One of the biggest groups of the time, Dire Straits had elevated the role of lead guitar so that it was as if though the band had two singers.*

SECTION 1

advertisement by Marshall which pictured Yngwie Malmsteen in front of six 4x12 speaker cabinets and six 100 watt amps:

"Yngwie J. Malmsteen hits the stage with wall to wall Marshall Stacks. One of the few legit electric guitar virtuosos on the planet, Yngwie explodes rock structures with a dazzling, laser-hot attack that takes no prisoners. From soaring, classically-influenced solo flights to the dark collective energy of his band, Rising Force, he insists on nothing less than the savage power and radiant tone that make original Marshalls an ongoing legend for our times ... Top pros like Yngwie depend on a backline of full-sized stacks for total performance power ..."

It was music as warfare. Or as guitarist Steve Stevens put it in *Guitar Player* April 1993, "There were a lot of great players in the '80s, but when the smoke cleared, you couldn't remember a single thing they played. Some of the super-fast playing got to be like a gymnastics event – you wanted to hold up a scorecard after the solo." Back issues of *Guitar, Guitar School, Guitar World, Guitar Player* and *Guitarist,* featuring as they do many now-forgotten Super Strat-wielding virtuosos of 1980s rock guitar, make sober reading.

1985-90: THE GUITAR SOLO: AN ALTERNATE HISTORY

In the later years of the 1980s it was clear that, contrary to New Romantic-era beliefs, the guitar was not dead. For rock traditionalists there were bands like Iron Maiden, Def Leppard, Kingdom Come, The Cult (in their *Electric* and *Sonic Temple* phase), and of course Guns N' Roses, who brought a new guitar hero in Slash, who used a Les Paul. But there was a noticeable division in rock guitar between bands who played heavier rock with the flashy, technical solos they felt obliged to incorporate, and the alternate/college-rock/indie scene represented by R.E.M. and The Pixies in the US, and The Smiths and The Stone Roses in the UK.

Johnny Marr (The Smiths) and Peter Buck (R.E.M.) both favoured Rickenbackers, a guitar with little guitar-solo pedigree. Neither was interested in guitar solos for the sake of them. Buck told *Guitar World* in February 1996 that he felt everything had been done solo-wise: "So many guys try to show off how good they are and wind up detracting from the song ... [When punk arrived] I was so excited – you could just write songs and not worry about the solo!" His tactic for avoiding solos was to write a bridge to the song instead: "A good bridge is there to tell you something lyrical or musical that you don't learn from the rest of the song. It widens the song harmonically, and adds a new perspective." (The same thing should be true of a solo). Buck's one-take wah-wah solo on 'Pop Song '89' (*Green*, 1989) was done almost as a joke.

Both Buck and Marr excelled at creating guitar textures and hooks, such as the harmonised high guitar phrases on The Smiths' 'How Soon Is Now?'. Marr told *Guitar Player* in January 1990, "There's a lot of guitar culture that I don't like at all. I find the traditional idea of the guitar hero to be really irrelevant to the 1990s. ... Being a soloist who wants to just display virtuosity is a dated philosophy, and I don't think there's any room for it in pop music. It's the last stand of late-60s/early-70s rockism, and it should have gone a long time ago." In *Guitar* (UK) in January 1997, looking back on The Smiths, Marr remembered how "I was desperate not to play boogie or blues leads. There was a million other guys doing that, and anyway, it really didn't have any poignancy for me. I still hear young players doing it to this day and … it just seems too easy."

Alternative guitar prospered in the hands of The House Of Love, The Chameleons, My Bloody Valentine, The Cocteau Twins, Curve, The Cure, Lush, Jesus & Mary Chain, and Red Hot Chili Peppers. Sonic Youth were one of a growing number experimenting with altered guitar tunings, which were to 1990 what tapping had been to 1980. These created many new chord voicings and made it hard to play traditional lead patterns, which in turn encouraged new approaches to the solo.

Other trends in popular music were making the solo on *any* instrument unfashionable. The new guitar hero was the DJ, armed with a pair of turntables, a box of vinyl, headphones, and a PA. Dance music had limited use for guitars or traditional instruments. Music was now being written on digital audio workstations and computers, with drum loops and sampling providing a new method for importing sounds into arrangements. Musical material was as likely to be treated by the frequency sweep of equalisation on a mixing desk. The melodic value of a solo was replaced by the stress on rhythm. Dance music was less interested in melody and harmony in comparison to mainstream songs. For the first time in the long history of popular music even vocal melody was displaced by rapping, and rappers became soloists. This was also true in nu-metal/rap hybrids, in which, in the mid-1990s, heavy guitar riffs combined with rapped sections. Trip-hop and ambient lounge acts, including Portishead, Gomez, Mercury Rev, Beck, Moby, and Air, had a highly selective approach to solos.

THE 1990S: GRUNGE AND BRITPOP

The most important event in the renewal of rock guitar in the early 1990s was grunge, which defined itself against the excesses of 1980s rock guitar. Bands like Nirvana, Pearl Jam, Soundgarden, and Smashing Pumpkins emphasised songs and riffs. The solos (if there were any) were shorter, simpler, slower, and bendier, or even ironic deconstructions of a guitar solo. These bands were more likely to explore altered tunings than to go 'shredding'. As Billy Corgan of Smashing Pumpkins told *Guitar World* in August 1995, in love with the electric guitar as he was, "If you look at the guitarists who are most noted for their playing ability, you will find that their reputations are inextricably tied to the great songs they have written, or at least reinterpreted in their own unique ways.

"We appreciate the guitar-playing skills of Eric Clapton, Jimi Hendrix, Jimmy Page and others within the context of their songs. The downfall of the Yngwie Malmsteen school of guitar-playing, which focuses almost solely on technical proficiency, has occurred because ultimately, no one really gives two shits about guitar playing in and of itself, except maybe other guitar players."

Soundgarden's Kim Thayil was even more forthright when he told *Guitar* (UK) in March 1994, "… that beedily-beedily-beedily shit. I can't think of anything more boring than listening to some guy do that. I'd rather hear the meat of the riff."

The milestone album was Nirvana's *Nevermind* (1991), and the singles 'Smells Like Teen Spirit' and 'Come As You Are'. Both approached the guitar solo in a similar way, mangling the vocal melody as the basis for a short, sarcastic break, a parody of the traditional solo, ironically stressing indifference to technique. On 'Smells Like Teen Spirit' the solo comes after the second chorus (2:53-3:34) and its last note fades into a feedback which threads the last verse. The guitar has phasing and chorus, and is in the middle range. The solo on 'Come As You Are' (2:00-33) plays over the main riff and draws on five notes from the verse melody. The solo on 'In Bloom' ventures into extreme noise on the bends which break up the scale phrases, with the hint of a dissonant augmented fourth toward the end (2:53-3:17). A faster lead guitar on standard patterns would have ruined these tracks.

After grunge the tide had turned. The solo was now to serve the song and not the other way round. In March 1995 no less a guitar soloist than Eddie Van Halen said, "Over the years I've come back to look at solos more as little pieces within the song … On the first record it was like, 'All right! I get to solo!' and I'd blaze without thinking. Now I try to plan my solos a little more, except there are still songs like 'Feeling', which is more old-style, totally spontaneous, whatever-comes-up reckless abandon. On a lot of songs I try to do something that fits the song as opposed to taking a gunslinger attitude and just blazing."

Songwriting was also paramount in the guitar bands of the UK associated with the Britpop scene of the mid-1990s: Oasis, Blur, Suede, Pulp, Ash, Supergrass, Stereophonics, The Verve, and Manic Street Preachers. Where Britpop revived the guitar solo, it kept it economical, as with Bernard Butler's phased solo on Suede's 'Animal Nitrate' and the solo on Ash's 'Goldfinger'. There are many guitar solos on Oasis songs, of which the pentatonic-based solo on 'Live Forever' from *Definitely Maybe* is simple but effective. Fixated on the mid-1960s, Britpop occasionally resurrected some of the stylistic traits of 1960s solos.

Attitudes varied, but there was now ideological opposition to the rock (or 'rockist') guitar solo. John Squire seemed to be swimming against the tide with extended solos in a traditional rock guitar style on The Stone Roses' second album *The Second Coming*. In 1992 Blur released their debut album *Leisure*. Asked about solos by Jon Lewin for *Making Music* in January 1992, bass player Alex James' blunt reply was, "solos are vetoed". In the band's later track 'Beetlebum' the guitar reiterates a single two-bar phrase all through a chord sequence on the coda (3:58-5:04) where another band might have been tempted to put a solo.

The success of Oasis in particular underlined the desirability of memorable songs. When in May 1996 US *Guitar* magazine carried a piece about Oasis and Noel Gallagher, it was in a general article about the 'return' of songwriting. The cover caption was telling: "Like it or not, songwriting is as important today as guitar playing … if not more." The editorial by H. P. Newquist said of Gallagher that "his commitment to writing songs with his guitar – not songs for his guitar – puts him at the forefront of players who use the instrument for something other than displaying chops." (The Pixies once advertised for a new bass player specifying "no chops".) Shred was dead, it seemed.

Another important album for its combination of remarkable songwriting and imaginative guitar-playing is Jeff Buckley's *Grace* (1997). Buckley was a very able rock guitarist, but the songwriter in him was the stronger, guiding force. Presciently, he spoke to *Guitar* (UK) in September 1994: "When we're jamming I do huge, huge solos and go off ... but for songs I'm more interested in finding melodies. They're more powerful. Every guitar player should know that ... The shredding shit is fine – but it will go, and nobody will care." He also had a laudable respect for the guitar itself: "The guitar is full of wonder, it's not an extension of my ego – I believe that it too has spirits flying through it and not just erudition and learning. The guitar is a mysterious instrument, but a lot of the mystery has gone or has been hidden."

Textural treatment of the guitar was a key element in the music of Radiohead's angsty ambient soundworld, as the band grew quickly from the neo-grunge of 'Creep' to the glacial beauty of the echoing guitar arpeggios of 'Let Down' and the ferocious guitar solos by Jonny Greenwood in 'Paranoid Android' (*OK Computer*, 1997). Radiohead have shown that the guitar solo can always work if the context is right and the approach is imaginative. 'Paranoid Android' wasn't complete until Greenwood added a fourth section as a fade out – a lengthy, intense solo, which alternates between being backwards and forwards. The solo section on 'Just' (*The Bends*, 1994) goes through three distinct and highly-contrasted sections: 1:55-2:06 has tremolo picking and unison bends, 2:06-20 is clean and harmonised; there's two seconds of silence, and then pure guitar noise, until about 2:36 when the chorus returns.

INTO THE 21ST CENTURY

"People thought the guitar would be dead by now, that nothing new would ever happen and that's rubbish. There's always going to be something different because it's context – sounds in context makes newness." Kevin Shields, My Bloody Valentine (*Guitar World*, February 1996)

Through the first decade of the 21st century, in the mainstream, the aversion to the more showy guitar solo generally remained. Even rock tracks like Feeder's 'Buck Rogers' (2001) avoid a guitar solo. For indie youth bands it remained tainted by association with older guitar groups on the heavier side of rock music. But there are many bands in the rock mainstream who have been very successful and whose songs include guitar solos, including Coldplay, Artic Monkeys, Franz Ferdinand, The Black Keys, Kings Of Leon, and Queens Of The Stone Age. Muse kept the progressive guitar solo alive and The White Stripes reconstituted blues-rock solos in a post-punk framework. In heavy rock, heavy metal, and contemporary progressive rock the guitar solo is alive and well, as can be heard in Avenged Sevenfold's 'Afterlife' and Alter Bridge's 'Blackbird'. These solos are more likely to cram in more techniques in a small space than in past decades, and their sound is also affected by being played over sometimes drastically detuned backing progressions.

But the song comes first. As Jonny Buckland of Coldplay said to *Guitarist* in October 2001: "It's quite fun to do the cheesy solos, but not on our songs. I play around with stuff, do a bit of improvising, but only around the melody ... George Harrison is one of my heroes, everything he did just made the song better. Just fitting the song, rather than, 'Look at me, spotlight please.'"

BASIC CONCEPTS AND APPROACHES TO SOLOS

The solo – and especially the guitar solo – is capable of delivering a thrill to match anything in popular music.

SECTION 2
BASIC CONCEPTS AND APPROACHES TO SOLOS

A well-timed, creative solo can lift a song at a crucial moment as much as a great vocal. Whether played by guitar or another instrument, it can make a great song even better. That's why songwriters need to know how they work. At its best the solo – and especially the guitar solo – is capable of delivering a thrill to match anything offered in popular music.

WHAT TYPES OF SONG HAVE A SOLO?

"I still do whatever the songs require; the song is king to me, and I just do whatever works within any given song." (Mark Knopfler, *Guitar*, September 1992)

A solo can occur in almost any type of song, whatever the genre. There are few styles where the presence of a solo would seem incongruous. More important is the choice of instrument for the intended solo, its timbre, and whether both the instrument and musical style of the solo suit the genre (instruments are dealt with in Sections Four and Five). Reggae songs don't have Van Halen-style tapping guitar solos; rap songs don't have clarinet or saxophone solos. MOR ballads don't often have electric guitar breaks, but they can work if played with enough sensitivity, as George Harrison's contributions to The Beatles' 'Something' and 'Let It Be' show, or Henry McCulloch's solo on Wings' hit 'My Love'. For the MOR genre it could be that a different instrument is needed, such as saxophone – as featured in the solo in T'Pau's 1980s hit 'China In Your Hand'. That songwriters still consider solos at all is largely due to the influence of the guitar in so much popular music since the 1960s.

WHY DOES A SONG NEED A SOLO?

After the typical song structure of verse/chorus/verse/chorus, there is often a need to have a third section:

■ to prevent the song becoming dull and predictable;
■ to introduce musical material that provides contrast;
■ to enable the verse and chorus to return and be heard afresh.

Even bands that resisted putting a solo into their songs sometimes recognised its musical value. R.E.M. resisted traditional expectations of rock bands, such as guitar solos, and came to prominence at a time in the mid-1980s when lead guitar solos were getting increasingly technical. Peter Buck told USA's *Guitar* magazine in January 1993, "Usually, I'd rather write a bridge. But sometimes you don't need one,

SECTION 2

everything that needs to be said lyrically and melodically and rhythm-wise is said during the verses and chorus. So on both those songs ['Stand' and 'The One I Love'] we knew from the beginning that some kind of solo was needed there."

It can be difficult to maintain the level of interest as a song starts its third verse, after two verses and two choruses. In weak songwriting, the tension and interest drop at this point and only recover on the return of the verse or chorus. If a third section is successful, it not only maintains the level of interest, it may even heighten the drama. If there's no third section (sung or solo) the song may need to finish earlier – thus leading to the sub-three minute song – as with a track like James Brown's 'It's A Man's Man's Man's World'. In some songs the middle section becomes merely an instrumental version of the verse or the chorus; this is sometimes ineffective because it doesn't introduce enough melodic interest or harmonic contrast, as opposed to a true bridge/middle-eight and/or solo.

The third section of a song can be created by several means:

■ a short link leading to a 'middle-eight' or bridge with vocals;
■ a similar length instrumental section with no featured instrument;
■ a solo, with or without the vocal middle-eight.

So the need in a song for a third section is sometimes satisfied by a solo. It is also possible to merge the middle-eight and the solo principles, as happens in Fleetwood Mac's hit 'Man Of The World'. In this eight-bar sequence, drama is created by new harmony – the appearance of an F♯m chord (III in the key of D major) for the first time in the song – coupled with an intensifying drum part, and Peter Green's three expressive lead-guitar phrases in between the vocals adding a soloistic element.

A third section can also be created from the chorus by changing its arrangement, either by altering the instruments or by re-mixing. This produces a barer statement of the chorus; a classic example would be voice over drums and almost nothing else. This can lead to a dynamic return of the full chorus.

Interviewed by UK magazine *Guitar* in September 1995, Peter Buck observed of R.E.M.'s 'Losing My Religion': "The bridge of a song is supposed to widen it either emotionally, lyrically, or rhythmically. This song was finished, so rather than come up with a bridge that wasn't going to tell you anything, we needed an instrumental hook. I didn't want a solo; a Fleetwood Mac type of breakdown seemed a nice idea. So I did this little riff on the mandolin while Michael hummed over it and re-did one of the vocal lines. It was a nice way to get into the third verse, which finishes the song without throwing a curve into the lyric process."

Unlike a vocal middle-eight, a solo takes the spotlight away from the singer and the lyric. It exists in a world of pure music, albeit coloured by the mood that the song and lyric have already established. In a song, solos function differently to the way they would in pure instrumental music. They are like actors already robed in the song's emotions. In this way a solo can express the feeling of the song, repeating the emotion from a different angle. On some instruments the soloist may be able to do things that a singer could not. Instrumental solos need not follow the same kind of pitch contour as a vocal melody. There may be wide intervals difficult for a singer to pitch, extremely rapid sequences of notes, sound-effects, full chords and parallel intervals,

SECTION 2

etc. As Billy Corgan of The Smashing Pumpkins told *Guitar* (UK) in August 1993, "I think I can express things on the guitar that I can't with my voice, so why not?"

A solo can:

- be a respite from the issues of the lyric;
- create anticipation to hear what comes next in the narrative of the lyric;
- provide a break from the vocals;
- bring one of the players not usually in the spotlight to the fore;
- be a kind of super-chorus, an intensification of the song;
- make explicit an emotion which has only been bubbling under or partly expressed by the singer;
- express those aspects of the song that cannot be expressed in words or are behind the words;
- melodically cover a bigger pitch range than a singer, or be louder, faster, more sustained;
- melodically link song sections;
- form an additional bridge or be a bridge in itself;
- be a melodic focus when the vocals cease;
- provide a contrast which benefits the other parts of the song;
- be a dramatic section that sets up the return of the verse and/or chorus.

The question is to what extent does the solo really draw on the music of the song or depart from it?

WHY DO SOME SONGS NOT NEED A SOLO?

Sometimes a song doesn't need a solo, and it is good for a songwriter to develop a sense of this. Billy Duffy told *Making Music* (October 1994) "On *The Cult* (1994) I was very reluctant to do any guitar solos at all. I was like, 'Why does every song have to have a guitar solo in it?' I grew up always thinking that was the case, but we'd led ourselves down a path – 'Oh, where's the guitar solo?' – I said, 'Let's not have one.' Stuff like that helps you change, and makes you work in different areas, so you use moods rather than going for the easy option – 'It's the guitar solo now so that'll kill 30 seconds.'"

A badly placed solo might derail a song, causing it to lose focus. To test this, try imagining the song without a solo and see if it loses anything. Digital editing makes the process much easier, since the solo can be recorded but later shortened, moved, or edited out altogether. A song might not need a solo because:

- it is short: a strophic or verse/chorus-based song of two to three minutes might not need to add a third section;
- the mood of the song, the theme of the lyric, or the effect of the chord progression, might not want to be disturbed;
- the chorus or verse are quite long in themselves;
- the middle-eight/bridge, where a solo might have been, is needed for more lyric content.

Valuable insights can be had by considering songs where there is no solo and posing the question: why did this work? Some songs are simple enough that they don't need one. Like his more famous 'Like A Rolling Stone', Bob Dylan's 'Positively Fourth Street' lacks a solo section. In fact, it doesn't even have a separate chorus, as the song uses the simplest of forms, the strophic verse-verse-verse (etc) structure. This enables Dylan to focus his lyric on a single emotion from which there is no respite.

Carole King's 'You've Got A Friend' is a slowish piano ballad that lasts 5:05. It takes 0:58 to reach its first chorus, and the chorus is longer than most. The end of the first chorus is reached at 1:38, the second verse starts 1:49, the ten-bar bridge lasts from 3:14-42. There isn't room for a solo, and the short link passages are dominated by her piano work which generates quasi-melodic elements. Another piano song example would be Jackson Browne's 'The Pretender', which has an extended verse with several sections. There's room for a solo but none occurs. Instead, there is a two-bar guitar fill that twice links to the chorus. 'The Pretender' is dominated by the quantity of statement and observation in its lyric. Other examples of songs whose lyrics can't be interrupted because of their narrative momentum are Don McLean's 'American Pie', Tracy Chapman's 'Fast Car', and The Eagles' 'Lyin' Eyes'. This is often true of lyrics with third person narrators telling a story, rather than those songs expressing feelings from a first person perspective.

Other songs that don't have solos for various reasons include Elton John's 'Saturday Night's Alright For Fighting', which elects to stay firmly on the riff to sustain its energy. The Byrds' 'Chestnut Mare' has a radically disjunct middle section that changes tempo, time signature, and has a new chord progression. Although there is no guitar solo, there are plenty of guitar fills. Blur's 'The Universal' has an orchestral chorus before the last vocal chorus, no bridge and no solo. A solo might have reduced the music's grandeur or been heard as out of genre. The solo function is left to the laconic, short trumpet break after the first chorus. The Rolling Stones' 'Angie' avoids having a solo during the instrumental passage where piano, strings, and acoustic guitar are playing, from 2:11-37, a recap of the song's intro.

The link passages in Neil Young's 'Only Love Can Break Your Heart' are left without any instrument adding a solo phrase. The bridge of The Police's 'Every Breath You Take' (1:43-2:14) has no solo because the vocal has done the job over the $\flat$VI-$\flat$VII chord change. What follows is an instrumental verse where a piano chord is struck on every other beat. Sometimes an instrumental passage where there might have been an explicit solo can have a curious tension. This absence effect is felt on the bridge of Roxy Music's 'Avalon' where there is no real solo instrument and this absence draws the listener in. It is only after the last chorus that a few saxophone phrases are heard and a backing vocalist scat-singing to the fade.

> *Sometimes an instrumental passage where there might have been an explicit solo can have a curious tension. This absence effect is felt on the bridge of Roxy Music's 'Avalon' where there is no real solo instrument and this absence draws the listener in.*

SECTION 2

Similarly, Squeeze's 'Cool For Cats' has a 16-bar instrumental passage on a single implied chord of Em. There's no true solo instrument, but instead a variety of synth sounds over a steady beat. A solo would have been too straight-forward. It saves the solo for the coda where the electric piano takes over from the vocal melody, the lyric's imagery having been used up.

Consider why there is no solo in Eric Clapton's 'Layla', since it seems the kind of rock song that would usually have one. The answer is that the intro and choruses are already dominated by multiple lead guitars playing the riff at three different octaves. That doesn't leave much space for a lead guitar to add anything else. More importantly, the gesture of a high wailing lead solo is pre-empted by Duane Allman's high slide. During the coda the slide line starts to improvise around the riff, constituting a coda solo. The single version of 'Layla' is an edit of an album version that has a long instrumental where piano comes to the fore.

There are songs that arguably didn't need a solo or where solos were not the best fit for the genre of song. Kate Bush's Number One single 'Wuthering Heights', has an arrangement based on piano and orchestra. The guitar solo appears as a coda to the final instrumental choruses, and is a surprise since it is not particularly in genre (this isn't a rock song). It also seems redundant, because Bush's high vocal has already carved out that musical territory. Her high pleading vocal can't be topped by the lead guitar, despite the solo being good on its own terms. If anything, the strings are doing more to make the coda lyrical. For her first two albums, Kate Bush relied on established arrangement styles; it would not be until her third and fourth that her arrangements broke the mould. For 'Wuthering Heights', she drew on the arrangements of the day, and guitar solos were common. Perhaps this is why her later re-recording of the vocal (for the compilation *The Whole Story* in 1986) seems misjudged. In it she trades phrases with the lead guitar in a way that compounds the original problem, and magnifies the fact that this solo doesn't evoke the imagined world of Emily Bronte's moors. Although tasteful, the solo takes us away from the lyric's vision of the moors, and back to a lead guitarist. By analogy I think of this as a reductive move from three dimensions to two.

THE '2-D' VERSUS THE '3-D' SOLO

In songs, a solo should generally not be used as an opportunity to show off technique. It may function this way in instrumental and improvised music, in musical genres where virtuosity is expected, or where a song is happy to be exhibitionist, content to draw attention to the performers, rather than the performers losing themselves in the material. Inappropriately technical solos, or solos which are out-of-place, wreck the imaginary world the song creates by replacing that imaginative content with a nut'n'bolts domain of self-conscious technique. They spoil the artifice of the song's imaginary world by drawing attention from background to foreground, from the inner world to the outer surface world of performer/performance. I think of this as the '3-D field' of a song. A show-off solo collapses the song into 2-D; the spectacle of the player eclipses the world of the song. A song about love, loss, or desire, becomes a spectacle of frets, string-bending, or piano keys. Great songs have little to do with great technique and therefore showing off technique in them is pointless.

Some songs can support a virtuoso solo because it fits their themes. The Spin Doctors' 'Two Princes' has a lively guitar solo that covers much of the neck and expresses the passionate nonchalance of the lyric – the show-off quality fits the exuberant persona of the character and thus the virtuosity is contained within the song. The solo is played over a verse and chorus (1:39-2:12), starting low and moving upward, alluding to part of the vocal melody but adding chromatic touches which indicate dare-devilry.

HOW LONG IS A SOLO?

"There's a solo on 'Hot For Teacher' that's not a regular length. When I was done with the solo we ended, you know what I mean? It ended up being like 13 bars instead of 12. To me it feels right." (Eddie Van Halen, *Guitar Player*, March 1995.)

Solo sections are often four, eight, 12, or 16 bars long. If they aren't, they add on a couple of bars – so an eight-bar solo turns into nine bars, a 12-bar solo turns into 14 bars. The main cause of such extensions is the need for a couple of bars' gap between the end of the solo and the next section, otherwise the transition is abrupt and the vocal may sound like it's tripping over. It may also be that the solo's climax involves a held note that lasts beyond the limits of the solo's end bar. The same transition issues can apply setting up an approach to the solo, with perhaps a few bars needed to link a second chorus to a solo, or a middle-eight to a solo. Give these apparently insignificant transitions some thought, because if they lack clarity of execution they can confuse the listener and ruin the effect of the solo that follows. The transition point can be a matter of harmonically setting up the solo, or scene-setting in some other way. In 'Stairway To Heaven' this takes the form of a pause and a fanfare. In David Bowie's 'Jean Genie' there is a dynamic scene-setting with the volume dropping a little before the solo starts. When practising it is a good idea to limit yourself to that length so you force yourself to come up with something memorable but short. Then practise an eight-bar solo where bars seven to eight are a crescendo into the main part of the song.

Occasionally a solo will last for an odd number of bars, which brings its own challenges. Radiohead's 'There There' builds tension steadily toward the explosion at 3:58-4:18 where there is a guitar solo that deconstructs some of the assumptions of a solo, complete with several chromatic descending phrases, a spikey arpeggio idea that has already been heard in the song, and what sound like unison bends to finish. The solo takes 11 bars and is played over an unusual chord sequence of Bm7-Dm7-Am-Em. The asymmetry is part of what creates an opportunity for the soloist.

The length of a solo will depend on many factors. Bear in mind the solo as a proportion of the entire song. If a song is about three minutes long a 10-20 second solo might be in balance. The solo's length might be shaped by what you want to say, but also bear in mind how long you want the spotlight taken off the vocal. How long a diversion or contrast do you want the solo to be? When do you want to return to the verse or the chorus and re-establish the central mood? You don't want the listener to go on such a detour that they've lost track of the song's basic emotional theme.

SECTION 2

CAN A SONG HAVE MORE THAN ONE SOLO?

In some cases a song might have more than one solo. If the solo is fairly short and uses the same couple of phrases, it can occur more than once and function as a link. This means it won't necessarily have the impact of a single dramatic solo two-thirds of the way through, but could fit. Songs that open with a short solo designed to grab the listener's attention with immediate melodic interest include Mott The Hoople's 'All The Young Dudes', Bob Seger's song 'On Main Street', and Thin Lizzy's 'Whiskey In The Jar'. This intro break can sometimes be a link occurring after the chorus and may even feature during the coda. In T. Rex's 'Jeepster' the mid-point A pentatonic major solo is repeated with a few variations for the coda. Solos themselves tend not to be hooks, although they may constitute a memorable part of the song.

The longer a song, the more chance there is for two solos and these may be effectively contrasts, possibly on different types of guitar, or played by two different guitarists. In Thin Lizzy's ballad 'Still In Love With You' (from *Live And Dangerous*), after two verses and the chorus line, the first solo arrives, played by Brian Robertson in an aggressive, echo-laden style. This solo raises the temperature of the ballad. After that the remaining verse quietens right down. The second solo, which is longer, is played with creamy, dark sustain by Scott Gorham, with a flowing legato style, less angular than Robertson's approach. At its climax a short coda is added in which the two lead guitars harmonise with each other.

A solo might have two distinct parts. The solo on Led Zeppelin's 'In The Evening' (*In Through The Out Door*, 1979) is a two-part example. The first solo is high-pitched, frenetic, mostly blues-scale (E G A B♭ B D) with much worrying away at the flattened fifth. It is played over the song's verse riff. At 4:22 a second front-pickup solo starts using a natural minor scale, fewer notes and more sustain. The backing for the second half of the solo is quieter, keyboard-dominated, and with richer chords. Thin Lizzy's 'That Woman's Gonna Break Your Heart' has a double section solo. The first solo has four phrases with held notes after the music has plunged into a new key. It then returns to the major key of the verse and the guitar style changes, with a rapid scale-based solo with echo so that the guitar harmonises with itself.

CAN A SOLO HAVE MORE THAN ONE SOLOIST? THE SOLO AS DUET

A solo can be turned into a duet in the following ways:

- Manually double-track the solo but leave slight deviations between them.
- Have two contrasted guitar or instrumental tones playing independent lines.
- Have two guitars/instruments playing in harmony.
- Have a guitar and another instrument playing the same solo in unison.

Instead of merely reinforcing the lead line, imperfectly double-tracking a solo creates more interest. This result occurs naturally if a player takes two passes at a solo having basically worked out what they want to do but without listening to the first version

SECTION 2

during the playback. This happens in Jeff Beck's 'Hi Ho Silver Lining' and adds character to the pop song. The solo is double-tracked but the two parts have slight differences, which adds to the richness and sense of misbehaving. The Beatles' 'Fixing A Hole' has a solo at 1:16-32 which is double-tracked.

A later step would be to have two guitars doing different things or actually answering each other. On the studio version of Led Zeppelin's 'No Quarter', Jimmy Page has one clean guitar, the other distorted, playing answering phrases. There are fine solos with two guitars dueting in Robert Plant's 'Come Into My Life' and Dire Straits' 'You And Your Friend'.

Mott The Hoople's 'All The Way From Memphis' has a guitar and sax soloing at the same time, including on the coda. The track is 4:54 in length with the first guitar/sax solo coming in 2:06-34. The second runs from 3:16-4:12, at which point the guitar takes over, the sax ending with high-pitched noises. The guitar solo has some wild bending in it.

WHAT IS A SOLO?

You might think that the answer to this question is obvious: a solo is a solo. Although many solos are self-evident, this isn't always the case. When a solo is based on the vocal melody and repeats a segment of it without changing, especially if the selected phrase is quite short, then it may be that this is better described as a riff or fill. Take, for example, Coldplay's 'Reign Of Love', where at 3:10 the guitar takes over the vocal from the last chorus and plays the same four-bar melodic phrase twice until the sung coda. This phrase is based on the earlier vocal melody. Is this a true solo? Or is it an example of part-playing? In a true solo does there need to be a degree of freedom and departure, of deviating from previously-heard patterns of the song material? Does a true solo carry the sense of an improvisation even when it isn't actually improvised? Does the listener need to feel the presence of a soloist rather than a team player? Does there have to be a sense that a spotlight of attention has fallen on a single player?

Another angle from which to consider this is whether it is the boundaries around the solo that partly determine why some musical events are perceived as a solo. In other words, a context can be made in which the listener hears whatever occurs as a kind of solo. An instrumental passage is not necessarily a solo. The entire group or backing has gone 'solo' insofar as there is no vocal, but the spotlight might not fall on any one instrument or player. Each may in the totality have a few short melodic scraps, but the significance is the total sound, not what one player does.

There is a closer connection between great solos and the songs in which they occur than is often understood. Good songwriting and recording direct all the musical parts and the arrangement to one end: expressing that song idea at its purest. For this reason, you can plan or improvise a solo that in itself is technically, melodically, harmonically, and/or rhythmically brilliant, and yet it won't add much to the song. The critical factor is that the solo must be an integral part of the song. The stronger the impression of this it can give, the more inevitable and powerful it will be and the more it will justify its inclusion. Conversely, the less organically related it feels to the song, the more it feels like an arbitrary 'bolt-on' or digression, the more redundant it will feel. This vital connection was often lost in the 1980s during the 'technique wars'. Aerosmith's Joe Perry told *Guitar* UK in April 1993, "To me, it's always finding what fits the song – sure I love to jam, I love to rock out, and down in my basement studio I'll lay down loads of guitar solos, but that stuff just bores me after any great length. The guitar solo should be another part of the song that actually says something."

The style of the song and its arrangement also play a part. With guitar solos in particular, this effect is increased the less guitar-orientated the genre. In songs that belong to a genre in which electric guitar is dominant (ie, most rock) the guitar solo is half-expected. In other styles, such as soul, singer-songwriter material, folk, chart pop, MOR, etc, a guitar solo is less expected and will therefore be more noticeable. Tony Peluso's solo on the coda of The Carpenters' hit 'Goodbye To Love' drew attention because it was a rock lead solo in an unexpected context.

The final impression a solo gives is dependent on many factors, and its effectiveness may have been compromised even before you have recorded a note. The sense of impressiveness doesn't come entirely from the soloist – it's how the stage is set for the solo. This includes such as aspects as:

- where the solo comes in the song
- how the solo has been prepared in terms of a prior link
- the dynamic level of the solo passage compared to what came before
- whether the solo is played over a chord progression already heard in the song
- whether the solo coincides with a key change
- what is happening harmonically and rhythmically in the backing.

In this sense, great solos spring not so much from virtuosity as from good songwriting technique. The great solo is almost always integral; it doesn't feel bolted on as an extra. It grows out of the song itself as a final expression of something in the spirit of the song, as though something in the song has decided to speak through the solo instrument instead of the vocalist.

Mark Knopfler of Dire Straits told *Guitar* (UK) in January 1993, "When I'm working on a solo I don't really know how it comes about. I think not being able to sing means the guitar becomes like a voice and you make it do things that you wouldn't do otherwise. Perhaps if you can't sing you push a little harder with your instrument, but I've never thought about that."

A TEST CASE: THE GREATEST GUITAR SOLO?

Magazines, internet forums, and blogs love 'Best of' rankings. *Guitar World* published an online 'Top 50' guitar solos. Those mentioned included Eric Clapton on The Beatles' 'While My Guitar Gently Weeps' and Cream's 'Crossroads' (1968), Brian May on Queen's 'Brighton Rock' (1974) and 'Bohemian Rhapsody' (1975), Elliott Randall's lead on Steely Dan's 'Reelin' In The Years' (1972), Jimmy Page on 'Whole Lotta Love' and 'Heartbreaker' (1969), Slash on Guns N' Roses' 'Sweet Child O'

Mine' (1987) and 'November Rain' (1991), Jonny Greenwood on Radiohead's 'Paranoid Android' (1997), B. B. King on 'The Thrill Is Gone' (1969), Randy Rhoads on 'Mr. Crowley' and 'Crazy Train' with Ozzy Osbourne (1981), Kirk Hammett on Metallica's 'Fade To Black' (1984) and 'One' (1988), Jimi Hendrix on 'Little Wing' and 'All Along The Watchtower' (1968), Ritchie Blackmore on Deep Purple's 'Highway Star' (1972), Don Felder and Joe Walsh on The Eagles' 'Hotel California' (1976), David Gilmour on Pink Floyd's 'Comfortably Numb' (1979), Allen Collins with Lynyrd Skynyrd on 'Free Bird' (1973), Paul Kossoff's solo on Free's 'All Right Now', Chuck Berry's 'Johnny B. Goode' (1958), Les Paul on 'How High The Moon' (1951), and Stevie Ray Vaughan's 'Texas Flood' (1983). The solo that topped the poll, and which often receives the accolade of rock's greatest song, was Led Zeppelin's 'Stairway To Heaven'.

Of course, there cannot be a 'greatest' solo, for the same reason there cannot be a 'greatest' song. Musical greatness is not a single pinnacle, like the apex of a pyramid. A better analogy for musical achievement would be a high-altitude plateau, reachable by many routes, connecting many peaks offering sublime yet divergent views. Expressivity takes many forms. But if there was a near-universally acclaimed guitar solo, presumably it would tell us something important about solos and songs (and not just "X is a great guitar player"). So, given it has enjoyed a special prestige for over four decades, what does 'Stairway To Heaven' reveal about the relationship of a solo to its host song? The answer supplies several important insights that apply to solos regardless of the instrument on which they're played.

Of course, there cannot be a 'greatest' solo, for the same reason there cannot be a 'greatest' song. Musical greatness is not a single pinnacle, like the apex of a pyramid.

As suggested earlier, one way to gauge the importance and relevance of a solo is to imagine the song without it. Try to think of 'Stairway To Heaven' without Jimmy Page's guitar solo, edited so that the 'fanfare' section's final G/B chord at 5:52 is followed by the first stabbed A5 of the last vocal verse at 6:43. It is not only hard because we're used to hearing it; it's difficult because it spoils the shape of the song. Without the solo, several important steps are missing from the dynamic build-up to the final verse. There is no longer any chance for the vocal to refresh itself by being absent. But more significantly it is also as though something not in the lyric has gone unsaid.

In some of the best solos, there is a feeling that the solo is enacting something in the theme of the song through the music. This is the opposite of the characteristic that makes solos sound like irrelevant, indulgent anti-climaxes, the chance for someone to parade their dexterity with scale patterns. While there is a consensus that Page's solo is magnificent as a set of phrases in itself, it also shines because of the musical context.

First, the solo has the D major 'fanfare' as a clear preparation, with its powerful irregular stresses. This section interrupts the steady 4/4 of the preceding verses, and its off-beat stresses make the return to a slightly faster 4/4 seem fresh. Second, the lyrical, bitter-sweet Am-Am/G-Fmaj7 sequence droned by the rhythm guitars is fertile support for a solo. The more expressive the harmony, the stronger the platform it provides. An A minor chord has the notes A-C-E; an F chord is F-A-C. Minor chords are traditionally felt to sound sad relative to major chords, which sound happy. The F chord here has a fourth note – E, a major seventh – making F-A-C-E. These four notes include the A minor chord. The major seventh chord is for this reason full of longing, fusing the sadness of the minor chord with the major chord's hope. The change from Am to Fmaj7 and back means the notes A, C, and E resonate in a luminous cloud behind and throughout the guitar solo, heightening its expressiveness. Even heard with only John Bonham's drums and Page's rhythm guitars, this progression played so powerfully combines the elemental and the ethereal.

The rhythm section do their bit also, with Bonham's thunderous fills and John Paul Jones laying down a Motown-influenced bassline, syncopating the root notes to create a groove. In an interview for *Bassist* in September 1999 he told me it was "syncopating against a straight beat – Motown was very Latin-influenced in that way … In 'Stairway' …. at the end there's three notes [ie, A-G-F], so you don't want to be piddling around while there's a great guitar solo going on that you can support."

The journey within the music of 'Stairway To Heaven' leads inexorably to the guitar solo. 'Stairway To Heaven' is not, in the crude sense, a song with a 'message'; its form and energy *are* the drama of the lyric acted out. The distinction can be clarified by comparing John Lennon's 'Imagine' and The Beatles' 'A Day In The Life'. 'Imagine' talks about a secular transcendence of what it judges outmoded beliefs, but it does not musically enact this. Dynamically subdued, it has no solo, and the music only generates a mild sense of imminent liberation at the E major chord in the bridge after the word "dreamer". (This is a 'reverse polarity' III^ in C major, using my symbol to indicate that it is major where minor would be expected; where I refer to a chord that 'reverses polarity' from major to minor, an 'm' is used after the Roman numeral.) By contrast, The Beatles' ambitious 'A Day In The Life' dramatises its shifting psychedelic perception through changes of voice, lyrical focus, instrumental balance, and tempo, along with two huge crescendos that in effect are pitch-blurring solos for orchestra. 'A Day In The Life' doesn't only talk about its theme of reality-shifting, it enacts it *within* the music.

Likewise, the guitar solo in 'Stairway' is the point of release for an emotional expectation that originated with the song. Its structure is sustained by a dynamic curve from quiet to loud, from folk pastoral to elemental rock, on which the guitar solo stands as a transcendent point. That which could not be lyrically said is expressed wordlessly in it. The '3-D' quotient in this solo is high. In his book on Led Zeppelin, *Hammer of the Gods* (1985), Stephen Davis wrote that the song "expressed an ineffable yearning for spiritual transformation deep in the hearts of the generation for which it was intended." Its guitar solo articulated that "yearning".

From this it can be seen that a good, even great, solo is a result of a combination of things:

- the notes of the solo itself, its melodic ideas and phrasing
- the harmony that colours and supports it
- the underlying rhythm

- the effect of it happening at the right point in the song's overall structure
- a length of solo proportionate to the song's overall duration
- fitting the mood and emotion of the music
- fitting the theme of the lyric.

In the light of the discussion of 'Stairway To Heaven', an interesting contrast is The Stone Roses' 'Tears' (1994) which is indebted to Led Zeppelin by virtue of its first riff resembling 'Your Time Is Gonna Come', a D passage reminiscent of 'Thank You', and for its electric guitar solo. It has two solos contrasted by timbre. At 2:40 there's an attractive acoustic guitar break, double-tracked before moving behind the vocals. From 3:24-45 there is a gapped rhythm, before the electric solo, over the same progression (Am-G-F) as the solo in 'Stairway'. There is nothing wrong with the lead playing, but the solo cannot prevent the song seeming less than the sum of its parts, with the return of the vocals an anti-climax. The song's overall architecture doesn't work well enough to make the 6:40 duration entirely convincing.

SECTION 2 | 37

PLACING THE SOLO IN A SONG

Great solos are not just about notes and scales. Their greatness is also about the stage you provide for them.

SECTION 3
PLACING THE SOLO IN A SONG

The musical context for the solo has much to do with how impressive the final solo might sound. This includes how the solo is prepared and where it comes in the song. What is its relationship to the overall structure of the song? What chords are used: same as in prior sections or different? Same key or different? New instruments? What about the pitch of the backing: does it leave room for the pitches of the solo instrument to come through? Does the backing have continuous rhythm or stopped rhythm with pauses?

As Phil Manzanera told me in a December 1999 interview, "Many people can play technically, but it's the context that makes a solo great. It's how you react to the context. One or two notes can sound brilliant, whereas on their own they're just two notes. Therein lies the craft. You go to a school and learn to play those two notes. But it's your experience, the music you listen to and where exactly you position those two notes. It doesn't have to be 50 notes."

Take the solo by Doug Boyle on Robert Plant's 'Anniversary' (*Manic Nirvana*, 1990). The whole arrangement builds the tension, including a crescendo, to the solo at 2:04-3:12. Boyle is not afraid to leave gaps between the lead phrases. He rises in pitch gradually and includes more notes, more passing notes, and changes of direction. The second climax of the song is one of Plant's patented wails from 3:43-50. From this point the track goes into a false fade; from 4:13 the original drum beat and chord sequence have gone. The song concludes with nightmarish sampled laughter and Plant's last despairing cry (the third climax) cut off echoing at 4:56.

WHERE DOES THE SOLO GO IN A SONG?

Timing a solo means not only how long it lasts but when it arrives. Be sensitive to the distance from the start of the song, from the previous chorus, and from the previous vocal ending. The vast majority of solos in popular songs come roughly two-thirds of the way through, linked to or replacing the bridge/middle-eight. Possible positions in a song for a solo are:

- the intro
- after the first chorus, where it links to/delays the next verse
- instead of a second verse, leaving only a second prechorus
- after the second chorus
- before or after the bridge/middle-eight
- as an instrumental chorus in a group of last choruses

SECTION 3

■ before a vocal coda
■ after the last chorus in the coda.

If the solo is short enough it can even be a repeated section of its own. The Beatles 'Get Back' is punctuated by eight-bar solos, at 0:39-54 (after the first chorus) on guitar, on electric piano at 1:12-27 (after the second chorus), and at 1:59-2:14 on guitar (after the third chorus).

Sometimes the position of a solo is affected by commercial considerations, as with a radio edit mix, where sections of the song or the solo, or both, are cut to make the song more radio-friendly. This creates differing single and album versions of the same track, and confusion for buyers of later CD anthologies of popular music. Radio-edits affected songs like Free's 'All Right Now', The Who's 'Won't Get Fooled Again' and 'Who Are You', and Ash's 'Goldfinger'. In the case of Led Zeppelin's 'Whole Lotta Love', the album track (5:30) has the guitar solo at 3:06-22, whereas the radio mix (4:50) edits the free-form middle section bringing the solo forward to 2:23-39 and giving it slightly more emphasis. In the radio edit of Boston's hit 'More Than A Feeling' the edit cuts out the second verse and chorus from the album version. Consequently the solo arrives earlier, after the first chorus, in the middle of the song, ensuring no loss of tension after the first chorus, with the solo then becoming a kind of double chorus. The chord progression is ten bars, and not taken from another part of the song.

Recounting for *Guitar World* how his solo in Queen's 'Bohemian Rhapsody' was created, Brian May said, "Freddie [Mercury] had the whole piece pretty well mapped out, as I remember, but he didn't have a guitar solo planned. So I guess I steamed in and said, 'This is the point where you need your solo, and these are the chords I'd like to use.'" The chord progression for the solo is based on the verse, but with a slight foray into some different chords at the end, to make a transition into the next section. It is arguable that if the guitar solo had come after the mock-operatic section it might have seemed an anti-climax.

WHICH PART OF THE SONG GOES BEHIND THE SOLO?

A key decision when working on a solo is to plan what section of the song will support it. Any earlier section of the song could be used as the harmonic backing for the solo:

■ A solo could be played over an intro, verse, pre-chorus, or chorus.
■ It could use an earlier section transposed into a new key.
■ It could use an earlier section in a different arrangement.
■ It could change the rhythm or the dynamic of an earlier section.
■ It could be played over an entirely new section.
■ It could use a section without any definite harmony.

A simple example is in songs that use a 12-bar (rock'n'roll or blues) sequence where the section is repeated one more time with the soloist improvising over it. Earlier song sections might be edited down to the right length, sometimes by omitting repeats – a verse that used a turnaround four times might feature as the backing for the solo by having that cut to twice. A pre-chorus that only lasts four bars might be repeated a number of times to make the backing for the solo.

For Jethro Tull's 'Aqualung', guitarist Martin Barre suggested playing the verse chords in half-time for the first part of the solo and returning to their normal timing for the rest of it. Moving from 4/4 to 12/8 without a change of tempo is also an interesting tactic to use in a solo. The song appears to slow down considerably, because the pulse that governed a quarter-note has become an eighth-note, which is only a third of a beat. A similar effect is created by half-time 4/4 where a quarter-note turns into an eighth-note, with two on a beat, so the music seems to be going half as quick.

If you don't want to recycle a section from earlier in the song the next option is to write a new third or fourth section. If the bridge/middle-eight has a vocal, then the solo might bring in chords previously unused, or have a new chord progression, possibly in a different key. If you use a key-change, think through how this section will connect with a return of the verse or the chorus if they are in the original key – sometimes they might come back in a new key of their own to avoid a feeling of let-down. This partly depends on which direction the modulation takes. Moving 'flatwards' from the home key can give a feeling of a drop in intensity, or a darkening; moving 'sharpwards', there is a brightening and a rise of tension (the reason why so many popular songs modulate up by a tone).

A solo's characteristics and function change as it occurs at these different points in a song.

THE INTRO SOLO

- helps establish an atmosphere and stylistic intention for the track
- reinforces the home key
- may grab the listener's attention by its sound or phrasing or melody
- creates anticipation by delaying the vocal entry
- if unaccompanied, delays both the harmony and the vocal entry.

The Temptations 'Just My Imagination' has a lead phrase on the intro, played three times in the first 13 seconds. The intro is rounded off with backing vocal harmony until 0:24 when the verse starts. B. B. King starts 12-bar songs such as 'Every Day I Sing The Blues', 'You Upset Me Baby', and 'Paying The Cost To Be The Boss' with a 12-bar solo. The Strawbs' 'Lay Down' has an effective short melodic intro solo. The Who's 'Who Are You' starts with a short blues solo accompanied by synth chords – a striking blend of genres – and 'How Many Friends' begins in F major with a short solo that uses the F mixolydian scale with an additional lowered third during its four phrases. The House Of Love's 'Shine On' begins with a distinctive repeated lead guitar phrase reprised with minor changes after the second chorus and bridge. David Bowie's 'The Prettiest Star' (*Aladdin Sane*, 1973) opens with a short guitar solo by Mick Ronson until the vocal comes in at 0:18. Ronson reprises this solo at 2:06 and then extends it (2:22-38), changing position with a glorious swoop at 2:26.

SECTION 3

The intro to Alice Cooper's 'No More Mr Nice Guy' signals the rebellious theme of the song with a six-bar solo after four riffs. Python Lee Jackson (Rod Stewart) opens 'In A Broken Dream' with an anguished, fuzzy guitar solo. Fleetwood Mac's 'Need Your Love So Bad' begins with an instrumental verse with a lead solo that lasts about 40 seconds. The first 35 seconds of Chris Isaak's 'Wicked Game' are dominated by a reverb and echo guitar using tremolo arm for the vibrato, which establishes the early 1960s references (ie, Roy Orbison). This solo returns after the second chorus. Wishbone Ash's 'Errors Of My Way' has the note F♯ held for 15 seconds, forming varying degrees of tension or consonance against the E minor progression underneath.

On Cast's 'Walk Away', after the acoustic guitar intro, there is a brief clean and reverby lead guitar (0:30-42) that precedes the first verse and helps to establish the reflective atmosphere. This lead guitar continues adding fills to the verses and chorus hook. It takes a full solo at 1:54-2:18, using a short ascending two-note idea and echo. The focus then shifts to the acoustic guitar. The Hollies' 'The Air That I Breathe' comes in with a guitar bend and turns into two lead guitars playing slow trills with flanging. At 2:09-20 there is another short, lyrical guitar solo with a single lead. The chord change goes from E to Em coming out of the chorus, the lead guitar coming in on the second beat, the vocal harmony held across it. The solo is repeated between the last two choruses. At 2:20-31 it is succeeded by an orchestral passage where the main melody is taken by French horns.

A pure form of the intro solo is one that doesn't repeat anywhere else later in the song, either melodically or harmonically or both, as with Mott The Hoople's 'All The Young Dudes'. Another distinctive form of intro solo is when a track starts with a single instrument, like the 34 seconds of solo piano on the intro of Al Stewart's 'Year Of The Cat'. A single instrument can set the entire context, and can possibly be self-contained enough to be a focus of interest as opposed to setting the scene for something that is happening. If the intro solo is extended, it can become a prelude to the main song, as in the case of the dramatic piano intro for the teen-tragedy of The Boomtown Rats' 'I Don't Like Mondays'.

SOLO BEFORE / AFTER THE FIRST CHORUS

A solo before the first chorus can function as a delaying tactic, so that when the chorus is reached it is more dramatic. The solo here becomes a substitute chorus – almost as though there are two choruses side by side. The solo might offer a musical comment on the issues staked out by the lyric in verse one. If the solo is after the first chorus, it can function as a link, a way of returning to the verse, but with more melodic interest than a link. It can combine with a link where there is a riff. If the chorus has changed key, this solo can also serve the purpose of returning to the key of the verse. The melody of the solo can act as a way of leading the modulation, rather than relying on the chord progression to do it.

At 1:00-07 of The Darkness's 'I Believe In A Thing Called Love', a brief solo is squeezed in which has a couple of harmonised phrases. This keeps the music full of event, before the return of the verse. There's no post-chorus sag. The main solo comes at 1:52-2:22, using pentatonic major phrases and taking advantage of the key of E major to put in some resonant open strings. There is a third solo break toward the end where you can hear trilling off the top string onto the open E from 3:00-06, ending on a very high note. Alice Cooper's 'No More Mr Nice Guy' has a second eight-bar solo on a link after the first chorus bringing in a pre-chorus, and replacing the second verse, an effective bit of song structure editing. The Who's 'Relay' has an extended solo before the second verse (1:17-56) which is far more than a link, but a full solo section. The band's 'Dreaming From The Waist' has a short solo (1:54-2:01) that effectively links to the second verse.

SOLO BEFORE THE SECOND CHORUS

If this is the first solo of the song it functions as a way to avoid the predictability of the second chorus arriving straight after the second verse. The harmonised lead break at 1:47-2:04 in Led Zeppelin's 'Ramble On' works brilliantly in terms of delaying the second chorus, increasing the anticipation.

SOLO AFTER THE SECOND CHORUS

This is a very common place to find a solo. Here it can function as a link to, or substitute for, a vocal bridge/middle-eight. In contrast to when a solo comes after chorus one, there is a sense here that it is possible for the song to go in a new direction. The Turin Brakes have a very sudden cut from the second chorus of 'Painkiller (Summer Rain)' to an A pentatonic minor guitar solo which contrasts with the rich E major chording of the chorus. The backing is sparse at this point, with almost no harmony; it is reduced to bass and percussion. The Eagles' 'New Kid In Town' is an example of an eight-bar solo after chorus two.

SOLO AFTER A VOCAL BRIDGE / MIDDLE-EIGHT

This type of solo is often set up by the new material – either musically, lyrically or both – which a vocal bridge uses. The solo then acts as a point of release, going further than the voice has gone with this new outlook. If it has a dramatic, high rising end this can either lead straight to a chorus, or a cliff-hanging moment of quiet where the volume goes right down and then the verse returns.

The Beatles' 'Day Tripper' has a 12-bar solo after its second chorus, where the solo is played over a B chord with a crescendo approach to a return of the riff and then verse three and chorus three. The solo on Thin Lizzy's 'Don't Believe A Word' is cleverly sandwiched between two short bridges, the song consisting of a riff and a verse but no separate chorus. The solo is played over the verse progression. Their 'Soldier Of Fortune' comes to a stop after its second chorus and then a martial-sounding snare-drum beat leads a tattoo section for the guitar with one single phrase harmonised. This section is at a slower tempo to the rest of the song.

S E C T I O N 3

SOLO BEFORE THE LAST CHORUS

This is similar to putting a first solo before the second chorus but creates a more powerful delay because having reached this late in the song the listener is no longer expecting a solo. The Who's 'Baba O'Riley' has a four-bar guitar solo (3:06-20) which links to the final choruses. Like the solo before a second chorus, it increases anticipation. In this instance the dramatic effect is heightened by the drums dropping out for this short break. This lead guitar continues behind the vocal.

SOLO BETWEEN REPETITIONS OF THE FINAL CHORUSES

Songs often end with multiple choruses. It is relatively easy to make one of these choruses instrumental and put a solo over it. The Vapors' 'Turning Japanese' does this between 2:54-3:15 where a twin-lead guitar break happens during the last choruses. Alternatively, you can combine a solo with a vocal chorus by having them going at the same time. The lead instrument could double the vocal melody, harmonise it, or play variations and answer phrases around it.

CODA SOLOS – SHORT

When the last chorus vocals have ended, a song reaches its coda (literally the 'tail' of the song). This might be a repetition of the chorus as instrumental or earlier sections of the song such as the intro or verse. This can be a good point for a solo. The coda is a place where things can be let loose. The discipline and demands of the song structure have been largely satisfied, and a solo can express a certain informality and relief, and perhaps a sense of transcendence of whatever the song has posited.

Examples of short coda solos include those on Jimi Hendrix's 'Little Wing' and Roxy Music's 'Street Life'. There's a solo from bass and organ on the coda of Deep Purple's 'Smoke On The Water'. At 2:24, Led Zeppelin's 'Immigrant Song' is so short there's no room for a solo on the studio version, but live Page would add a solo to the coda, as can be heard on *BBC Sessions* and *How The West Was Won*. Jefferson Airplane's 'Somebody To Love' has a coda solo from 2:25-56 (ie, to the end of the track) which is about one-sixth of the entire track. The second solo in Oasis's 'Live Forever' happens in the coda over an Am-F. It enters on a bend (3:46-4:30 end), each phrase punctuated by a three-note descending phrase. The coda of Tom Petty's 'American Girl' has a two-note phrase played over D-E-G-A twice, which then turns into fast triplet pull-offs to the fade at about 3:28.

A short guitar solo can function as a link from the last chorus into a vocal coda, as happens on David Bowie's 'Time'. The last chorus begins at 2:41, and after once round the progression, Mick Ronson's lead guitar enters at 2:55, at first playing spaced intervals and then breaking into a lyrical counter-melody which intensifies the emotion of the vocal before coming centre stage from 3:20-56.

CODA SOLOS – LONG

In some songs a coda is stretched out quite considerably. Long coda solos can take a precisely arranged form, as with The Eagles' 'Hotel California', or they can have an improvisatory quality, as with Prince's 'Purple Rain'. For a 1960s freak-out coda solo try Love's 'Your Mind And We Belong Together' (2:40-4:18), which takes up almost the last third of the track. A famous example is Lynyrd Skynyrd's 'Free Bird' where the guitar solo coda starts at 4:56 over a four-bar chord progression. It has two lead guitars, which mostly coincide but sometimes deviate, and many bars of repeat licks. Fading out at around nine minutes, the solo at the end of 'Free Bird' lasts almost half the song's length. It developed so singer Ronnie Van Zant could have a break, and was extended to make the song longer in concert. By the time of the 1976 live album, *One More From the Road*, 'Free Bird' lasted up to 13 minutes.

In the Isley Brothers' 'Summer Breeze' there is a solo just before the last hook-line from 3:50-4:16 that features gargling notes via the tremolo arm. At 4:16 the solo takes off in a high-pitched flowing style with many bends, just as the guitar had on their hit 'Who's That Lady'. It pretty much stays in one high position with many repeat licks until the track ends at 6:05, so the last third of the song has a guitar solo. A similar effect is achieved on David Bowie's 'Moonage Daydream' where Mick Ronson plays a solo on the coda, which consists of long sustained notes until the fade. Hurricane #1's 'Step Into My World' has a long solo that occupies the second half of the song from 2:43 to the end of the track at 4:58. There are two lead guitars that sometimes coincide and then move apart. Led Zeppelin's 'Sick Again' has a middle solo and a coda solo.

Two Roxy Music songs show just how expressive a coda solo can be, albeit in different ways. 'In Every Dream Home A Heartache' pauses for a moment, during which Bryan Ferry delivers the punch-line of the entire lyric, and then Phil Manzanera delivers a rip-snorting freak-out guitar solo which is an art-glam tribute to Hendrix. This solo is played over a progression not used before in the song. His guitar is phased, but after the track's false fade-out the music returns with the whole band going through the phasing effect. By contrast, after two verses and choruses, 'More Than This' (lasting 4:12) reaches a long instrumental coda at 2:52 using the verse progression. Manzanera shows amazing self-control in confining his lead guitar to only an occasional phrase, showing that such a coda need not have a spotlit soloist. This extended coda is all about atmosphere.

There are extended coda solos by David Gilmour on Pink Floyd's 'Another Brick In The Wall' and 'Comfortably Numb'; in the former, the solo adds something that neither the melody nor the vocals have spelt out, perhaps a sense of regret or loss. Few coda solos are as dramatic as Jimi Hendrix's 'House Burning Down' where, after

> *Fading out at around nine minutes, the solo at the end of 'Free Bird' lasts almost half the song's length. It developed so singer Ronnie Van Zant could have a break, and was extended to make the song longer in concert.*

playing some blues-rock lead, the guitar is suddenly isolated to describe the spaceship mentioned in the lyric flitting backwards, forwards, near and far in the stereo image.

Coda solos can also re-balance the emotional content of a song by offering an extra statement, perhaps with a different solo instrument. Aztec Camera's 'Somewhere In My Heart' has a saxophone coda solo. Bruce Springsteen's 'Thunder Road' has a Duane Eddy-style lead guitar paired with saxophone. There's also saxophone on the coda of 'Dancing In The Dark', offering consolation after the bleakness of the main lyric.

HOW DO YOU WRITE A SOLO?

"One way is to conceive what it is you want to accomplish – you hear it in your head before you record it. That's a technical way of going about it. Then there's the absolute spontaneity of a first take – not locking into anything, but just going for the magic of what happens when you really nail something." (Joe Walsh, *Guitar Player*, April 1988.)

The short answer is that you don't necessarily write a guitar solo; you could *play* it rather than write it. Some solos are improvised completely, some are developed during the recording process, and some are planned carefully beforehand. There are pros and cons to each approach. The improvised solo has the possibility of a greater sense of risk and danger, but the planned solo may win on the basis of the ideas.

The composed solo
There are various advantages to planning a solo in advance. On the large scale, it provides an opportunity for lateral thinking, so you can identify what the obvious approach would be and then try to invent something less predictable. It makes it easier to alter the backing progression's length, chords, or rhythm before you record and to work out how to tackle awkward chords and transitions, etc. Ritchie Blackmore's solo on Deep Purple's 'Highway Star' was written note for note before it was recorded, partly because he wanted it to sound baroque. Kirk Hammett worked out the first and last solos on Metallica's 'One' in advance of recording.

The improvised solo
Playing a solo at its most spontaneous means improvising to the backing track. Cue the solo section, press record, wait a bar or so (however long you need to feel the tempo and sense where you are musically) and then play the first thing that comes to you. You can prepare for this to some extent either by thinking beforehand about what you want to play or at least working out some elements – like how to begin and end, leaving the rest to chance and inspiration. This is less pure than the wholly unplanned first take.

If you're lucky and/or a good player, and sufficiently in tune with the song as a whole, this may give you something inspired straight away. When Robby Krieger played the solo on 'Light My Fire' (*The Doors*, 1967) he only had two tries at it and the album version was edited for the single. To get attuned I recommend listening to the song from the very beginning, rather than starting a few bars before you begin the solo. It may take a couple of minutes to reach the point where the solo will go but it is time well spent because it helps internalise the song's feeling. The tension of waiting for the solo to come up can also provide a little edge.

The special quality of the 'first take' solo is that it is unselfconscious and largely intuitive. It often has a sense of danger because the player may be on the edge of his or her technique, in terms of the gap between what they can invent and the speed necessary to know how to execute it. First-take solos can also have a sense of discovery, because the player does not know what is going to happen. Elliott Randall's lead on Steely Dan's 'Reelin' In The Years' (*Can't Buy A Thrill*, 1972) was a single, continuous take. Randall said, "The whole solo just came to me, and I feel very fortunate to have been given the opportunity to play it."

Looking back on his early Sun Records solos for Elvis Presley's sessions, Scotty Moore commented "... they were all completely off the cuff. I never sat down and played the same thing twice. You might get a bass riff or something, as a hook for the song, but the songs were strictly *ad lib*. Even now I'll go back and I can't play note for note what I played then; I can get the general feel of it but I can never go back and hit it note for note." (*Guitar*, November 1992.)

Record producers have often sought this sense of spontaneity by asking the guitarist to run through a few times to set tone and levels, cunningly not mentioning that they've pushed the record button. In this well-known studio scenario, the guitarist tells the control room, "OK, that's fine, I'm ready now," only to get the reply, "Thanks, that's great, you're done." This happened with the slide work on 'Rocky Mountain Way', where Joe Walsh thought he was warming up and they were only setting levels, when he was actually being recorded. The first take was the one that was used.

Sometimes the thing to do to get round a block is to stop thinking about a solo and just play. When Randy Rhoads worked on a solo for Ozzy Osbourne's track 'Mr. Crowley', for the 1981 *Blizzard of Oz* album, he tried for hours and got nowhere. Ozzy told him that everything he was playing was rubbish and sent him back in with the instruction to "play how he felt". He did a take, and when he listened to the playback both he and Ozzy felt it was a great solo. However, it should be pointed out that Rhoads had considerable technical knowledge and years of experience as a player and teacher. All this was at the service of his intuition and could be thus drawn on spontaneously.

A similar thing happened to Freddie Stewart during the recording of Sly & The Family Stone's album *Stand!* (1969). Stewart had rehearsed a solo but in the studio spent up to four hours trying unsuccessfully to play it. His bandleader stepped in and told him to go home, sleep, and come back the next day. The break enabled him to forget the ideas he had rehearsed but that didn't work, and he played something fresh that did.

Sometimes the right guitar sound/effect for the mood of the track provides inspiration in itself. When Kirk Hammett was recording the solos on 'One' from *And Justice For All* (1988) he decided on a clean tone for the intro solo, and once it was found on an ADA preamp he got the right ideas quickly.

First takes are also likely to have extraneous noises, mistakes, wrong notes, phrases where the timing is slightly off, etc. If you get a good one that is 95 per cent right, these days digital technology can tidy it up. Unlike in the days of analogue recording, you don't even have to live with the mistakes. Your next step might be to repeat the process several more times, without listening to the earlier takes.

SECTION 3

The composite solo

"Being a producer helps – I tend to make decisions as I go. If there are five tracks of a particular solo, I'll wipe the tracks I don't like. If it sounds good, you have to go with it, or you'll be forever going round in circles." (John Paul Jones, December 1999.)

Modern recording technology makes it easy to copy the best phrases from a number of takes and make a single composite solo. David Gilmour of Pink Floyd used this on 'Comfortably Numb': "I banged out five or six solos. From there I just followed my usual procedure, which is to listen back to each solo and make a chart, noting which bits are good. Then, by following the chart, I create one great composite solo by whipping one fader up, then another fader, jumping from phrase to phrase until everything flows together." Notice that Gilmour describes here a process of creating the composite in real time at the mixing desk. With digital technology this can now be done with copy and paste.

One further step is to learn this composite and then re-record it in one take, which may smooth out any differences in tone and phrasing that a composite might have. As Kirk Hammett told *Guitar World* in October 1994, "On *Metallica* I recorded six or seven different guitar solos for almost every song, took the best aspects of each solo, mapped out a master solo, and made a composite. Then I learned how to play the composite solo, tightened it up and replayed it for the final version." When Eric Johnson recorded his Grammy award-winning 'Cliffs Of Dover' (*Ah Via Musicom*, 1990), the solo ended up being a composite of many guitar takes, even including some played on a Gibson 335 and some on a Fender Strat. Despite the obvious change in tone, he decided to leave it as it was.

Recording Megadeth's *Youthanasia*, guitarist Marty Friedman tended to improvise in the studio, get a basic idea, then revise each part of it, polishing what had originally been spontaneous ideas. Producer Eddie Kramer once said that, contrary to his freewheeling image, Jimi Hendrix more often than not had carefully planned what he was going to play before a recording session. This was true of 'All Along The Watchtower', for example.

Whether you improvise or plan solos, there is a further question of when in the process of making an album the solos should be done. When bands make records there is a decision about whether to record all the solos in one go or do them track by track. I think most of the time leaving them all to the end is not the best approach because then the soloist has to come up with great ideas again and again. It is easy to end up repeating yourself. It's probably better to record one solo at a time while you're tuned into the particular vibe of a song.

THE SOLO AS NARRATIVE

"If you're playing a solo, start off with something simple and let it build, let it crescendo and let it resolve." (Gary Moore, *Guitarist*, Summer 2004.)

Whether you are planning or improvising, one way of thinking about a solo is via the metaphor of narrative. Seen in this light, making up a solo is like writing a story. A story has a beginning that grabs the reader's attention and presents a riddle or problem, something that must be answered or figured out. The story proceeds with a series of events, some expected, some not. The pace of events may slow or quicken; there may be a rising sense of conflict, and conflict creates drama. Out of that drama comes the possibility of an exciting climax and a need for resolution. The challenge for the soloist is to find the musical vocabulary to achieve this, and also to consider how this narrative matches that told by the lyric, for songs already have a story that is partially told by the lyric.

STARTING A SOLO

A solo should make an impact – grab people's attention. There are various ways to achieve this and not all of them have to do with the soloist. Think of a spotlight on a stage. It could be turned on first and the soloist could step into it. In a song this would mean that the musical context changes before the solo starts. This could be achieved by:

- a key change
- a chord that has not been used
- a distinctive rhythm motif
- a rise or fall in dynamics
- a change in the arrangement
- a drum fill
- a sudden stop
- a vocal cue
- a sound-effect
- a pre-solo phrase, such as a rising or falling scale.

Aerosmith's 'Cryin'' has a brief solo at 2:44-58 that features an abrupt change of key and a brief pause which demarcates the entry of the lead guitar. It also has a brief harmonica solo over the instrumental chorus, which is then joined by lead guitar, and the lead continues during the vocal return in this last chorus. As the song fades the vocal is pulled back from the chorus and the lead guitar comes back to the fore.

Some guitar solos start with an arresting noise. This could be a fast phrase, a bend whose pitch is varied, an unusual guitar effect, a pick-scrape, a chord, or coming in very high, as is the case with the solo on Starship's 'Jane' (2:07-39), where the second phrase is a flurry of notes. This solo ends on its highest note, which blends with the high note of the vocal re-entry. The coda sees the return of the lead guitar playing in between the vocal reiteration of the title.

Dodgy's homage to The Who, 'In A Room', has a short dramatic solo with an attention-grabbing pre-bend on the second note, reached by an unexpected drop of almost a sixth from the first note. Pre-bends are often attention-grabbing because in the vocabulary of lead guitar we are used to hearing notes bending up in pitch, rather than going down. The solo on Patti Smith's 'Because The Night' (1978) starts with rapid picking of a single note at 1:52-2:08 and finishes with a distinct syncopated ascending scale.

Adding a guitar effect to the solo may be enough in itself to provide a memorable

SECTION 3

start. Jimmy Page's solo on Led Zeppelin's 'In The Evening' (*In Through The Out Door*, 1979) starts with a highly depressed tremolo arm that is suddenly released, making a springy bang of crazy rising pitches (at 3:43 and 4:01) during the solo which lasts to 4:21.

'Black Magic Woman' by Fleetwood Mac has a long middle solo coming after two verses, ie, twice through a 12-bar. It is memorably introduced by a sustained high minor triad ghosted in with volume pot and reverb.

Another effective musical device is to repeat a phrase near the beginning of a solo, a good way of drawing people in because it gives them the feeling they can follow what's going on. Starting with a melodic phrase obviously derived from the vocals also has the virtue of familiarity, as does using a melodic fragment from a famous (but preferably out of copyright) tune.

BASIC SOLO IDEAS

Once you commence the solo you can draw on a range of musical techniques to develop its opening idea. These include

- straight repetition of phrases
- repeat licks – in a single position
- repeat licks moving diatonically (in key) or chromatically (out of key)
- repetition with variant endings
- constructing phrases on aaab, a1a2a3b, abab, a1b1a2b2 patterns
- transposition of phrases by octave up or down
- transposition of phrases by intervals that match chord changes
- contrasting major pentatonic phrases with equivalent pentatonic minor ones
- shaping the solo as a climb from low to high pitch, or high to low to high
- cascade runs – harmonised or single (or with echo)
- using a dynamic curve from soft to loud, or loud-softer-loud
- playing lots of notes
- playing very few notes (the minimal solo)
- using call and answer phrases, including at the octave
- using call and answer phrases with another lead guitar or second solo instrument
- working with rhythm ideas.

Many of these ideas are illustrated in Sections 8-11. If the solo is played with a repetitive riff backing, if the gaps are big enough between the riffs the lead phrases can go in those gaps (an example would be Mountain's hard rock classic 'Mississippi Queen'). Conversely, a lead phrase could be answered by a few beats of chordal playing, as on All About Eve's 'Tuesday's Child' (*Scarlet And Other Stories*, 1990), where lead phrases are fitted in between the arpeggiated chords of the chorus.

Phrases answer phrases. Ascending answers descending and vice versa. A phrase can be inverted around a central pitch. A phrase can contrast a bent note with the same pitch fretted normally. Short-value phrases contrast with long note-values.

Phrases start in different positions in the bar, including offbeats. The same phrase can be played first on the beat and then syncopated. Phrases can be repeated wholesale at a higher or lower octave and then subjected to slight variation. A phrase can be transposed up a fourth for chord IV from I. The Cult's 'Wild Flower' has a solo (2:08-2:35) that concludes with a call-and-answer octave transposition idea. The Manic Street Preachers' 'La Tristesse Durera' has a solo that includes several examples of a phrase being answered at the octave (2:29-34, 2:42-46).

Dynamics are always important. Guitar solos are associated with louder dynamics – the high, screaming note idea. But the listener can be seduced and drawn in by playing at a softer level. This is especially effective in ballad material. Two examples are Eric Clapton's solo on 'Bell-Bottom Blues' and Ryan Adams's solo toward the end of 'Harder Now It's Over'.

Repetition with variation is a good rule for solos. Try an A phrase with four different answers (A B1 A B2 A B3 A B4). Answering phrases can be contrasted by additional colour such as palm muting or, if there is time, a change of pickup or the switching-on of an effect. Staccato is relevant, compared to legato playing. Never be afraid of repeating a phrase – it gives the listener the pleasure of recognition.

PHRASING IDEAS

Transposition and sequence
This is where a short phrase is transposed up or down in pitch with its basic shape kept intact, in a kind of melodic development. It also incorporates pushing the phrase into a new key, with or without the addition of the necessary accidentals. The Strokes' 'Alone, Together' uses the idea of alternating two notes and pushing this up or down (2:30-50), having started with fourths on the top two strings. Motorhead's 'Ace Of Spades' has a frenetic solo on blues scales in three parts (1:32-52) on the chords Ab-Bb-Ab, the scale being transposed (the band detuned a semitone). Bruce Springsteen's 'Adam Raised A Cain' uses the technique of answering a lead phrase in a different octave at 2:12-2:22.

AAAB / ABAB phrasing
In this phrasing, an initial idea is played three times and then answered by something new, or two ideas alternate. The guitar solo on The Skids' 'Into The Valley' uses the 3+1 formula twice, with the second '1' at a higher octave and changed. From 1:07-23 the solo on The Beatles' 'Drive My Car' uses the 3+1 formula: the first three phrases the same, the fourth different and rising and played by slide.

The minimal solo
"... Eddie Van Halen can pretty much play circles around anybody existing. But Albert King can blow him away with two notes. I have nothing but respect for Eddie; I can't even comprehend what he does. But why would anyone want to play like that? After two or three solos, it's a blur." (Joe Walsh, *Guitar Player*, April 1988.)

Rock critics have sometimes joked about guitarists who allegedly play one-note

SECTION 3

guitar solos. Is this possible? As a 1960s session guitarist, Jimmy Page did what was effectively a two-note solo on Tom Jones's 'It's Not Unusual'. A solo made of only a couple of notes can work. Guitarists such as Leslie West and Paul Kossoff squeezed as much as they could from a few notes, and as a lead player Bruce Springsteen likes to worry away at a couple of notes in one or two positions. Playing a good solo doesn't mean you have to play lots of notes.

Speaking to *Guitar Player* in December 1994, Walter Becker of Steely Dan described the idea for his solo on 'Cringemaker', from *11 Tracks Of Whack*, as "like what you'd hear on an old Chess record where the guy found a good note on his guitar that day and just wailed away on it from beginning to end. There are so many great guitarists who can play a million notes on something. You can't make a striking impression by doing that anymore. It's almost easier to get people's attention by doing less. It's so much fun to play this blues lick. Why play anything else when you find one that really fits?" Or maybe three of the same note might be enough, as Guitar Gable does in Slim Harpo's 'I'm A King Bee'.

The most celebrated example of a minimal guitar solo is Neil Young's 'Cinnamon Girl'. For almost four bars it stays on the note D – actually a unison because the song is in double drop-D tuning (DADGBD) so you hear the D fretted at the third fret second string plus the open top string. The notes C and B sneak in just before the riff. It works because the chords move through D5-Am-C-G and the harmony thus changes the single note. Peter Buck of R.E.M. told *Guitar* (USA) in January 1993 that "I love Neil Young solos – they're not technically flashy but they're so powerful and non-clichéd."

Elvis Costello's 'I Want You' has a solo consisting of two notes an augmented fourth apart, melodramatically expressing the psychotic tension in the lyric. Buzzcocks' 'Boredom' has a two-note solo playing E and B, the first and fifth of the scale, repeatedly, ending on an out-of-key B♭. The coda solo in T. Rex's 'Baby Strange' is based on four notes, as are those in 'Raw Ramp / Electric Boogie' and 'Mambo Sun'. The Beatles' 'Back In The USSR' has an eight-bar solo over the chord sequence I-IV-♭III-IV – using a four-bar phrase and repeating it. R.E.M.'s 'The One I Love' has a minimal solo after the second chorus, a phrase played three times and then extended and answered. It has no bends and uses E pentatonic minor (1:46-2:01). Coldplay's 'Lost!' has a guitar solo based on a two-bar phrase played four times with a drone note at 2:23-45 just before a chorus. In 'Violet Hill', after the second chorus, the guitar solo at 2:13-37 consists of a one-bar phrase eight times over the verse sequence. Bruce Springsteen's 'Candy's Room' opens with a single phrase played four times against four different chords, so each chord gives the phrase a different quality.

Other minimal solos include The Lemonheads' 'The Great Big No', Lloyd Cole & The Commotions' 'Perfect Skin', The Ramones' 'I Wanna Be Sedated', and Buzzcocks' 'Boredom'. The coda guitar solo freak-out on Love's 'A House Is Not A

There are so many great guitarists who can play a million notes on something. You can't make a striking impression by doing that anymore. It's almost easier to get people's attention by doing less.

Motel' begins with the guitars playing only D and E notes. Slade's 'Mama Weer All Crazee Now' has a solo after the second chorus of a single bent-note phrase at 2:00-03 leading straight into verse three. Norman Greenbaum's 'Spirit In The Sky' at 2:00-15 has a simple distorted low-pitched solo using five notes and contained within a fifth – heavy emphasis on the flattened seventh in A. At 3:18 there is a sequence of four unison bends on G which develops into a slow phrased pentatonic minor solo in A to the fade.

The MC5 cover of 'Tutti Frutti' (1970) has a guitar solo over one 12-bar from 0:44-58 which is an interesting variation on a 1950s rock'n'roll solo with a descending single note line to get to bar five's chord change. The entire track hardly lasts 90 seconds. 'Teenage Lust' has an interesting solo that ends with two unison bends (1:16-33) where a single phrase is repeated with slight changes and an answering phrase.

Talking about the solos on 'Don't Stop' and 'The Chain', Lindsey Buckingham told *Guitar* in September 1992, "… you can get a lot of rhythm going within one note, by leaving it for about as long as you can".

Draw on the vocal melody

Some solos can develop by taking phrases from the vocal melody. On The Doors' 'Love Her Madly' at 2:30-56 the electric guitar takes a solo based on the vocal melody, developing a two-note motif. Springsteen's 'Further On (Up The Road)' uses part of the vocal melody for the solo.

THE SOLO AS DUET

A solo can use two distinct guitar sounds. The entire solo section might also consist of two short solos back-to-back. Ozzy Osbourne's 'Shot In The Dark' (song duration 4:16, solo 0:32 at 2:34-3:06) has a 16-bar solo split between two guitar sounds. The first solo is eight bars of overdriven slide over a new chord change of C-Bb. This is arpeggio-based. Then the lead plays scale-based fast runs in A minor over a descending bass riff line for eight bars. The last two phrases feature tremolo-picking and the solo finishes on its highest note. The initial impact of the second solo is the change of tone, bending, and speed.

Bryan Adams' 'It's Only Love' starts with a solo (0:12-32, eight bars on F pentatonic major) after one riff and is played over two of the riff. The second solo of four bars returns after verse two (0:50-1:00); the third solo comes at 1:19-37, and then there's a bridge. The riff returns after a pause. At 2:10 the guitar starts alternating phrases with the two voices. There's a final solo at 2:46 to the end. It is an interesting example of a song that is punctuated by soloing from the start.

Queen's 'Who Wants To Live Forever?' (song duration 3:54, solo 0:26 at 2:08-34) has an eight-bar solo in E minor. The backing sequence is new for the song, changing Em-C four times. The solo starts, with subtle playing, increasing the drama by adding more notes but not much dynamic lift and ending with a chord. For the first lead phrases there are three repeating counterpoint phrases.

U2's 'The Fly' (song duration 4:26, solo 0:40 at 2:27-3:07) has a solo where The Edge dirties up his original sound. It lasts 18 bars, with its backing at first based on the riff and then the chorus chord sequence. It uses wah and echo on a falling E major scale. Because the vocal is half-spoken during the verse, the lead solo is a kind of outburst.

'Black Magic Woman' by Fleetwood Mac has a long two-part solo in the middle coming after two verses, ie, twice through the 12-bar (0:58-1:42); the first part is quite high-pitched, and second time round the 12-bar more reverb is added. At 2:08 the tempo goes into double-time for the vocal coda, the guitar playing answers to the vocal. Santana's version of the same song has a guitar to start the song, which lasts 40 seconds, and then a further one as it traverses the verse progression that ends at 1:07. At this point the electric piano has a solo.

ENDING A SOLO

"Once I know where I'm going to end up, I think backwards: how long do I have to develop the solo? Gradually I think back to the beginning, and then I just go for it. Since I know where it's going to end up, it doesn't really matter where I start as long as the solo develops." (Joe Walsh, *Guitar Player*, April 1988.)

The ending of a solo is important, both in terms of how it completes the solo, and how it connects with the remaining part of the song. Sometimes a solo requires a few bars to wind down or sustain over before the progression of the next section can proceed. On 'Don't Stop' by Fleetwood Mac, the lead solo after the second chorus (1:33-53) requires an elongation of the final chords to create dynamism and tension. The standard way to end a solo is to put the highest notes at the end. A solo that puts the highest notes early on can give itself a tough challenge to whip up the drama a second time. This often bedevils extended live solos, where there can be a feeling of anti-climax after the first batch of high notes if they are right at the top of the fretboard.

David Bowie's 'Space Oddity' has a solo at 2:42-3:02, introduced by a squirt of Stylophone. It consists of clearly-defined clean guitar phrases, detached and unhurried, out of this world. The very last phrase ends the solo on a weird noise caused by a detuned last note. A similar solo is played over the coda starting at 4:14, ending on a high repeatedly picked note and then a pick slide. Also worth hearing is Mick Ronson's short solo from 1:26-41 on 'Life On Mars'. This has very distinctive phrases, including double-tracking, wide interval skips, and a chromatic ending – approaching the resolution note by semitones. It also shows the contrast of ascending and descending phrases.

THREE DIMENSIONS OF THE SOLO

Another perspective with which to approach the solo is to consider solos as having a melodic, harmonic and rhythmic dimension.

The melodic dimension
The melodic aspect of a solo is its hummability. Many players talk about whether you can sing a solo and say that this is a useful test of its success as a melody. The prime

element is to shape the solo so that it has a strong tune. This may explicitly recall the melody of the song or develop out of it. It is good practice to attempt to hear the solo melody before you play it, rather than moving on a pattern and allowing your fingers to dictate what you play. Fretting up and down a string rather than across the fretboard can help this. Factors that help to make a solo melodic include:

- a powerful reciprocal interaction with the harmony
- partial use of arpeggio ideas
- ensuring scale-patterns are obviously subservient to the melody
- avoiding obvious guitar licks and patterns
- sparing use of guitar effects
- some wide interval leaps
- clearly defined phrases, and variation of phrase.

The harmonic dimension

This is the aspect of solos that most players probably think about more than any other, partly because it relates to the fear of playing a wrong note in a given progression. The harmonic aspect of a solo comprises:

- the underlying chords
- whether the solo will fit those chords
- what those chords do to the soloist's notes on this scale or that.

In many songwriting situations a single scale in a couple of positions on the fretboard is enough to carry the solo through the chord changes. If the chord progression features any non-diatonic or altered chords, then adjustments to the scale may be needed at those points. This could require a change of scale, or possibly just the alteration of a bend from a semitone to a tone. These altered chords could include 'reverse polarity' or 'flat degree' chords, chromatic chords, or chords that are in key but have altered notes such as the flat fifth, etc. A key change in the middle of a solo would also require additional notes.

The most useful scales are the major, the mixolydian (major scale with a flattened seventh), the aeolian (natural minor) and dorian (natural minor with a raised sixth), the harmonic minor, the melodic minor, and the pentatonic major and minor with their respective blues scales. To determine what scales are needed for a given chord sequence, check for any non-diatonic chord (out of key) or altered chord. Any chord that is diatonic will be covered by a major or pentatonic major scale, assuming the key is major. More details of this are given in Section Seven. The simpler a chord sequence, the easier it is to play over, but it can be harder to play something memorable. A chord sequence with a few unusual chords and changes is harder to play over but offers opportunities for striking melodic turns.

The harmonic dimension also refers to the rate of movement of the chords, their sequence, and whether important chords are displaced or withheld (these songwriting techniques are described in detail in *The Songwriting Sourcebook*). For example, what is described in that book as a turnaround – a four-chord sequence like C-Dm-F-G that is repeated a number of times – might call for a different approach;

or the energy of it might suggest some soloing ideas. The displaced chord sequence, which comes in on a less expected chord (ie, not I or V) often has more forward movement than one that starts on I. Chord inversions can also affect solos, partly because they create movement but also by colouring the third of the chord if it is placed in the solo (ie, playing the note E over a C/E first inversion is not the same as playing over a root position C chord).

If you want this particular effect, harmony can be incorporated into a solo by playing:

- full chords
- double-stops and triads
- arpeggio figures
- consecutive thirds and sixths
- relevant open strings added to fretted notes.

Solos that make extensive use of these techniques can lay out the harmony fully enough that harmony instruments in the mix can be either reduced or removed altogether.

The rhythmic dimension

Of melody, harmony, and rhythm, it is the rhythmic dimension of a solo that is least thought about. Focusing on it means thinking about:

- the rhythmic value and effectiveness of phrases
- the duration of notes
- the use of accents and staccato
- which beats a phrase starts and ends on.

Rhythm can have considerable impact in itself, and attending to rhythm can give a soloist's lines greater force. If a solo lacks rhythmic tension it may be uninvolving. This has nothing to do with volume. An intense solo can be played quietly, not just loudly. But languid phrasing can disarm a phrase's melodic power. The rhythmic dimension of a solo is affected by tempo, the type of beat and also by time signature – it is much harder to play a solo in irregular time signatures.

Lead players concentrate too much on scales and not enough on the rhythm of what they play. Consider the use of triplet figures, including quarter-note triplets (six in a bar of 4/4). Play with rhythmic conviction – always know where you are in relation to the beat. If you fog it you will sound out of time and your lead will lose energy. A simple phrase played with conviction will be better than a complex phrase played out of time. Rory Gallagher once said he thought the solo "should bleed out of the rhythm parts".

When accentuating a solo's rhythmic element, the player should listen carefully to what the bass and drums are doing at that point. A solo can ride the rhythm of the song, take advantage of a riff, or duck and weave in the spaces in-between. An example of tying the solo into the drums is the guitar break in Led Zeppelin's 'I'm Gonna Crawl' (2:41-3:52). This Jimmy Page solo climaxes with a battering rhythm (3:30-45)

SECTION 3

where the guitar and drums are on the same heavily accented rhythmic figure.

First phrases in particular need to be considered in terms of where they are in the bar. The obvious beat is the first downbeat, but it can be effective to come in on the last beat of the previous bar, as happens for the first solo in Oasis's 'Live Forever' (at 1:46-2:31) after two choruses. The first phrase of the short guitar solo on Dodgy's 'In A Room' has great rhythmic value, an interval jump, and comes in on an offbeat (2:30-45). Each guitar phrase is punctuated by synth brass. It is preceded by a bridge that is dynamically below the level of the previous chorus, where the drums drop out, and has shifted key centre from the home key of A minor to A major. So the impact of the guitar solo is caused by a change of key, a jump in dynamic level and the satisfaction of a return to the song's main riff, last heard ending at 1:29.

HANDLING LINKS AND FILLS

Songs often have links – sections between vocals – where the soloist can play a few phrases. These fall short of directing the spotlight away from the central mood and material. Their character is different to the solo proper, as they seek to be complementary. Guitar fills are often played during a verse, inserted between vocal phrases, or sometimes even quietly underneath the vocal. A good fill can add interest to an arrangement without commanding the centre ground. In certain styles, putting in the right fills becomes part of how you build up a sense of that style – think of the sixths in Atlantic soul in the playing of Steve Cropper. These fills also add melodic interest, like those on the intro of Aretha Franklin's 'Respect', or throughout Robert Palmer's 'Barefootin''.

A short solo might constitute a link, though a pure link does not require any particular melodic material – rhythm and harmonic progression, or a riff, can be enough. A solo primarily introduces competing or new melodic material. One or two phrases add interest to a link. Take care these do not collide with the start or end of a vocal melody line. Some phrases can blend in underneath with the use of careful mixing. If such a link recurs enough times during a song it may reduce the need for a designated solo.

A good fill can add interest to an arrangement without commanding the centre ground.

SONGS WHERE THE GUITAR HAS EQUAL BILLING

As mentioned in Section One, there are some songs where the guitar takes equal billing with the singer, no longer confined to just a solo section about two-thirds of the way through, but weaving in and out of the entire track, or with significant melodic sections all to itself. Examples of this hybrid include Jimi Hendrix's 'Still Raining, Still Dreaming', Dire Straits' 'Sultans Of Swing', 'Brothers In Arms', and 'You And Your Friend', and Robert Plant's 'Big Log'. Throughout The Stone Roses' 'I Wanna Be Adored', the guitar has a major role. Long cascading pentatonic minor runs dominate the intro, with an octave counter-melody for the hook-line. Where there would have been a solo on the D-C chord change, the main guitar mostly plays chords (3:04-24), with a few lead phrases buried in the mix. The band's 'Ten Storey Love Song' also has the guitar playing a very prominent melodic role throughout. The lead guitar counterpoints the vocal melody, at times playing harmonies with it. The Who's 'How Many Friends' has a lead guitar woven throughout it. Pete Townshend tends to be more celebrated as a rhythm guitarist and a songwriter, but he has played many fine melodic lead breaks when the harmony he is playing over allows him to avoid the pentatonic minor, or play it against a non-blues chord progression.

Television's 'Marquee Moon' (10:36) is dominated by its lead guitar. The climax, just before the chorus hook-line, is taken by the guitar playing a scale phrase three times with an extension. The vocal then comes in. The first solo (2:58-3:15) has three phrases. There is then a third verse and chorus and then a long solo (4:52-9:11) that starts low down and slowly builds upward. It is remarkable that a new wave song should devote almost half its length to a guitar solo. Almost devoid of bends, it studiously avoids rock guitar clichés, drawing instead on the alternate 1960s guitar tradition that is not virtuosic. It goes into thirds toward the end, again building up until 8:13 where a stop rhythm riff enters. At 8:42-9:11 there is an attractive series of chords with chirruping lead phrases.

SOLOS AND OTHER INSTRUMENTS

The guitar is a good choice for playing a solo – but it's not the only option. Maybe another instrument will suit the song better.

SECTION 4
SOLOS AND OTHER INSTRUMENTS

Songs And Solos is primarily about solos played on guitar. Nevertheless, it is important for the songwriter to be aware of the possibilities offered by other instruments if a song is going to have a solo. This section reviews the use of instruments other than guitar for solos on chart hits and album tracks. The songwriting guitarist can learn much from listening to the style and effect of solos recorded by other instruments. Think of the way songs like Gerry Rafferty's 'Baker Street' (saxophone), Elvis Presley's 'Heartbreak Hotel' (piano), Elvis Costello's 'Shipbuilding' (trumpet), The Moody Blues' 'Nights In White Satin' (flute), and Bruce Springsteen's 'The River' (harmonica) are marked by solos on those respective instruments.

Almost anything can be used as a solo instrument; the choice depends on many factors. The characteristics of certain instruments lend themselves to certain kinds of solo. So consider what instruments are conventionally used for the song according to the genre to which it broadly belongs. Which musical elements do you want the solo to give to the song? Do you want soaring melody, full chords spelt out, or something that emphasises rhythm? Do you want to use a novelty or unusual instrument to surprise the listener, or change the sound of what would have been a familiar instrument into something unfamiliar? Does the lyric suggest an appropriate instrument? Dire Straits' 'Sultans Of Swing', Chuck Berry's 'Johnny B. Goode', and Bread's 'Guitar Man', have lyrics about a guitar-player – so it would be peculiar if their solos were not on guitar. Something about the emotion or theme of a song might be compromised if the solo is placed on an unsuitable instrument, almost as much as if it is badly phrased or executed. This is one reason why guitar solos do not feature equally in all genres of popular music, and why electric guitar solos using string-bending and distortion are not often heard in MOR ballads – they have the wrong 'vibe', even if the notes fit.

But it's possible to undermine expectations by giving a solo passage to an instrument not usually heard in that genre of music. It risks confusing the audience, and could even be comical, but might result in a memorable twist. In this connection, consider putting an acoustic instrument solo into a mainly electronic mix, or *vice versa*. The contrast of the 'organic' with the high-tech can be expressive. The violin that appears as a solo instrument in The Korgis' 1980s hit 'Everybody's Got To Learn Sometime' make an unexpected and poignant contrast with the synth-dominated arrangement.

Choosing a solo instrument is also shaped by a 'politics of association' linked to musical instruments. This already existed among orchestral instruments in the classical tradition because several hundred years of composing and performance have linked certain instruments with particular styles, musical gestures, and emotions. If popular music as it currently exists goes back almost 60 years, it is unsurprising that by now the instruments played in this musical tradition have accumulated similar symbolic associations. Part of being a songwriter, arranger, and/or producer is the manipulation of these associations to signal extra-musical meaning to potential audiences, as much as haircuts, clothes, and artwork. These are gestures over and above specific musical content. This topic is discussed in my book *Arranging Songs*, in the context of gauging the effect of choosing instruments for an arrangement. But the principles are also true of instruments chosen for a solo; perhaps more so, since a solo draws attention to itself in a way arrangements often don't.

In the February 1995 *Making Music*, Noko of dance band Apollo 440 commented on the associations of certain sounds and what they might evoke: "People who play guitar now, play in a much more gestural way. It's like its sound and the cultural resonance of its sound are part of the reason for the music they choose to make. The expression of personality within the actual confines of the instrument itself, or the playing of the instrument is almost less important." He gave the example of what happens when a guitarist chooses a Hendrix sound or riff: "It's like the using the instrument as a cultural trigger: to make people feel the way they did when they first heard the guitar on 'Voodoo Chile'." He also cited the wah-wah guitar from Isaac Hayes' 'Theme From *Shaft*' (1971) "which delivers an image of that film, and every other film of that era, into the tone and ambience of a track, every time it's used".

Another example of an instrument which will do this is the Coral sitar guitar, which is linked with the latter 1960s, as it emulated the then fashionable sound of the Indian sitar. However, recording with the Coral sitar in the 21st century now evokes a particular historical moment (the 1960s hippie counter-culture) and thus might be heard as kitsch or ironic – more Austin Powers than Indian guru. Similarly, the twangy echo and tremolo favoured by Duane Eddy and The Shadows now signifies the early 1960s – the world evoked in *Mad Men* and the James Bond films – and is used as such in adverts and film soundtracks.

In rock, associations attach to various electric guitars. In the mid-1960s the Fender Stratocaster became less 'cool' because of its association with early 1960s guitar groups such as The Shadows. Jimi Hendrix's use of a white Stratocaster when he emerged in late 1966 reversed that. Hendrix, along with Ritchie Blackmore and Robin Trower, gave the Strat a new, psychedelic identity. In the early 1970s the hippest electric guitar was probably the Gibson Les Paul, owing to glam-rock guitarists such as Marc Bolan and Mick Ronson, technical players such as Jan Akkerman and Robert Fripp, and rock players like Jimmy Page, Peter Green, Paul Kossoff, and Pete Townshend. In the later years of the 1970s the Les Paul was largely rejected by punk and new-wave bands. Paul Weller with The Jam single-handedly made Rickenbackers fashionable for the first time since about 1965. Elvis Costello's early albums have guitar breaks coloured by his use of a Fender Jazzmaster (a Les Paul on those songs would have been unthinkable). It's no accident that many players of the early 1980s who took rock guitar in new directions – The Edge, Van Halen, Mark Knopfler, and John McGeoch – didn't use Les Pauls.

Later, Slash's adoption of a sunburst Les Paul with Guns N' Roses was a coded evocation of the sleaze of the hard rock of a classic era. In the early 1990s, Kurt

SECTION 4

Cobain's grunge ethic expressed itself in his choice of guitar, a hybrid Fender called a 'Jagstang'. Hand in hand with these choices went attitudes toward guitar solos and whether they were desirable or not.

Narrowing this question of associations to a purely musical/timbral focus, it can be seen that instruments carry symbolic meanings that colour what they play. Take this into account when selecting an instrument other than a guitar to play a solo. Choosing a saxophone to play a solo instead of a guitar makes a significant difference. In the case of 'Baker Street', previously cited, the opening saxophone phrases that became the song's trademark were originally written on guitar, but sound so much fuller on saxophone.

Some instruments may be the preferred choice in certain genres. Guitar dominates rock; piano and saxophone, rock'n'roll; saxophone, strings and other orchestral instruments, MOR; saxophone, trumpet, vibraphone, piano, double bass and drums, jazz; harmonica, mandolin and fiddle, folk. Blues, soul, and rhythm & blues often have organ solos. Pop music, MOR, Broadway hits, jazz tunes, etc, are more likely to use classical instruments, such as a violin or cello solo. Orchestral sounds can be approximated, if you don't play them and can't hire a professional, by samples triggered from a keyboard or on computer using sequencing software, a MIDI keyboard, and a sample library.

Let's have a look at some possible solo instruments, taking keyboards first.

KEYBOARDS

Among the potential solo instruments in the category of 'keyboards' are acoustic and electric piano, clavinet, various types of organ, harmonium, mellotron, and monophonic or polyphonic synthesizers. The sounds of these instruments are widely available from digital workstations, sound module hardware, and sample library software.

Acoustic piano
The acoustic piano has a wide range of associations for a solo, from sophisticated elegance and classical rhapsody to energetic glissando-driven rock'n'roll energy; from swinging jazz and blues to the modern reverb-laden minimalism of motifs that only employ a handful of notes. Unlike many soloing instruments, the piano need not be confined to a melody line of single notes; it can thicken a melodic line with octaves, double octaves (both hands), and by adding chords and bassline. As a solo instrument it can cover more musical ground than almost anything else and reduce the need to have much else going on harmonically and melodically during the piano solo. Even if only playing a single-note melody line it can be effective, as in Nick Drake's 'Northern Sky' (1:46-2:15), where its percussive cool is contrasted with a warmer organ sound.

The 1950s saw a number of successful singers who were anchored to their pianos, notably Fats Domino who had 58 hits during the 1950s, of which 18 sold a million, including 'Ain't That A Shame' and 'Blueberry Hill'. In uptempo rock'n'roll, performers like Jerry Lee Lewis and Little Richard pounded away at the bass-notes of chords with the left hand, with the right hand throwing out octaves, fast melodic phrases, note clusters, and chords. The piano lent itself to rock'n'roll partly because of its percussive timbre, and also because there was no better instrument (with its classical pedigree) for a teen rebel to subvert.

A piano solo fits naturally in a song where piano is dominant in the arrangement. Bruce Hornsby & The Range's 'That's The Way It Is' is piano-dominated, so there's no surprise when it takes a solo at 2:15-58 (43 seconds of a track that lasts 4:50) after the second chorus, and returns after the last chorus. The sprightly combination of chords and single notes creates a mildly jazzy musical statement impossible on any other single instrument.

A 'classical' (ie, a generic romantic piano concerto style) approach is demonstrated by David Sancious's long piano solo introduction to Bruce Springsteen's 'New York City Serenade' (*The Wild, The Innocent, And The E Street Shuffle*, 1973). Acting as grand scene-setting, this solo is harmonically far more complicated than the actual song, which is based on a simple four-chord turnaround. There is a dramatic 25-second piano intro for The Boomtown Rats' 'I Don't Like Mondays'. The 'classical' style is felt in the dramatic big octaves that stud Dusty Springfield's 'I Close My Eyes And Count To Ten' and the octaves over a pedal note that open Elton John's 'Someone Saved My Life Tonight'.

One of the most celebrated piano solos on a rock album is Mike Garson's on the title track of David Bowie's *Aladdin Sane* (1973). Virtuoso technique is placed, as it should be, entirely at the service of the imagination. Over a two-note A-G backing derived from the chorus, Garson lets rip with an explosion of splintered phrases, demented octaves, and hammering off-beat chords, as if Edward Scissorhands were playing *avant-garde* jazz. The rigid, incessant backing gives his abandoned playing a tension it would have lacked in a jazz or contemporary classical framework. This solo voices the decadent brink-of-World War III paranoia that Bowie's apocalyptic but brief lyric only hints at. The solo evokes and mangles the high culture associations of the piano to imply that that very culture is mad and cannot save civilization.

On a smaller scale, the distinctive tone of a 'honky-tonk' upright piano, rather than the huge black Steinway of the concert hall, evokes low-life bars and clubs. It has also provided songs with memorable solo breaks, as on 'Dream A Little Dream' by Mama Cass of The Mamas & The Papas, where it is based on the verse, and the group's hit 'Dedicated To The One I Love'. It can also be heard on Thunderclap Newman's 'Something In The Air', for the dark vaudeville of The Doors' 'People Are Strange', on The Band's 'Rag Mama Rag', and the pastiche of The Beatles' 'Rocky Raccoon'.

Carole King's 'I Feel The Earth Move' has a piano solo punctuated by a few lead guitar phrases toward its end that answer the piano twice. She starts the song with a chorus, verse, chorus, with the piano taking over at 1:01, in a chordal style interspersed with octave melodic phrases. Tori Amos's 'These Precious Things' (*Little*

> *The piano lent itself to rock'n'roll partly because of its percussive timbre, and also because there was no better instrument (with its classical pedigree) for a teen rebel to subvert.*

SECTION 4

Earthquakes, 1992) at 3:06-16 has a raucous piano break of four cascading descending runs after the bridge.

The Moody Blues' 'Go Now' has a 15-bar piano solo in a style that provides contrast to the otherwise heartbroken chorus and verse (1:56-2:18, over two minor chords). Cat Stevens placed a beautifully melodic piano solo in 'Sweet Scarlet' (*Catch Bull At Four*, 1972). Nashville Teens' 'Tobacco Road' has a 10-bar piano solo on the main riff in opening rapid triplets (1:04-18). Session player Nicky Hopkins played great piano on many rock tracks. One memorable solo by him occurs on The Who's 'They Are All In Love' (*The Who By Numbers*, 1975), where its elegant regret contrasts with the sarcastic lyric barked by Roger Daltrey. The solo is effectively set-up by a chord shift out of key as the solo begins (1:32-2:10).

Electric piano

Instead of acoustic piano, another option is the rounder tones of an electric piano. This features in many Supertramp songs, and on Elton John's 'Daniel'. Randy Crawford's 'One Day I'll Fly Away' has a short electric piano break (2:22-50) that enters in a different key to the previous chorus and modulates again when the strings take over after a few bars. Family's 'In My Own Time' has a high-pitched electric piano solo. The Monkees' 'I'm A Believer' has an eight-bar electric keyboard solo in the middle. The Zombies' 'She's Not There' has a nine-bar electric piano at 1:38-55, comprised of fast scale runs but going into chords at the end; it is preceded by a second of silence. Spirit's 'Fresh Garbage' has an electric piano solo at 1:12-2:20 (track length is 3:10) where it plays the ♭VII-I two-chord vamp as well as improvising a lead line. This section is in triple time, unlike the 4/4 of the main part of the song. There is a simple electric piano melody for a solo on Badly Drawn Boy's 'Silent Sigh' (1:36-52), which has piano as its main accompaniment; this solo is given more space on the coda. There are electric piano solos by Ray Manzarek on 'The Crystal Ship', from The Doors' first album, and 'Riders On The Storm'.

Organ

The organ is associated with churches, with ritual, and religion. Often played during ceremonies that mark the great passages through life, it is a natural choice for gospel and also for that strand of secular romanticism that runs through popular music in love songs in which romantic experience substitutes for religious experience. As such, it can be used to sanctify a song. Less percussive than the piano, it can also be gothic and spooky. Church organs have to be played *in situ*, but technology developed smaller models that could be moved, including organs such as the Farfisa, the Vox, and Hammond.

In 1960s pop music the high-pitched organ was used for solos, as at 1:37-48 on The Monkees' 'A Little Bit Me, A Little Bit You' before another chorus, and on The Beatles 'I'm Down'. This sound was resurrected in the 1980s on Tasmin Archer's 'Sleeping Satellite', which has an unusual break, with the Farfisa organ at 2:50 as the second solo that precedes the last choruses. The middle-eight break consists of a few organ phrases and then some vocal effects. The Style Council's 'Speak Like A Child' has an organ solo followed by a few synth string phrases – an example of a 'baton-pass' solo where the solo is shared by two consecutive instruments. This solo comes out into a repeat of the short middle-eight passage.

The organ is a foundation sound of gospel-tinged soul and rhythm & blues. The solo on The Animals' 'House Of The Rising Sun' was played on organ (a 14-bar verse sequence from 1:54-2:26), and organ dominates the coda of the song. Crazy Elephant's 'Gimme Gimme Good Lovin'' has an organ solo at 1:07-20 which adds rhythm & blues grit. Steppenwolf's 'Born To Be Wild' has a 20-bar organ solo over a static E chord (1:34-2:07) which turns into a crescendo at the end.

The romantic, sanctifying aspect of the organ colours Led Zeppelin's untypical ballad 'Thank You', which ends with a coda featuring an organ solo buttressed with occasional chords from electric 12-string and bass. Jeff Buckley's 'Lover, You Should've Come Over' has a pipe organ solo intro that sets a powerful atmosphere. George Michael's 'Faith', driven by a Bo Diddley rhythm, starts with 38 seconds of organ solo fading in – an example of the songwriting technique of the 'false' intro in terms of the mood, drawing on gospel associations to sanctify the song and illustrate its title. It is set at a slower tempo than the main part of the song and comes to a cadential ending that sets the scene. The greatest 'sanctifying' organ solo in pop history is surely that played by Gary Brooker on Procol Harum's 'Whiter Shade Of Pale'. There the organ plays the main melody for the intro (first 27 seconds), returning at 1:44-2:10 after the first chorus and again after the second chorus at 3:27-3:50.

The other-worldly effect of the organ assisted the gothic vibe of some of The Doors' songs, including 'Light My Fire', whose central section starts with an organ solo, and 'Break On Through', which has a 16-bar organ solo. Pink Floyd's early hit 'See Emily Play' has a brief organ solo on its intro before the first verse. Later there is a 16-bar solo on the chord of A minor (1:31-2:01), with guitar effects over the top and a hypnotic octave bass underneath. Brian Auger, Julie Driscoll, and the Trinity's 'This Wheel's On Fire' fades out on a coda organ solo for the last 27 seconds of its 3:27 length. Sparks' 'This Town Ain't Big Enough For The Both Of Us' has an organ break at 1:31 (for eight bars) moving into a guitar solo with gunshot sound effects and then straight into the verse.

The gothic organ solo also features in early 1970s progressive rock. Bands like Deep Purple, Atomic Rooster, Argent, Yes, Emerson, Lake, and Palmer, and later Supertramp featured organ solos, with or without a guitarist. This approach was given a new twist by punk group The Stranglers; the organ solo on 'No More Heroes' is preceded by a long guitar solo at 1:25-50, a stream of almost continuous eighth-notes moving in scale form. The organ solo (1:50-2:28) is in single notes. It dovetails straight into the verse in a manner that means we don't initially notice we've moved out of the solo section; this is a very effective join and worth studying. The vocals come in just a little bit later.

Clavioline

The late 50s and early 60s can be evoked by the sound of a Clavioline. The Clavioline was invented in 1947 and featured on a hit record in 1953 – the first electronic instrument to do so. Modified to what Max Crook called a Musitron, it can be heard on his distinctive solo in Del Shannon's 'Runaway' at 1:10-38 over the verse progression. This comes after the first chorus and leads into the second. The Tornadoes' 'Telstar' used the Univox Clavioline, and it can also be heard on The

Beatles' 'Baby You're A Rich Man' and The White Stripes' 'Icky Thump'. For funk, turn to the clavinet, a 1970s keyboard that starred on Stevie Wonder's 'Superstition' and John Paul Jones' solo on Led Zeppelin's 'Trampled Underfoot'.

Harpsichord

The harpsichord has a sound that is too brittle and short-sustained to lend itself much to solos, but it did enjoy a supporting role as a late 1960s psychedelic instrument (see Jeff Beck's 'Love Is Blue' and Pink Floyd's 'See Emily Play'); certainly it was more in keeping with the era than piano, which was perhaps ideologically too bourgeois. On The Beatles' 'In My Life', George Martin famously played a baroque-styled solo on a piano and then speeded it up to sound like a harpsichord (1:28-46). See also 'Fixing A Hole' and the pastiche baroque fills of 'Piggies'.

Digital technology means that new sounds for solos can be created by layering patches. Crowded House's 'Four Seasons In One Day' (1:44-59) has a solo passage featuring two instruments, one of which sounds like a harpsichord and the other possibly oboe, giving an arcane sound.

Synthesizer

Like electric guitar in the early 1960s, synths carried an air of space-age modernity in the late 1970s and early 1980s. Early primitive analogue synths were monophonic, capable of only playing one note at a time, and were restricted to playing solos and melodies. At this stage in rock history, synth solos had an earthy quality about them that helped to define the groups who used them as distinct from guitar-based bands. Curved Air's 'Backstreet Luv' has a synth solo on the intro. Roxy Music's debut hit single 'Virginia Plain' has a synth solo made of octaves from 2:12-34, punctuated by chords from the whole band. Edgar Winter Group's 'Frankenstein' has two synth solos with plenty of pitch-bend effects in addition to a guitar solo. Funk bands also used synths. Ike & Tina Turner's 'Nutbush City Limits' has a high-pitched synth solo (1:38-2:03 in a track of about 2:55). Genesis put a synth solo on their hit 'Follow You Follow Me' which starts out as a single line and then is harmonised in thirds to build up to a climax.

By the end of the 1970s synths were becoming polyphonic and capable of chords. They later became capable of playing more than one sound at a time, either by dividing the keyboard between the two sounds or layering them so that any single key created a blend of two sounds. Blondie's 'Call Me' (1980) has a solo that layers several tones including organ and synth. It comes in after the second chorus and leads to a chorus.

All these keyboards have become vintage in their turn and can now be enjoyed and used via sample libraries. This technology was embraced by bands such as Pink Floyd, Tangerine Dream, and Kraftwerk who were less interested in short songs. As synth technology developed, the range of sounds that could be triggered became enormous. This further increased in the late 1980s with the advent of sampling, where any sound could be captured, played at any pitch, and subjected to further sound processing.

Avoidance of prominent guitar solos became ideological in New Wave and New Romantic songwriting in the early 1980s. Both were committed to writing short songs. The former grew out of punk opposition to self-indulgent progressive supergroups; the latter disliked the guitar as an old-fashioned sound compared to the developing technology. Synths were from this point a central feature of dance music. Had Nik Kershaw's hit 'Wouldn't It Be Good' been recorded five years earlier it would almost certainly have had a guitar solo in the middle. As it is, a guitar is playing in the solo but it is overlaid with synth brass sounds. The track length is 4:24 with the 40-second solo occurring at 2:44-3:24, beautifully and melodically phrased on the major scale.

This marks the period where orchestral instruments are more likely to be emulated by synths than recorded from traditional instruments. Thus China Crisis's 'Christian' (1982) opens with a synth flute melody of eight bars over a II-I chord change taking up the first 22 seconds of the track. This is the solo as an intro in itself. It returns as a link to the first chorus at 1:03 and throughout.

WOODWIND INSTRUMENTS

This group of potential solo instruments includes piccolo, flute, oboe, clarinet, and bassoon, which are part of an orchestra's woodwind section. To them we can add recorder, penny whistle, and harmonica.

Flute, oboe, and clarinet

These instruments sometimes feature in 1960s pop songs. The flute can lend a song a cool and sophisticated sensuousness to a song. Throughout The Four Tops' 'Reach Out, I'll Be There', flute and piccolo are heard playing a high melody in octaves on the intro and the chorus. Along with James Jamerson's bass part, this is very much part of the sonic signature of the song. The Moody Blues' 'Nights In White Satin' has a flute solo (2:06-50) after its second chorus, over a new chord progression announced by a drum 'flam'. A guitar solo here would have ruined the mood, which is ethereal and distant. Jethro Tull's 'Living In The Past' (1969) – one of the few hit singles written in 5/4 time – has a flute solo intro until 0:39, which returns after the first verse and chorus. There's a freer solo on the coda that departs from the melody. The Mamas & The Papas' 'Creeque Alley' also has a flute solo (2:22-58).

The flute has classical and Arcadian associations, and in the latter role became associated with the hippy counter-culture's stress on returning to Mother Nature. There's a hint of flute or recorder on The Flower Pot Men's 'Let's Go To San Francisco'. The Sandpipers' 'Cast Your Fate To The Wind' has a flute throughout and a solo. A flute or recorder is also heard playing a counter-melody on The Beatles' 'Inner Light'. It plays a part in the sensual psychedelia of West Coast 1960s band Love, whose 'Orange Skies' has a flute part throughout (the solo comes in at 2:06-26). 'She Comes In Colours' also has a flute solo at 1:30-44, where the melody is doubled by a harpsichord. This solo passage is reprised for the coda and the song ends on a flute trill (associated with bird song). The flute also provides melodies on Love's classic album *Forever Changes* (1967).

Low-pitched standard flute, or the lower-voiced alto flute, increases the sense of coolness in this register, becoming threatening in the right context, as it is on John Barry's theme for *The Ipcress File*. The arrangement needs to be fairly quiet and spacious for the instrument to come through as a soloist. At the other extreme, high-pitched lines can be assigned to a piccolo, whose trebly, shrill tones will pierce most arrangements, and communicate unrestrained gaiety and exuberance.

The oboe evokes English pastoral, innocence, loss, and nostalgia, and has a plaintive sound excellent for pop ballads. The plaintive quality is obvious in the solos on the intro and after the first chorus on The Carpenters' 'Superstar'. It is generally heard playing fills or backing the vocal melody. Honeybus's 'I Can't Let Maggie Go' has an oboe playing a brief solo and Glen Campbell's 'Galveston' has a few oboe fills toward the end. It is also heard on The Casuals' 'Jesamine' (1968), Rod Stewart's version of 'Handbags And Gladrags', and throughout 'I Got You Babe' by Sonny and Cher, where it adds a two-note phrase in the chorus.

The clarinet is friskier, with a distinguished pedigree in jazz (think of the extraordinary upward glissando with which George Gershwin commenced his famous concert piece *Rhapsody in Blue*). It can be heard on The Beatles' jazzy 'When I'm Sixty Four' (compare Brian May's woodwind pastiche played entirely on electric guitar on 'Good Company' from Queen's *A Night At The Opera*, 1975).

Bassoon

In pop records the bassoon is used for a comic or novelty sound, as on Sandie Shaw's Eurovision hit 'Puppet On A String', but rarely gets a solo. This is a pity, because its higher range is huskily erotic; metaphorically, it is the woodwind equivalent of the sandpaper vocal cords of the blues singer. Harpers Bizarre's cover of Simon & Garfunkel's '59th Bridge Street Song' has a bassoon on the right channel playing an accompaniment in unison with the bass. At 1:32 there is an unaccompanied harmony vocal finished off with a few woodwind exchanges including the bassoon being answered by a flute. Sonny and Cher's 'I Got You Babe' seems to have bassoon playing a couple of bass notes on the intro. Smokey Robinson's 'Tears Of A Clown' has a bassoon playing a bass part, and each time after the hook-line playing a high-pitched run.

Recorder

The recorder and penny-whistle evoke a child-like innocence, partly by sound and their limited range (which tends to be high-pitched), but also because they are played by children as they are technically easy. Being wooden, recorders symbolise the hand-crafted and organic. The Association's hit 'Windy' has a penny-whistle playing the chorus melody as a solo from 1:08-22. Either piccolo or recorder adds fills to Manfred Mann's cover of the Bob Dylan song 'The Mighty Quinn'. The Beatles' 'The Fool On The Hill' has a short recorder solo (1:24-36) double-tracked; it returns with McCartney doing vocal ad libs later. Here it stands for pastoral innocence – the idea of the Pied Piper – and perhaps comments on the naivety of the central character. It was sufficiently redolent of the song to be alluded to in 'Glass Onion', where there is a tiny burst of recorder just after Lennon mentions it (1:28-32).

Harmonica

The harmonica is an outdoor, campfire, traveller's folk instrument. You can carry it in your pocket even when you don't have room for much else. It enables a singer-guitarist to to play a solo on something other than the guitar while the guitar creates the harmonic background. Harmonica features in blues music and in protest folk in the early 1960s because of Bob Dylan's use of it. This was imitated by others, such as Donovan, whose hit 'Catch The Wind' adds a harmonica solo (2:01-34), with the song ending only about 20 seconds later. In the 1960s there were even instrumental hits carried by harmonica, such as Stevie Wonder's 'Fingertips' and Mr Bloe's 'Groovin' With Mr Bloe'. John Barry's theme for the film *Midnight Cowboy* is played by double-tracked harmonica, and on the fade-out one takes an *ad lib* solo.

The mournful wail of the harmonica was used to great effect on Bruce Springsteen's ballad of people falling on hard times, 'The River', where it sounds from the depths of poverty, and on the acoustic blues version of 'Born In The USA'. It plays a short solo on the intro of 'Thunder Road'. It can also sound lovelorn, as in Neil Young's harmonica breaks on 'Out On The Weekend' and in 'Heart Of Gold', where it is first heard on the intro, returns again after the first chorus and before the second verse, and is heard again at 2:15 after the second chorus. On R.E.M.'s 'Find The River' it takes the solo role rather than a guitar.

In uptempo songs the harmonica can spill over with exuberant joy. Stevie Wonder's early Motown career was enhanced by his use of harmonica, notably the harmonica solo on 'For Once In My Life' at 1:28-2:03 after two verses and a key-change achieved by a four-bar link. The high-pitched line brings a certain sweetness to the track. In Van Morrison's 'Bright Side Of The Road' (1:38-2:00) the harmonica supplies a jaunty upbeat brightness to express the song's happiness – it comes after the second chorus and leads to the bridge that connects to the last verse.

The harmonica is sufficiently piercing that it can hold its own in an electric rock context, as it does in Led Zeppelin's 'When The Levee Breaks', where it is swelled with reverb, and 'Nobody's Fault But Mine', which has a harmonica solo as well as a guitar solo.

There is a harmonica solo on The Doobie Brothers' 'Long Train Running' and, borrowed from the blues, The Beatles chose a harmonica to play the opening motif of their first hit single 'Love Me Do' (1962), which also has a 12-bar harmonica solo; the harmonica also contributes to early Beatles tracks such as 'From Me To You', 'Thank You Girl', and 'I'll Get You'. It lends a blues toughness to The High Numbers' (soon to be The Who's) single 'I'm The Face' and takes a solo that is followed by a double-stop guitar solo over a 12-bar pattern.

BRASS INSTRUMENTS

This group comprises French horn, trumpet, saxophones, flugelhorn, trombone, tuba, and euphonium. It is unlikely that you'll find a French horn section (normally four players) taking a solo, and it is probably only a comedy track that would choose to have a tuba or euphonium as a solo instrument. Thunderclap Newman's

> *In uptempo songs the harmonica can spill over with exuberant joy. Stevie Wonder's early Motown career was enhanced by his use of harmonica, notably the harmonica solo on 'For Once In My Life'.*

SECTION 4 | **69**

'Something In The Air' is wonderfully eccentric in arranging a song about revolution by combining open-tuned guitar with honky-tonk piano and tuba. The coda solo in T. Rex's 'Rip-Off' is played by a flugelhorn.

French horn

The French horn has a serious, magisterial quality, and is historically associated with the outdoors and hunting. In popular music it is used parodically to evoke pomposity. The Beatles 'For No One' has a four-bar French horn solo around 50 seconds in, adding to the sarcastic spirit of the song. But Brian Wilson made a superb arranging decision when he gave the opening motif of The Beach Boys' 'God Only Knows' to the French horn, where it is majestic and heartfelt. It features playing a few phrases on ELO's early '10538 Overture'. There's a couple of seconds of a French horn section toward the end of Wizzard's 'See My Baby Jive'. There's a French horn sound on The Pretenders' 'I Go To Sleep', on the intro and returning throughout as a motif. It fits the dreamy, detached theme of the lyric, and romantic longing.

Trumpet

The piercing quality of a trumpet cuts through most arrangements. It can wear a jazz guise, especially when played quietly and with a mute, conjuring up an atmosphere of urban nocturne; or suggest spaghetti Western or Latin American festivity; it can evoke pomp and circumstance in a classical fanfare-like style. Muted trumpet can also be the focus for a sense of eroticism and naughtiness, as it often is in the earlier James Bond soundtracks.

For an example of a fanfare, The Waterboys' 'The Whole Of The Moon' has a trumpet solo section after the second chorus (1:59-2:18). The trumpets echo each other and then finish with a run of descending triads. The fanfare is in keeping with the declarative romanticism of the track. The trumpets return on the last choruses, along with a saxophone that takes a coda solo. There is a brief trumpet section fanfare used as a link in The Herd's 'From The Underworld'. The Manic Street Preachers' 'Ocean Spray' has a trumpet solo for eight bars coming after an eight-bar instrumental following the second chorus. This instrumental is A♭-Fm-Gmaj7 but the trumpet plays over Em-Am-D-G indicating a key change.

The Beatles famously included a higher-pitched piccolo trumpet in 'Penny Lane', played by David Sinclair to give an English baroque feel, somehow sanctifying the British suburban psychedelia of the lyric. It comes in at 1:09-25 before the second chorus and plays two more *ad lib* phrases over the last chorus.

A trumpet can also stand in for a military bugle. Elvis Costello's 'Shipbuilding' uses Chet Baker's trumpet solo to suggest urban desolation and also historical parallels between the plight of workers and soldiers during the Falklands conflict in the early 1980s and the experiences of their forebears in earlier decades. Belle & Sebastian's 'I Fought In A War' has strings and trumpet taking over an instrumental passage at 2:07-36. The trumpet returns after the last chorus for the coda.

Latin American flavours attend the use of the trumpet fills in Dave Dee, Dozy, Beaky, Mick & Tich's 'Legend Of Xanadu'. The trumpet plays a part in the sensual psychedelia of West Coast 1960s band Love, when the band are doing a more Latin-influenced track. In 'Alone Again Or', after the second chorus line and guitar break, there is an instrumental verse with the trumpet playing the lead (1:48-2:12) with help from the strings. Similarly, the trumpet break on 'Maybe The People Would Be The Times Or Between Clark And Hilldale' hits a single note repeatedly with scat-singing accompaniment.

The romantic, subdued trumpet features on Burt Bacharach classics such as 'Walk On By', where it plays crucial answering phrases. A trumpet section plays a melancholy role on Gene Pitney's '24 Hours From Tulsa'. The short trumpet break in Blur's 'The Universal' (1:25-37), after the first chorus and then repeating its phrase into the second verse, fits the languid Bacharach-imitating groove. Muted trumpet plays a short solo in The Four Tops' 'Walk Away Renee' (1968) at 1:23-39, providing a rather mournful sound doubled an octave lower by another instrument. There is a relaxed, insouciant trumpet solo on B. J. Thomas' cover of 'Raindrops Keep Fallin' On My Head'.

The Jam included a trumpet phrase during the dub reggae section in their hit single 'Going Underground'. Another hit that used a trumpet break was The Fortunes' 'You've Got Your Troubles' (solo at 1:59-2:13) in a song where the brass section is prominent in a supporting role throughout.

Trombone

The trombone sometimes appears as a solo instrument. A trombone solo on The Kinks' 'Dead End Street' evokes Northern English working life. Muted trombone plays a melody on the intro of Sandie Shaw's 'Always Something There To Remind Me'. There's a short trombone solo on The Specials' reggae ska track 'A Message To You Rudy' from 1:34-52, after the first verse and chorus, which adds to the good humour of the track. A few more phrases appear on the coda right on the fade-out. A trombone section plays a short chordal fill at various points in the song.

Brass section

Solos can also be taken by a brass or horn section, which traditionally consists of a number of trumpets, trombones, and saxophones. These are often heard playing throughout soul and rhythm & blues tracks released on labels such as Stax, Atlantic, and Motown in the 1960s and 1970s. Often they would have a solo passage playing chords or in unison, as in Wilson Pickett's 'In The Midnight Hour' (1965), where they get eight bars, or, for a six-bar solo, in Arthur Conley's 'Sweet Soul Music' roll-call of soul greats. On Otis Redding's version of 'My Girl', the brass section solos after the second chorus (1:29-51) over a new chord progression and facilitates the key change that brings in the last verse and chorus a tone higher. It is worth comparing this with The Temptations' version at Motown, where the melody in this bridge section (1:33-51) is in the strings, giving a sweeter effect.

In an American context the brass section recalls the big bands of the 1940 and 1950s, and by extension Broadway and film tunes, and therefore the glitz of big nights out in the city. This association is evoked by the brass on Petula Clarke's 'Downtown'. In a British context brass sections are more likely to evoke nostalgically either military brass bands or the cultural landscape of the Northern working class. *The Who By Numbers* has a track, 'Blue, Red, and Grey', which draws on the same sound, setting ukulele against a (possibly synthesized) brass section.

The languid funk of Stretch's 'Why Did You Do It?' has the brass section take a solo at 1:58-2:32; this also features solo brass sax on the right of the mix, then trumpet on the left. There's a brass section break in Otis Redding and Carla Thomas's 'Tramp', where for several phrases the guitar joins in, playing thirds.

SAXOPHONES

"Ultimately, my guitar playing came to be about fitting in with the ensemble. Then Clarence came along with his saxophone. He's sort of a force of nature, so if I wanted to hear a solo, I let him do it …" (Bruce Springsteen, *Guitar World*, October 1995.)

This quote explains why, with the late Clarence Clemons a central figure in the E Street Band, it's not surprising that Springsteen's repertoire has many songs with prominent saxophone breaks instead of guitar solos, including 'Born To Run'. The saxophone (actually a family of soprano, alto, tenor, and baritone models) can be earthy, raucous, breathy, and sensuous; hence it is favoured for rock'n'roll, rhythm & blues, and blues, as well as MOR love songs. Even when played with virtuosity, that virtuosity doesn't draw attention to itself in the same way as it does with electric guitar; the saxophone therefore doesn't lead to as much risk of collapsing the '3-D field' the song has projected. The saxophone is a perennially popular soloing instrument, featuring on hits from all decades of recent popular music.

With its fluid pitching and rasp, the saxophone can imitate vocal phrasing very effectively. A saxophone solo could almost be a second singer taking over, as can be heard on tracks like Dion's 'The Wanderer', The Coasters' 'Yakety Yak', and playing prominent riffs between the vocal lines on Etta James's 'I Just Want To Make Love To You'. Saxophone plays *ad lib* lead throughout Sting's 'If You Love Somebody Set Them Free' and 'An Englishman In New York'. In the former, it sounds exotic; in the latter, urban and sophisticated. There is an out-and-out jazz break in this song for the sax with rapid walking bass. It has the coda solo to 'Fortress Around Your Heart'.

Classic rock'n'roll sax breaks can be heard on 'This Little Girl' by Gary U.S. Bonds, where sax trades phrases with the guitar during the short solo. Dion's 'The Wanderer' has a typical 1950s sax solo at 1:40-2:06 which substitutes for a bridge and arrives after two verses and two choruses. On Georgie Fame's 'Yeah Yeah', a sax plays every other vocal phrase with the voice on the verse, with a solo at 1:32-53. There is a short sax solo on Wizzard's 'See My Baby Jive' in keeping with its evocation of early 1960s Spector-produced pop. At 3:26-33 in T. Rex's 'Get It On', there is a short saxophone section solo leading to the final choruses, fitting the song's 1950s rock'n'roll origins. David Bowie's 1973 cover of 'Sorrow' has a short, unassertive sax solo at 1:09-24 and his 'TVC 15' has a coda solo by saxophone. Roxy Music put a 12-bar sax break early in their cover of 'Let's Stick Together', and 'Do The Strand' features the sax playing an alternate melody in parts answering each line of lyric. Other songs with saxophone solos include Lenny Kravitz's 'Let Love Rule' (2:18-3:08), and Martha & The Muffins' 'Echo Beach' (1:22-39), leading back to the guitar riff and verse, with a longer sax solo at 2:21-42 linking to the final chorus.

The saxophone often soloed on soul tracks such as Etta James's 'I Just Want To Make Love To You', growling for eight bars at 1:53-2:11 just before the bridge. Eddie

Floyd's 'Knock On Wood' solo at 1:43-52 consists of the sax section playing a phrase and moving it up in sequence three times before rounding off with a fourth phrase. The Isley Brothers' 'This Old Heart Of Mine' has a short, deep sax break at 1:34-43 after the second chorus. A saxophone section takes a short solo on Carla Thomas's 'B-A-B-Y' at 1:41-52 after the vocal bridge, and The Supremes' 'Baby Love' has a saxophone section solo at 00:59-1:12. Motown in the 1960s had a resident saxophone master in Junior Walker who, with his group The All Stars, had several hits that featured the instrument, including 'Shotgun' and 'Road Runner'.

For an insight into romantic saxophone solos try Joan Armatrading's 'Love and Affection' and George Michael's 'Careless Whisper'. Dusty Springfield's 'The Look of Love' features a solo that shows the saxophone at its most gentle and sensual to match the breathy quality of her vocal; only at the last chord does it play a more vibrant leaping phrase. In a similarly quiet mode is Stina Nordenstam's hit 'Little Star' with a soft saxophone solo using a certain amount of chromatic notes, and the sax solo that starts Tears For Fears' 'The Working Hour'.

There are prominent lyrical sax solos on Supertramp's 'The Logical Song' and T'Pau's 'China In Your Hand', where the sax solo is based on the chorus chord sequence. This sax solo suits the romanticism of the song, more emotionally crushed and less hysterical than a guitar, whose effect might have been too brash – as can be heard on live versions. The positioning of this solo is very effective, coming at what seems an early conclusion after two verses and two choruses at 2:24. Initially it seems the final chord I is fading on the piano. But it is overwhelmed by a vocal sample that unexpectedly swells in volume. During this five-second pause the sax plays a few notes to introduce its solo at 2:28. The solo's start is powerfully reinforced by a loud chord IV supported by a thumping bass drum. The solo also benefits from the underlying chorus-derived chord sequence displacing chord I into its centre (the chords proceed IV-V-I-IV-VI-V and repeat).

The saxophone can also communicate good-time humour. There are saxophone solos on many Madness hits (they had a flying saxophonist in the video for 'Baggy Trousers'), with their debut hit 'One Step Beyond' being a saxophone-led ska instrumental. There was a 20-bar minor key sax solo toward the end of 'Embarrassment'. Ian Dury & The Blockheads also made use of saxophone solos on tracks such as 'Hit Me With Your Rhythm Stick'.

Although it does not play a solo, the saxophone defines the sound of Gerry Rafferty's 'Baker Street', opening the song with a distinctive four-bar phrase which, when combined with a slide descending guitar chord, makes a powerful hook. The urban rhythm & blues association it draws on in 'Baker Street' is also relevant to the use of the saxophone in The Boomtown Rats' 'Rat Trap' and tracks such as Graham Parker & The Rumour's 'Heat Treatment' where, at 1:58-2:12, the saxophone's solo happens on a key change from G major to C major.

PERCUSSION BREAKS AND DRUM SOLOS

In songs a drum solo or percussion break has its uses in refreshing the listener's ear for pitch and harmony. The logic of having a drum solo on a track is that it brings the rhythmic element of popular music right to the fore. Drum solos foreground the role that rhythm plays in popular music: if it is all about a beat, why not strip it back to the beat? They also stem from virtuoso display – the drummer wishing to show that he was more than just the person holding the beat. An example of the former would be The Dave Clark Five's foregrounding of drums on 'Bits And Pieces'; of the latter, Led Zeppelin making a track out of a drum solo by bookending the solo with two bursts of guitar riff on 'Moby Dick'.

A short drum break can make an effective link. On The Beatles' 'The End', Ringo Starr provides a drum solo to link the start of the track to the triple guitar solos (0:19-34), and from on 'Birthday' there's drum break at 0:42-56. Mitch Mitchell's drum breaks play an important role in Jimi Hendrix's 'If 6 Was 9', adding strength to the quietly-spoken manifesto of personal freedom.

Blackfoot Sue's 'Standing In The Road' has a percussion break at 1:54-2:18, after the second chorus; this percussion break occurs again before the coda. John Kongos's influential 1971 hit 'He's Gonna Step On You Again' has a similar percussion break (2:22-40) where the arrangement is stripped down to the drum and percussion track with the looped voice repeating the title. This section also functions as the intro and coda.

Cozy Powell's 'Dance With The Devil' starts with only percussion. Its first guitar riff is heard at 0:38 seconds, and at 1:47-2:03 the mix switches back to solo drums. Golden Earring's 'Radar Love' has a short drum solo that acts as a link from the second chorus to the instrumental bridge (2:30-39) continuing its rhythms at that point. The Who's original version of 'The Kids Are Alright' puts the focus on Moon's drums at 1:58-2:15 (some of this was edited out of the UK single). There are also short drum breaks in 'Won't Get Fooled Again' and at the coda of '5.15'.

A percussion break might feature more exotic instruments, including pitched percussion. The Hollies' 'Carrie Ann' opens with congas and a fishstick before the first verse, and, most unusually for 1967 British pop, has a percussion solo played on Jamaican steel drums from 1:38-54. Peter Gabriel's 'Intruder' (2:20-43) has a sinister solo break played with two marimba sounds, one left, one right.

HARP

The harp is rarely used as a soloing instrument. Its tone is beautiful but with little penetrative power. Single-note ideas and harmonics work at soft dynamic levels; octaves and chord ideas have more body, but it is vulnerable to being swamped by other instruments in a mix. The exception is the dramatic, sweeping (and clichéd) harp glissando which is effective at adding a touch of magic to significant musical transitions.

In popular music the associations of the harp are to do with romance, sentiment, the ideal, and tender feelings. A harp provides typical arpeggio ideas for the intro of The Beatles' 'She's Leaving Home', which prime the listener for the pathos of the song's narrative. It is also heard on the first verse of P. P. Arnold's 'The First Cut Is The Deepest'. You can hear harp fills in The Temptations' 'Just My Imagination', where it has a role in the link to the bridge at 2:25-33 and even briefly on the coda. Here it is the other-worldly associations of the harp (voted instrument-of-choice by most angels) that sustain the dream motif of the song.

Solo harp (the smaller Celtic instrument, not the large orchestral harp) is more likely to be found on folk records: see Alan Stivell in particular, whose harp can be heard on Kate Bush's 'Never Be Mine', used as a link to the choruses which form the coda. Players such as Ruth Wall, who has worked with Goldfrapp, and her electronically-treated harp have shown new possibilities for the instrument yet to be explored in popular music. A magical web of sound can be created by treating a harp with multiple-repeat echo.

STRINGS

The bowed-string family offers many possibilities for solos in a song. It comprises solo violin (acoustic and electric), viola, cello, and double bass. In addition, a solo section might be scored for a group of strings, from a quartet (two violins, viola, and cello) to a larger chamber group up to an orchestral string section. These can be approximated by using digital versions from a keyboard or samples. Strings offer a great number of articulations, which make them very adaptable, from pizzicato to many types of bowing. The character of strings associates them with on-the-sleeve emotion, sincerity, and directness. A violin will generate different arpeggio and melodic ideas from guitar because the strings and notes are laid out differently.

Violin

The acoustic violin signals something folk, organic, or classical. The electric violin signals something more modern and possibly rebellious than its acoustic equivalent. The electric violin has a rougher sound, can project better in a rock context, and be treated with various effects. Slade's hit 'Coz I Luv You' features an electric violin solo for 16 bars over a verse and chorus. The rhythm playing is very disciplined up to 1:10-38, where the violin really takes off, the guitar playing small fills. The solo returns at 2:39 and continues to the fade. The arrangement was repeated for the follow-up, 'Look Wot You Dun'.

The acoustic violin signals something folk, organic, or classical. The electric violin signals something more modern and possibly rebellious than its acoustic equivalent.

Notable players worth investigating for their violin solos are Papa John Creach, who played with Jefferson Airplane, Hot Tuna, and Jefferson Starship, and Graham Smith, who played with String Driven Thing, Magna Carta, and Van Der Graff Generator. The coda of The Who's 'Baba O'Riley' is dominated by an extended electric violin solo, which exudes a certain otherness, in keeping with the elusive spirituality of the track. East Of Eden's 'Jig A Jig' was an instrumental featuring folk violin, and other examples will be found on albums by bands such as Steeleye Span (see 'King Henry' on *Below The Salt*, 1971), Fairport Convention, The Wonder Stuff, The Waterboys, and The Levellers.

In mainstream songs, solo violin is heard on the intro to 'Come On Eileen' by Dexy's Midnight Runners, and playing Spanish-sounding phrases on the false intro of ELO's 'Living Thing' over B♭m-C (IVm-V in F major, the song being in C major). This violin break is recapped after the first chorus as a link to verse two. In these, and in Van Morrison's 'Bright Side Of The Road', the violin represents a Gypsy freedom. Bob Dylan's 'Hurricane' (from *Desire*) has a violin part throughout. As previously cited, The Korgis' hit 'Everybody's Got To Learn Some Time' has a violin solo, which is unexpected, given that the track is synth-based.

Rod Stewart's hit 'You Wear It Well' has a violin solo at 1:50-2:12, with the vocal coming back in over its final notes. The violin is also heard playing a phrase after the title phrase is sung. The violin's association with sincerity and innocence is relevant here because the singer is trying to establish this sincerity in the lyric. U2's 'Drowning Man' (*War*, 1983) and Kate Bush's 'The Fog' (*The Sensual World*, 1989) both have powerfully expressive parts for solo violin, in the latter instance played by Nigel Kennedy, duetting with lead guitar by Alan Murphy.

A popular string articulation is pizzicato, where the string is plucked rather than bowed. On violin and viola the note is short and percussive, and lends itself to rhythmic figures with rests in between. There are pizzicato strings on Andy Williams' 'Can't Get Used To Losing You' and Siouxsie & The Banshees' 'Overground', despite the vast contrast in genre. Cockney Rebel's 'Judy Teen' has pizzicato violin throughout. The violin takes over the solo from an electric piano that starts at 1:54.

Viola

For the use of viola in a rock context, see early recordings by the Velvet Underground. 'Venus In Furs' has viola playing throughout. The viola is tuned a fifth lower than the violin, (CGDA instead of GDAE), and has a darker, more mellow tone because of its bigger body. To get an idea of its pitch range mapped onto the guitar, its open strings are the guitar's fifth string, third fret; third string open; second string, third fret; and first string fifth fret. John Cale played a viola counter-melody throughout Nick Drake's 'Fly'.

Cello

The cello is celebrated for its intense higher register and rich lower tones, and as a soloing instrument it has many possibilities. Solo cello has an emotive appeal, especially if a melody is placed on its top 'A' string. The cello can be heard on some of the songs of Nick Drake. There is a solemn cello melody on the intro of Embrace's 'Fireworks', with a voice singing along and matching the pitch – bearing out what is often said about the cello being closest to the human voice.

Double bass

Solos played by double bass are usually pizzicato, and often heard in 1950s rock'n'roll and jazz. They have the effect of re-focusing the listener's ear on low frequencies and rhythm, so that when everyone comes back in there is a dramatic effect. There is a prominent double bass part in The Cure's 'The Love Cats'.

String sections

A solo could be given to a melody played by a string section of some kind. Group strings can create a feeling of grandeur, as on the intro to 'Dazzle' by Siouxsie & The

Banshees, or Madonna's 'Frozen', which has the strings providing a solo section (3:17-53), using Eastern-sounding scales, the violins playing in octaves. Many listeners will associate a string section with film music, and therefore a cinematic impressiveness. After 1980, string sounds are increasingly likely to be synthesized or sampled rather than played on the original instruments.

The Shirelles' 'Will You Still Love Me Tomorrow' has a violin section solo after the second chorus and bridge (1:59-2:12). Gene Pitney's '24 Hours From Tulsa' has a string section break at 1:24-40, with trumpets helping out playing the verse melody. Ben E. King's 'Stand By Me' has, at 1:52-2:25, a 16-bar instrumental break with the high violins taking a solo between choruses; some of the lower string parts are just audible. The Drifters' 'Save The Last Dance For Me' has high violins take the melody for a solo passage. Dionne Warwick's 'Walk On By' has a solo section where the melody is taken by the strings, at 1:42-55; the strings express the emotion that the trumpet hides as if it is putting on a show.

Chris Farlowe uses strings on the intro of 'Out Of Time' and continues their melody during the first verse. This is repeated as the break going back into the last choruses. The strings play a single melody in octaves. There are prominent strings on Green Day's 'Good Riddance (Time Of Your Life)' that in effect provide a solo section. Manic Street Preachers' 'A Design For Life', after the second chorus, has a string break rather than a guitar solo (2:54-3:21). Lou Reed's 'Perfect Day' has a piano solo supported by violins (2:22-37). In Sister Sledge's 'Thinking Of You', after the second chorus at 2:30-50, rhythm guitar and string melody have a solo section as the rhythm section drops out except for congas.

Mention should be made of the Mellotron string sound, which strongly evokes the mid-1960s and psychedelia. The string tone is fuzzy and the pitch can fluctuate, but it can sound haunting if the amount of reverb is increased.

SOUND EFFECT SOLOS

As recording technology improved during the 1960s, and multi-tracking developed, it became possible for solo instrumental sections to be made up of sound effects. Sound effects are a way of graphically illustrating the song's lyric. The break in The Lovin' Spoonful's 'Summer In The City' has city noises and a high-pitched bass guitar pattern, repeated without sound effects later in the song. The Beatles helped pioneer this approach, assisted by producer George Martin, who had already produced comedy records for the Parlophone label, which would have had sound effects. 'Yellow Submarine' has sound effects where there might have been a solo. 'Being For The Benefit Of Mr Kite' has a section imitating carousel sound effects in the solo sequence (1:00-26). The middle section of Alice Cooper's 'Elected' is taken by sound effects, voice broadcasts, and brass. The solo passage on The Police's 'Synchronicity II' (2:43-3:05) consists of feedback and pitch-bend noises, and comes after the lyric has described the emergence of the monster from Loch Ness.

Duran Duran's 'Hungry Like The Wolf' creates an instrumental passage after the second chorus where there are solo phrases from guitar, synth, heavy breathing, drums and bass, the idea being to create an open space that somehow has tension.

(2:14-42). The Electric Parade's 'Silent To The Dark', after a third chorus, has an instrumental break of various samples including a slowed-down drum rhythm, held keyboard chords, and reverbed guitar notes. This is over a chord sequence that would normally offer itself as a must for conventional soloing (ie, Am-Am/G-D/F♯-Fmaj7).

10cc's 'I'm Not In Love' uses sound effects in the central solo. The piano plays a delicate solo melody with lots of reverb. There are vocal sustained chords, some bass fills, the voice repeating "big boys don't cry", and then, towards 2:40, the gradual climax of the vocals: one of the more complex uses of harmony in pop history.

VOCAL (HUMMING, SCAT, WHISTLING)

Singers can use their voices as an instrument by forgetting about words and simply singing pitches. This is a time-honoured tradition in jazz. Guitarist George Benson sang scat solos with his guitar on the album *In Flight* (1976). There are sections in The Turtles' 'Happy Together' which erupt into "ba-ba-ba", presumably copied from groups like The Association and The Beach Boys. This was so much a signature of 1960s easy listening and lounge music that later parodists of this genre invariably draw on it.

The saxophone solo in The Beatles' 'Lady Madonna' is accompanied by scat singing in lieu of a full brass section. 'Blackberry Way' by The Move has a scat-sung short instrumental sequence. The Monkees' 'Pleasant Valley Sunday' has a scat-singing break instead of a solo at 1:50-2:05. On Roxy Music's 'Avalon', following the last chorus, after a few saxophone phrases one of the backing vocalists scat-sings a solo until the fade. There is scat-singing in the middle section of 'What's Going On', for which there is an extended section on an Am chord and then B, which takes the song away from the E major key. This is reprised at the end of the song. There are two of Marvin Gaye's voices as well as other voices talking. Gaye is clearly imitating jazz instruments some of the time. In a more melodic style is Julianne Regan's wordless vocal solo on 'Severina' by UK band The Mission (1:43-2:10, and from 3:22 on the coda).

One of the most unusual vocal-based solos in a song occurs in U2's 'Miss Sarajevo' when the operatic voice of Luciano Pavarotti takes over the song.

One of the most unusual vocal-based solos in a song occurs in U2's 'Miss Sarajevo' when the operatic voice of Luciano Pavarotti takes over the song. The effect is disconcerting and very much as the solo has switched from vocals to a solo instrument, because suddenly there is a trained voice singing in another language (2:36-3:59), in a song that lasts about 5:15.

A whistled phrase can give a solo section an air of insouciant and filmic melancholy. Three instances are Roxy Music's 'Jealous Guy', Peter Gabriel's 'Intruder', and Otis Redding's 'Sitting On The Dock Of The Bay', in which he whistled over seashore sound effects in the coda.

Occasionally a solo section might contain a speaking voice. In early 1960s pop songs of a melodramatic kind, there were sometimes spoken intros or spoken bridge sections.

The gesture was intended to be a switch into intimate confession, but it often comes across as kitsch and manipulative. At the very least, shifting from the sung voice – where the power of melody gives the human voice extra lift – to the spoken feels like a loss of power and a descent from the poetic to the prosaic (see Elvis Presley's 'Are You Lonesome Tonight' or Smokey Robinson & The Miracles' 'Come Round Here'). Simon Dupree & The Big Sound's 'Kites' is perhaps a little more interesting, with its spoken Japanese in the middle section.

COMBINING SOUNDS

A solo need not use only one instrument. It can feature a combination of sounds playing at once, or a sequence of instruments. The flute puts in a brief appearance in unison with an organ melody in The Herd's 'I Don't Want Our Loving To Die'. Love's 'Stephanie Knows Who' has a solo shared between a freak-out guitar and saxophone (0:59-1:27), taking up a fair chunk of the track's 2:33. The Beatles' 'Revolution' combines fuzz guitar with electric piano at 1:52-2:11. 'Birthday' has a solo from 1:28-48 where a treated honky-tonk piano interjects phrases in the gaps in the guitar riff. The solo in Foreigner's 'Cold As Ice' (1:32-1:46) uses a steep climbing run repeated, with the last few notes trilled in harmony. There is an earlier shorter solo with synth keyboard. On Kings of Leon's 'Pyro' there is a short solo (2:31-46) where the guitar is doubled at a higher octave by a synth or keyboard sound as it plays a four-bar phrase twice.

Examples of songs which have two solos back-to-back on different instruments include The Beatles' playful 'For You Blue', where an extended ironic blues slide solo with queasy vibrato is followed by the piano adding a second solo 12-bar. The 12-bar format lends itself to this type of configuration. 'I'm A Loser' has at 1:15-36 a 16-bar solo, first eight bars taken by harmonica, then guitar doing a conspicuously 1950s rock'n'roll solo based on dominant seventh chords. The harmonica solo acts as a coda with the guitar solo fading. The Beatles 'It's All Too Much' combines a fairly static lead guitar solo with a trumpet fanfare-type break. It starts with a burst of feedback pitch-wavering with a tremolo arm. 'I'm Down' has a 12-bar solo on guitar in a pentatonic minor style, and the same later on electric keyboard (Vox or electric piano).

In Paul Young's cover of Crowded House's 'Don't Dream It's Over' there is an organ solo from 1:45-2:08 followed by guitar at 2:08-24. Coming after the second chorus this takes the place of a vocal middle-eight and has a slightly different chord progression to anything else in the song. The organ break is a cool, soulful single-note melody; the guitar is clean and chorused with some nice jazzy turns that take advantage of the chord changes. In The Police's 'King Of Pain', after a vocal middle-eight, there is a guitar solo at 2:58-3:14 which uses part of the vocal melody, before a keyboard takes over playing four phrases into the last verse. Pink Floyd's 'Money' has a sax solo before the guitar solo. Teenage Fanclub's 'I Need Direction' combines a chordal organ solo (2:44-3:01) with a Duane Eddy guitar solo (3:03), played very low down and stressing the second of the scale against the chord.

These two solos are sometimes separated. In The Doors' 'People Are Strange' the guitar solo (0:55-1:09) uses blues pentatonic phrasing and ends with a dead stop and a second of silence. There is an upright piano solo at 1:31-47 after the second chorus. This piano has been heard throughout expressing the jaunty but sinister atmosphere. Deep Purple's 'Highway Star' has an organ solo and then further on in the song a guitar break. Gene's 'We Could Be Kings' has an arpeggio-based piano solo at 2:52-3:12, the coolness of which contrasts both with the rocky guitar-dominated chorus that precedes it and with the guitar solo that follows immediately to 3:15-24. The Mission's 'Tower Of Strength' combines a string-section melody with an echoed guitar playing many downward slides (2:24-43 strings, 2:44-3:03).

Carole King's 'It's Too Late' has an interesting middle section that is divided into a triple solo. At 1:35-52 the piano and guitar play a melodic solo in unison, with vocal harmonies decorating some of these phrases. From 1:52-2:10 a lead guitar plays a solo. From 2:10-37 a saxophone takes over. Then there's a last verse and a chorus, and the piano and guitar return for another instrumental section before the short vocal coda finishes things off. The song lasts 3:50 and the middle solo section lasts a minute. The handing round of the solo material suggests mourners over the relationship, each trying to understand or explain in their own way.

Al Stewart's 'Year Of The Cat' has a solo section after two choruses and a bridge. It begins with a cello section at 3:07 and then full strings at 3:22. An acoustic guitar takes a Spanish-type solo and then at 3:52, with a change of key, a distorted lead guitar comes in and solos higher until 4:10, at which a saxophone enters soloing until 4:29 when the vocal returns. So this middle section has four solo instruments. The sax returns for the coda at 5:34 and plays all the way to the end at 6:30.

SOLOS, GUITARS, AND GUITAR EFFECTS

Just a painter uses many brushes, a guitarist can use a variety of guitars and tones for a solo.

SECTION 5
SOLOS, GUITARS, AND GUITAR EFFECTS

Sometimes putting an effective solo on a song means choosing the right type of guitar, if you've decided a guitar solo is needed. Guitars not only produce a range of varied tones, they feel different to play. If it feels different, a guitar is likely to make you play a different kind of solo. Which guitar sound you choose might be decided by how many guitars you have to choose from, though digital modelling guitars such as the Line 6 Variax and the Roland VG-8/MIDI pickup system approximate more guitars than most players could afford.

Guitars come in three main types: the nylon-string 'classical' or Spanish guitar; the steel-string 'folk' acoustic (6- or 12-string); and the semi-acoustic and solid-body electric (6- or 12-string). To some degree these are not only physical entities but even certain types of solo. This section discusses the implications of choosing any of these for a guitar solo. It also surveys some related stringed instruments such as the ukulele, mandolin, the Coral Sitar, lap-steel guitar, baritone guitar, and bass guitar. It also looks at the range of guitar effects and techniques.

ACOUSTIC GUITARS

The nylon-string 'classical' guitar solo

Symbolically, the classical guitar stands for something natural, organic, sincere, and passionate, and is culturally associated with the warm climes of the Mediterranean. It is old, rural, pre-rock, Latinate, not American and not blues. It featured on Mason Williams' instrumental 'Classical Gas' (1968), which has a 20-second intro of unaccompanied classical guitar, and on John Williams' 'Cavatina' (theme from *The Deer Hunter*). The practical effect can be heard by comparing The Doors' 'Light My Fire' with the cover by Jose Feliciano, who routinely used a nylon-string guitar. All these associations hover behind a classical guitar solo, and are triggered not by the notes of the solo but by the choice of instrument itself. How strongly they emerge depends on the character of the music. In fact, if the backing goes too much against these the classical guitar will sound out of place. It is difficult to imagine a Sex Pistols or Guns N' Roses track with nylon-string guitar on it! Whereas a classical guitar on a Santana recording would not be so surprising.

Compared to its electric cousin, a classical guitar cannot pitch as high, nor execute high fast runs. Without a cut-away to the body fretting the highest notes involves an awkward stretch. It has limited sustain, and string-bending is largely ineffective. Chord-strumming has some percussive effect but there's a woolly edge to the sound, even if played with a pick and not the fingers. An effective idiomatic style involves slow to medium tempo melodies with vibrato, slides, hammer-ons and pull-offs. The vibrato is especially expressive on the lower three strings between the fifth and 12th frets, and moving the plucking hand closer to the neck and over the soundhole accentuates this dark, velvet tone. The other two tones are the neutral position just off the soundhole, and a brittle 'ponticello' close by the tailpiece. Rapid articulations of a single note can be produced by a 'tremolando', in which all the plucking fingers are involved, but this is an advanced technique. Some of these characteristics can be offset by models that have a non-traditional shaped body and/or a pickup.

In popular music, the romantic sincerity of the classical guitar was evoked on The Beatles' 'And I Love Her', where a ten-bar nylon-string solo is linked to a startling semitone key change from F#m to Gm. It is also used to finish the song. To cite some other 1960s examples, the nylon-string guitar on Dave Dee, Dozy, Beaky, Mick & Tich's 'Legend Of Xanadu' helps the intro build the cod-Mexican melodrama and supplies fills through the verse. The intro to Tommy James & The Shondells' 'Crystal Blue Persuasion' has a short classical guitar break, with fills in the second verse and during the bridge.

A similar emotional signature is evoked by classical guitar solos on 'Lady Grinning Soul' from David Bowie's *Aladdin Sane* (1973), complete with a blast of authentic tremolando finger-picking, Chicago's 'If You Leave Me Now', and The Go-Betweens' 'Streets Of Your Town'. Sting's much-covered 'Fields Of Gold' has a Spanish guitar solo with a lower octave doubling to give the upper note more body. His 'Fragile' is dominated by sixths played on classical guitar, with a solo at 1:52-2:38.

There is a recognisable type of solo that draws self-consciously on the melodic vocabulary of Spanish guitar, which is sometimes transferred onto a steel-string acoustic. This 'Spanish' solo is typified by ornate pull-off figures, rapid tumbling scales with foreshortened time-values, and often uses the Phrygian mode (see Section Six) because of its connection with flamenco. There's an example on The Monkees' 'Valleri'. Jeff Beck played such a 'Spanish' solo on Mick Jagger's 'Just Another Night' on the album *She's The Boss*. Nothing else had been satisfactory, so they put light-gauge electric strings on a Gibson J200. This could be compared with the nylon-string guitar that provides the solo on the first eight seconds of The Beatles' 'The Continuing Story Of Bungalow Bill'.

The steel-string acoustic solo

Symbolically, the steel-string acoustic guitar also stands for something natural, organic, and emotionally direct, culturally associated with the people (hence 'folk' guitar), the rural landscapes in which they work, and, in the American context, country and blues. Compared to a classical guitar, the steel-string pitches a little higher, and has more volume, cut, and sustain. It has some bending capability, which can be increased by lighter-guage stringing. Chord-strumming is authoritative, percussive, and brighter than the classical, whether played with a pick or fingers. Side-to-side vibrato is less effective than up-and-down. Decorations such as slides, hammer-ons, and pull-offs are brighter in effect and add colour. Non-traditional body shapes have a cutaway, and some an integral pick-up. The steel-string guitar can solo in non-standard tunings and with a bottleneck slide. If the instrument is not

SECTION 5

providing a 'Spanish' solo, there are three other generic approaches for an acoustic solo: a solo on the vocal melody, phrases with bluesy bent notes, or a chromatic jazz style.

On Wayne Fontana & The Mindbenders' hit 'Pamela, Pamela' (1966), an ode to childhood, the acoustic guitar gives a feeling of innocence that the more worldly electric could not. It solos at 1:10-24 on the main melody. There is a key change in unison with the organ and a return to the original key with the next verse. Led Zeppelin's romantic ballad, 'Thank You' (*Led Zeppelin II*, 1969), has an acoustic steel-string guitar solo supported by organ and electric 12-string (1:53-2:18) after the second chorus. The light arrangement and romantic sentiment suit an acoustic solo better than electric. Another Led Zeppelin ballad, 'All My Love', has an acoustic solo after a synth solo.

Paul Weller's 'Wild Wood' is an acoustic ballad with acoustic guitar solos at 1:08-21 and 2:10-23. Soul Asylum's 'Runaway Train' starts an acoustic guitar solo at 2:26-56 that features single notes and chords and gradually fades away from being a solo and returning to texture. Judie Tzuke's 'Stay With Me Till Dawn' has an acoustic guitar solo. The Unit 4 + 2 hit 'Concrete And Clay' has a prominent acoustic guitar. The solo occurs at 1:23-36 but there are fills throughout. Its style is Spanish but the instrument was probably a steel-string, judging by the brightness of its tone.

12-string guitar

"... I was already into tunings, so the idea of taking strings off and putting strings on and using weird tunings and capos on a 12-string fitted well. The other thing about 12-string is it stops me noodling in a kind of bluesy fashion. And that's a trap that lots of guitarists fall into." (Johnny Marr, *Total Guitar*, May 1995.)

Sometimes six-strings aren't enough when it comes to a solo. In which case, try a 12-string. As a soloing instrument a 12-string is an odd beast. Its defining characteristic is that any single melody line will be automatically turned into octaves if played on strings six to three (assuming the third string has been strung with an octave). It is hard to bend strings or move very quickly on a 12-string. Arpeggio and partial chord ideas can work well. Examples would include The Byrds' 'Turn, Turn, Turn' at 2:03-2:39 over a verse, and The Who's 'I Can't Explain' which has two 12-string chordal solos at 0:59-1:06 and 1:34-48. Harmonics on electric 12-string can be effective.

The instrument survived in indie bands. Teenage Fanclub used it ('I Need Direction' sounds like a car-crash between The Byrds and The Association). The Stone Roses' 'Waterfall' has a short 12-string acoustic guitar solo link before going to a Stones-ish scale-based solo for the coda. Travis's 'Coming Around' has a 12-string solo at 2:00-18 based on long scale-based phrases. This recaps the mid-1960s sound of The Byrds. K. D. Lang's 'Constant Craving' has a 12-string solo in a fairly chordal texture, the melody line almost buried: country style but with very thick vocal harmonies.

The Beatles recorded 12-string solos on 'Nowhere Man', 'What You're Doing', 'You Can't Do That', 'I've Just Seen A Face', and 'I Should Have Known Better'. 'I Call Your Name' has an eight-bar solo from 1:09-25, an uneasy translation of Chuck Berry-style phrases onto the 12-string where string-bending is harder. 'Any Time At All' has a ten-bar 12-string guitar solo after verse four. 'A Hard Day's Night' has an eight-bar 12-string solo after verse three, doubled with either another guitar or piano.

There is a very short 12-string guitar solo on The Bluetones' 'Slight Return' at 2:02-11, which is in a Beatles mode, and another for the coda which changes from single-note lead to chordal. Echo & The Bunnymen's 'The Killing Moon' has a 16-bar solo after the second chorus at 1:56-2:34 with a new chord progression, and uses a 12-string electric playing an ascending four-phrase idea.

OTHER STRING INSTRUMENTS

Mandolin

The mandolin is a popular instrument in folk music, with a high, chiming timbre. It has little volume, body to its tone, or sustain, though an electric version takes care of the volume issue. It can carry a melody, as it does in jigs and folk reels. If used for a solo it is a good idea to double-track it. It is tuned in fifths (GDAE) the same as a violin, and this lends itself to melodic ideas that arise from its different note-patterns compared to the guitar, which is mostly tuned in fourths. It can be heard on Rod Stewart's 'Mandolin Wind' and 'Maggie May' (from *Every Picture Tells A Story*, 1971), R.E.M.'s 'Losing My Religion', and The Fleet Foxes' 2009 debut album (see the mandolin break on 'Blue Ridge Mountains' at 2:03-23).

Coral sitar

The Coral sitar was invented in the 1960s by session player Vinnie Bell for the Danelectro brand but sold under this other name. It was reissued in 1991, just in time for Britpop's obsession with the 1960s. This solid-body electric had an extra set of 13 drone strings intended to mimic the Indian sitar. Largely due to George Harrison, Ravi Shankar, and the fascination with the mystic East, the sitar signified the counter-culture and psychedelia. The Coral sitar offered a shortcut to make records sound hip. It was used on Traffic's 'Paper Sun' and The Supremes' 'No Matter What Sign You Are'. It can also be heard on the left of the mix on The Delfonics' 'Didn't I (Blow Your Mind This Time)', during the instrumental version of the hook, where it plays part of the melody, on Joe South's 'Games People Play', and on The Smashing Pumpkins' 'Luna'. On Steely Dan's 'Do It Again', from *Can't Buy A Thrill* (1972), it provides a 30-bar solo.

Baritone guitar

The baritone guitar was first built by companies such as Danelectro in the 1950s. It has a longer scale-length to facilitate a much lower tuning that puts it roughly half-way between guitar and bass guitar. The most common tunings are ADGCEA, BEADF♯B, and CFB♭E♭GC, which are a fifth, a fourth, and a major third lower than standard tuning. This means standard guitar scale patterns and chord shapes will work on the baritone; they just sound lower. It was sometimes used by Duane Eddy (on his album *The Twang's The Thang*, 1960) Brian Wilson (on 'Dance, Dance, Dance' and 'Caroline, No'), and on film soundtracks that required an extra-twangy tone. Rock groups such as Staind and Machine Head in the 1980s, exploring detuning, sometimes used baritone models. They are also played by Pat Metheny (see *One Quiet Night*, 2003) and Ani DiFranco.

SECTION 5

Lap steel guitar and pedal guitar

The lap steel guitar and pedal guitar are favoured for solos in country music. They are usually tuned to a major chord, possibly with an additional note such as a sixth, and played with a metal bar, creating a glassy vibrato comparable to a bottleneck. They can add a desolate beauty to a track because of their sustain, if treated with reverb. Gerry Rafferty's 'Right Down The Line' has a solo (2:18-35) with reverb to bring out the sense of space. Matthews Southern Comfort's 'Woodstock' has a similar steel solo before the choruses, and it can also be heard on Led Zeppelin's 'That's The Way' (*Led Zeppelin III*, 1970). You can hear a full lap steel solo in the country song 'Hickory Wind' by The Byrds at 2:03-16. The sound of these instruments can be approximated in standard tuning by certain types of bend on the top three strings, where a triad is sounded with two static notes and a third that is bent into the chord.

BASS GUITAR

The usual role for bass guitar is to support the foundation of the harmony by playing root notes. The problem for the bass guitar as a lead instrument is its pitch, being low where people are not accustomed to focus; low-pitched melodies are less likely to grab the listeners' attention. This almost subliminal quality to the bass was used effectively on Crosby, Stills, Nash & Young's 'Déjà Vu' (1970) where there is a bass solo from 3:15-52, with more bass fills coming after. It could be said that the submerged nature of the bass solo fits the altered consciousness theme of the lyric, which is about memories of past lives. If the arrangement were sparse enough, the electric bass could do more than just play roots, as it does in the highly imaginative arrangement of David Essex's 'Rock On', using stereo echo.

A bass solo can work if the arrangement is sparse, and picking can help give the notes more attack. Great players have nevertheless at times made it an instrument of solo interest. The design of the electric bass, moving away from the double bass and toward the guitar – giving it pickups and frets and playing with a plectrum – also gave it the potential to be a solo instrument. The electric bass guitar could be recorded easily and pushed up in the mix. An early example of its new role would be The Association's hit 'Windy', which starts with the melody being played on solo bass guitar before guitar and harpsichord double it. In the 1970s there would be eight-string basses, played by Chris Squire (Yes) and John Paul Jones (Led Zeppelin), that would lend the bass solo even greater penetration.

By changing the tone settings on an amplifier, even sending some of the signal to a guitar amplifier/speaker set-up rather than just a bass amplifier/speaker, the bass guitar could cut through more. Modern bass tones tend to favour a bright and toppy sound that is closer to the guitar. Percussive 'slap' techniques favoured by Mark King of Level 42 in the 1980s drew attention to the bass. Jaco Pastorius's chorused, fretless bass played a soloistic role on albums such as *Hejira* (1976) by Joni Mitchell, where it suited the sparse acoustic guitar ballads.

Interplay with the guitar in a dual solo can work well. The most famous early bass guitar solo on rock record was John Entwistle's break on The Who's 'My Generation' from 0:55-1:20, where the bass guitar's phrases were interleaved with lead guitar

SECTION 5

before the lead guitar takes the last eight seconds or so. At 1:50-58 on Van Morrison's 'Brown-Eyed Girl', the bass guitar plays a solo/link. On some Motown records, James Jamerson almost gets a bass solo, like the four-bar link on Stevie Wonder's 'I Was Made To Love Her'.

Once heavy rock and progressive rock had instilled the idea that each member of the band was a potential virtuoso and no longer a mere backing musician, there was the prospect of bass solos being expected. Deep Purple's 'Fireball' has a distorted bass solo (1:49-2:05) complete with bent strings. This is followed by an organ solo from 2:14-30 and the return of the vocal. Bass solos were rare during the punk and new wave years but Elvis Costello & The Attractions' 'Lipstick Vogue' (*This Year's Model*, 1978) has a bass solo during the song's middle instrumental part.

SOLOS AND GUITAR EFFECTS

"Whether it's a fuzztone, a wah-wah pedal, whatever, if it's really happening it becomes part of the instrument. I don't think about playing through an effect. I think about playing the whole thing." (The Edge, *Guitar* UK, December 1995.)

Interplay with the guitar in a dual solo can work well. The most famous early bass guitar solo on a rock record was John Entwistle's break on The Who's 'My Generation'.

Since effects can alter the sound of the guitar considerably, they influence the type of guitar solo you create. A player naturally adapts phrasing to what sounds good with a given effect. No-one puts a guitar through a chorus and/or flanger and wants to solo with Chuck Berry double-stops and unison bends. The beneficial influence of guitar effects is that they force you away from the finger-patterns and ideas you often play, because those may sound ineffective. But a phrase that's uninteresting with one processor could sound inspiring with another. A guitar effect may come as an amp setting, an effects pedal, a multi-fx unit, an outboard sound processing unit attached to the mixing desk, or software on a computer. Robin Guthrie told *Guitar Player* in April 1996, "God, I've got a big cupboard at my house with at least 150 old effects pedals, even original units still in the boxes. I've got lots of Colorsound stuff still in the box, and at least 25 Electro-Harmonix units. That's what I've used since I started playing guitar…"

Sometimes it's only when you get the right effect that the right solo for a track falls into place. Occasionally, it may even spark a whole song. When Joe Satriani wrote the title track of his 1987 album, *Surfing With The Alien*, his guitar was running through a wah-wah pedal into a 100-watt Marshall. Then he decided to plug in an Eventide 949 harmoniser. He was so impressed with the resulting sound that it triggered the song idea, and within 30 minutes he had the song melody and the solo.

Effects and changes of guitar tone can differentiate parts of a solo. When Jimi Hendrix played three solos back-to-back on 'All Along The Watchtower', he gave each one a contrasted tone and style. He used a cigarette lighter to play the initial slide solo, with delay added later. The second solo combined wah-wah and a mellow pick-up sound; the third was built from chords and a brighter pick-up, climaxing with an upward run of unison bends. A more recent example is the solo section on

S E C T I O N 5

Radiohead's 'Just' (*The Bends*, 1994), which goes through three distinct and highly-contrasted sections: 1:55-2:06 has tremolo picking and unison bends, 2:06-20 is clean and harmonised, there's two seconds of silence, and then pure guitar noise until about 2:36 when the chorus returns.

Fingers or pick?

There is one guitar effect doesn't need batteries or plugging in. A solo can have a new character if it is played with fingers and thumb, rather than a pick. If you try this as you're inventing the solo you are likely to write a different lead break, because you will want to maximise its potential. Note that picking with fingers:

- changes the sound of single notes
- enables percussive effects by snapping strings against the fretboard
- enables the player to roll chords or triads with thumb and two fingers.

Playing with fingers was an important part of Mark Knopfler's style. The solos on Dire Straits' 'Sultans Of Swing' and 'Lady Writer' used a thumb and the first two fingers to strike the notes. On 'Sultans Of Swing', his Stratocaster was a model with a three-way switch that had to be jammed into place to create the sound of the intermediate second position on Strat with a five-way switch. This pick-up selection combines well with the finger technique. Listen to the subtle sense of touch it produces on the middle solo in 'Where Do You Think You're Going', from *Communiqué*, at 1:43-54. On later tracks such as 'Brothers In Arms', 'Money For Nothing', and 'You And Your Friend' striking the strings with the fingers pulls new tones from an overdriven Les Paul. On Metallica's 'The Unforgiven', Kirk Hammett used a Stratocaster and played with his fingers to emulate the Knopfler sound.

The guitar solo on T. Rex's 1970 hit 'Ride A White Swan' was played without a pick. Several notes toward the end of the solo have a 'rounded-off' quality, probably the result of being struck by the thumb, creating a fleshly tone that isn't as sharp-edged as it would be with a pick.

Other tones for a solo can be extracted by holding a pick but angling the first finger so that the string is actually played by the flat upper surface of the finger nail. If this is done with the very tip of the nail the string slides off and hits the edge of the pick. This is one way of getting 'pinch harmonics', where notes suddenly leap higher than their pitch.

A variety of tones result from playing with picks of different thicknesses and materials. The most famous instance is Queen guitarist Brian May's sixpence, which he exploited for its serrated edge. As a general rule a hard pick is good for solos and a thinner one for rhythm parts. A hard pick gives a louder note and bends less, which is helpful if playing at speed. A thinner pick puts up less resistance, facilitating rhythm.

Pitch-bend or tremolo arm

An integral guitar device that might shape a solo is the tremolo arm or 'whammy bar'. Early in the electric guitar's history the tremolo arm added a gentle vibrato to notes, as can be heard on The Beatles' 'Baby's In Black', which has a halting six-bar solo using tremolo arm. The effect was taken further in the main guitar part of The Misunderstood's 'Children of the Sun'.

Later guitarists got more extreme effects by pushing the arm far enough to make the strings slack. Tremolo-arm effects are magnified when used in conjunction with other guitar processors. Jimmy Page with The Firm on 'Cadillac' combined tremolo arm with chorus and feedback to get a particularly sleazy sound. The definitive exploitation of what it can do was by Jimi Hendrix during his epoch-defining deconstruction of 'The Star Spangled Banner' at the 1969 Woodstock Festival. The tremolo arm has dramatic potential because of the way it unsettles the pitch of chords, especially if, as happens less often, it is pulled up rather than pushed down. Vernon Reid uses the tremolo arm effectively during his solos on Living Colour's 'Cult Of Personality' (1:35-46 and 3:01-55), siren wails alternating with very fast runs. Alex Lifeson's solo on Rush's 'Limelight' also makes clever use of tremolo to make the pitches surprising.

The solo (3:42-4:42) on All About Eve's 'Rhythm Of Life', played by Marty Willson-Piper, is a memorable solo drawing on a range of sound effects, including tremolo arm dips and bends, echo, whammy bar, toggle-switch feedback, quasi-whale noises, wide bends, and pinch harmonics. It shows the power of a good initial creative decision: to create tension by pitting a soundscape against a precise, arpeggiated progression. The underlying chords invited a standard rock guitar solo of predictable scale runs and bends. Instead, Willson-Piper chooses to paint with sounds. Only with the last phrase does he play a standard scale run to lift the solo's climax into the chorus.

Related to the tremolo arm is the Parsons White B-Bender, a mechanical device which turns the upper strap pin (the one nearest the neck) into a lever pulling a spring inside the body of the guitar to which the B-string is attached. Pulling down on the strap raises the pitch of the B-string, creating idiomatic bends for blues and country songs. Jimmy Page used it on two albums by The Firm and also for a solo on Robert Plant's 'Heaven Knows' (*Now And Zen*, 1988). The device allows for shapes that would be difficult to finger otherwise. Page also let rip with the B-bender on the coda to Led Zeppelin's 'All My Love' (*In Through The Out Door*, 1979), though some of this comes after the fade on the commercial release.

The possibilities of using pitch-bend effects were considerably increased by the invention of pedals such as the Digitech Whammy pedal, which enabled a player to drastically alter by foot the pitch of anything played, and without any of the tuning problems linked to extreme tremolo arm depression. Listen to Rage Against The Machine's 'Calm Like A Bomb'.

Choice of pickups
A guitar solo's tone is influenced by the selection of pick-up:

- Neck pickups provide rounded, mellow, sombre tones.
- Bridge pickups provide more cutting, trebly, bright tones.
- A Stratocaster with a five-way switch offers a further two so-called 'out-of-phase' sounds.

These tonal variations can be enhanced by:

■ choosing guitars with single-coil, mini-humbucker, or double-coil pickups
■ using tone controls on the guitar to dial back the treble frequencies
■ using the guitar's volume to reduce the drive on the pickup.

Solos have sometimes been inspired by a specific pickup tone that shapes the musical content. One instance – Mark Knopfler's early fondness for switch positions two and four on a Stratocaster – has been cited. Another would be the front humbucker 'woman tone' popularised by Eric Clapton on Cream's 'SWLABR' or 'Sunshine Of Your Love', and also used by Paul Kossoff with Free (see the solo on 'The Stealer'). On Cream's 'I Feel Free', during the solo, it's obvious when Clapton changes the pickup for the last phrase. This sound was much emulated. It can be heard on The Guess Who's 'American Woman' where two short solos introduce each verse, and at 2:49-3:31 where the solo gradually ascends in pitch. It can be heard on the twin lead fill in Led Zeppelin's 'Ramble On' (1:47-2:04); for the solo on Deep Purple's 'Smoke On The Water' (2:57-3:47); in The Stooges' 'I Wanna Be Your Dog' (at 2:39-3:04), where there's a solo combining fuzz and front pickup, and in Paul Kossoff's lead soloing with Free.

Other examples include The White Stripes' 'Seven Nation Army', with its slide solo played on the front pickup, the prominent lead throughout Manic Street Preachers' 'Motorcycle Emptiness', and The Stone Roses' 'Made Of Stone' (2:37-3:07), which has a front-pickup solo with a few double-stops.

Slide guitar

"Slide is really great for creating soundscapes – just moving the slide about on the strings, not really playing specific notes. You can hear that a lot on *Four Calendar Café*." (Robin Guthrie of the Cocteau Twins, *Guitar Player*, April 1996.)

Slide guitar (or 'bottleneck') where the player puts a glass or metal tube on a finger of the fretting hand is often associated with rock, blues, and acoustic styles. It offers:

■ complete control over pitch
■ notes to be flattened to any desired nuance
■ smooth pitch glides to approach or leave a note
■ emulation of the fluidity of a voice
■ many types of vibrato.

The sound depends on what the slide is made of – metal, brass, or glass. Chris Rea originally played with a brass slide; Johnny Winter, a piece of metal pipe narrow enough to fit his little finger; Mick Ronson, a cigarette lighter. Only a guitarist who plays and listens to a good deal of slide guitar is likely to register subtle differences stemming from the material of the slide; most listeners are only aware of the pitch-bend effects. Playing slide is harder on a low-action guitar, with increased fret noise a result.

Much slide playing in standard tuning sticks to single-note melody phrases, or thirds (on strings two and three). Double or triple tracking can thicken the sound.

This is evident on the double-tracked solo with slide and fuzz on Led Zeppelin's 'Tangerine'. The Smiths' 'Panic' has a short slide break at 0:48-1:02 with multi-tracked parts heightened with ghostly echo/reverb. There's an eight-bar slide solo on The Stereophonics' 'Have A Nice Day', after the second chorus. Two independent high-pitched slide guitar lines can create a poignant, 'weepy' sound, as on Wishbone Ash's 'Rock'n'Roll Widow', where the slide guitars also harmonise on a planned melodic phrase and solo in A minor after the second chorus.

Chordal effects are possible, even in standard tuning:

- The open top three strings make a minor triad.
- Open strings two, three, and four make a major triad.
- This means any major or minor triad is available in any key.

Open tunings make chordal slide playing fuller and easier (bold letters indicate strings that are re-tuned): open G (**D**G**D**GB**D**) and open D (**D**ADF♯A**D**) are popular for acoustic playing; open A (EA**EAC♯**E) and open E (**E**BEG♯BE) suit electric playing (higher tension).

A chordal slide solo may stand out better if the harmonic instruments supporting it are thinned out or moved into a higher or lower register (this is especially worth considering if the solo is on acoustic guitar).

Slide guitar solos can be heard in recordings by Ben Harper, Ry Cooder, Chris Rea, Bonnie Raitt, George Thorogood, and Lowell George with Little Feat. Stealers Wheel's 'Stuck In The Middle With You' has a slide solo where another lead guitar is also playing country licks. Pink Floyd's 'Wish You Were Here' has a muted slide solo (2:40-3:14) on acoustic which doesn't overpower the acoustic guitar backing and the synth brass chords; this slide idea is reprised before the fade. Turin Brakes' 'Future Boy' has an intro with a short solo of double-tracked acoustic slide guitar in unison with banjo; part of this solo is brought back as a link. Coldplay have a slide guitar on 'Yes', where there is a solo at 2:07-28, a four-bar phrase played twice.

Blues-rock bands frequently include slide guitar solos. ZZ Top's 'Tush' starts a slide solo at 0:48-1:29, after a single vocal verse. Thirty seconds later another solo starts, over a 12-bar sequence. Since the entire track is only 2:12, almost half of it is slide solo. Ron Wood added slide solos to Faces tracks like 'Stay With Me' and 'That's All You Need'. U2's 'Bullet The Blue Sky' shows how intense slide playing can become in a rock context.

Slide guitar solos can complement a lyrical pop style. In Eric Clapton's 'Layla', Duane Allman's high slide part is juxtaposed with the main guitar riff and adds much sweetness. George Harrison's 'My Sweet Lord' has a high slide guitar solo double-tracked. Notice the phrase repetition and harmonising (0:16-30) on this. It is significant that the start of this solo coincides with the first appearance of the key chord after the initial II-V changes. The middle slide solo benefits from the lift-off provided by the key change and the entry of a fuller rhythm section. The second solo is 2:39-54 and also harmonised towards the end. Harrison's influence as a slide player in non-blues contexts is considerable, as can be heard in songs like 'Day After Day' and 'No Matter What', by fellow Apple group Badfinger. A similar style of slide break can be heard on Todd Rundgren's 'I Saw The Light' (*Something/Anything*).

SECTION 5

The quasi-vocal quality of a slide guitar suits Carly Simon's 'You're So Vain', where there is a solo 2:01-26 after the second chorus. Notice how this solo worries away at a high single pitch when it starts. The slide comes back on for the last two phrases and ends with an off-the-fretboard glissando. The slide's unrestricted pitching is a suitable musical mirror of the unrestrained hedonism of the song's subject.

Slide guitar benefits from liberal application of reverb and/or echo. This can be heard with a glassy, clean tone on 'Wicked Game', Chris Isaak's homage to late 1950s songs, on the extended intro to Mountain's 'Pride And Passion', and during the languid slide solo of Led Zeppelin's 'What Is And What Should Never Be', whose break starts with single notes (1:47-2:11), shifts into chords, and finishes with a single note phrase at 2:29 and a downward glissando that has increasing reverb added to it to 2:41. The band's 'When The Levee Breaks' demonstrates what can be achieved by combining slide with an open-tuned electric 12-string.

Slide guitar solos of a non-blues character feature in some psychedelic songs that need bold sound effects. Since a slide does not rely on frets to create its pitches (though frets still assist the player to stay in tune), it increases the length of the fretboard and puts in reach a range of higher notes over the pickups, terminating only when the slide hits the bridge. Early Pink Floyd tracks such as 'See Emily Play' and 'Saucerful Of Secrets' (live version, 1969) have off-the-fretboard slide with added echo for psychedelic freak-out solos.

Harmonised slide lines can be impressive, especially if the glissandoes are also harmonised – something that harmonised twin lead can't reproduce. This is heard on the intro and during the solo (1:58-2:14) of Bread's 'Guitar Man', where swooping slide guitars grab the attention. Harmonised slide guitar is also featured during Fleetwood Mac's 'Albatross'.

Finally, even if the main solo instrument is something other than guitar, consider the use of slide to play short answering phrases to the main lead. This idea is used during the lead solo on 'Stairway To Heaven', where slide guitar plays a sighing three-note phrase at 6:24, 6:29, 6:34, and 6:39.

> *Harmonised slide lines can be impressive, especially if the glissandoes are also harmonised – something that harmonised twin lead can't reproduce.*

Volume pedal

The volume pedal has always been overshadowed by its cousin the wah-wah pedal (in fact, many who try it are disappointed, with a feeling of "Is that all it does?"). But as shown by Lindsey Buckingham's solo on Fleetwood Mac's 'Dreams', Dire Straits' 'Brothers In Arms', The Beatles' 'Yes It Is' and 'I Need You', the intro of The Who's 'Bargain', and Johnny Marr's playing on The Smiths' 'Well I Wonder', volume pedal effects can add a haunting touch to a solo. It works best in quieter songs and where the arrangement is sparse, as the pedal robs the notes of their attack, as by definition the volume swell is quiet and then increases. Its appeal means that you hear guitar chords without their expected percussive pick-strike. Techniques such as pre-bends, tremolo arm dips, and echo and reverb strengthen the impression the volume pedal makes. Distortion gives the effect greater emphasis.

Though the effect is achieved most easily with a pedal, some players get volume swells with the guitar's volume pots alone, by curling the little finger of the plucking hand around them. This is often called 'violin-toning'. The sequence is: turn the volume on the guitar off, strike a note, then quickly twist the volume pot back up. For this to work best the guitar amp must be set high enough so a small turn on the pot from '0' to '1' or '2' results in a surge of volume. If the guitar is too quiet the effect is not heard fast enough and requires too wide a turn of the pot. At high volume it is possible to free the picking hand to control the volume pot by hammering notes with the fretting hand rather than striking them. On the first live track on Mountain's part-studio/part-live album *Flowers Of Evil* (1971), you can hear Leslie West using violin-toning to play a guitar duet with himself, creating the illusion of two guitars by way of the contrasted tones.

There's an extremely restrained solo using violin-toning by Jan Akkerman on 'Focus (Vocal)', the opening track of the Dutch band's debut album *In And Out Of Focus* (1971). The solo on Television's 'Venus' begins with violin-toning that makes the guitar sound at first like a synth (2:11-40) before making use of chord tones.

Echo and delay

"For the solo in 'Save Me I'm Yours', I tried thousands of things. I tried a wah, thirds, fifths, slide, all types and then eventually settled on that repeat delay effect. We put it into Pro Tools and had it fire from all directions. It's picking up the tempo of the song and then it doesn't bludgeon you. Sometimes you have to think about these things. People assume you always do it off the cuff." (Steve Mason, Gene, June 1997.)

This solo cited by Steve Mason in 'Save Me, I'm Yours' (2:25-47) occurs over a III-VI-IV-V change in E and only uses about three notes, mostly repeating the same phrase, but the echo makes a huge difference to the expressive impact.

Echo/delay is one of the earliest effects to be applied to guitar in the recording studio, dating from the 'slapback' echo of 1950s guitar (20-50ms). Early analogue devices were limited and tended to colour the original note. Analogue tape delays caused each successive echo to degrade and distort. Modern digital units are cleaner and provide fine control over all parameters that govern the sound, including matching echo to tempo. Some emulate the imperfections of analogue tape echo. Many amps now come with a 'loop' facility allowing a performer to record a repeating phrase or a few chords, enabling other music to be created over the top. The amount of memory on such loops has increased considerably.

The main control parameters for delay are:

- how many repeats (feedback)
- how loud the repeats are in relation to the original note (echo level)
- how much time passes between the original note and the echo (delay time).

Echo can be used in several ways during a solo. A very short single delay thickens the note and gives an impression of sustain, but doesn't draw attention to itself as a distinctive effect. A longer delay, or multiple delays, makes more of an impression in its own right. If a delay is long enough, the solo can begin as a single line and develop into a double line from one guitar's input. A solo that moves stepwise up or

SECTION 5

down a scale can create consecutive thirds and/or fourths moving in parallel and in key.

The second solo on Thin Lizzy's 'That Woman's Gonna Break Your Heart' is a good example of how a correctly-timed delay will create a solo in thirds from a single guitar. The unexpected addition of an echo long enough to be easily heard after the original note can be very dramatic, as with the first lead phrases toward the end of Bad Company's 'Feel Like Makin' Love' (3:37-5:10). More generally, applying a relatively short echo to a lead guitar solo is one way of turning it into stereo (panning hard left and right) rather than positioning it somewhere in the centre of the mix.

The longer the echo, and the more repeats, the more challenging it is to play a solo with long phrases, because the phrases will partly obscure the echoes and result in sonic confusion. To get the best out of this approach, you can restrict the number of chords in the underlying harmony and the speed with which they change. It can also be fruitful to limit the number of echo repeats, and reduce their volume in proportion to the original signal, or send the echo to a separate track and then edit out any echoes that interfere.

Some examples of echoed solos include The Flamin' Groovies' 'Shake Some Action'. It has a 24 bar solo that runs from 2:22-48, multi-tracked and in stereo. It flows into the main guitar riff and returns for the coda. The solo on Royal Trux's 'Stevie' has two echoes, one left, one right, at different times. The intro lead to 'You Ain't Seen Nothing Yet' by Bachman-Turner Overdrive, which also follows each chorus, is treated with a stereo echo. On the third occasion the opening phrase develops into a melodic solo (2:01-33) and cuts out into a prechorus. The solo is briefly reprised for the coda fade. Billy Duffy's solo on The Cult's 'Soul Asylum' (*Sonic Temple*, 1989) has slinky echoed phrases and long-held bends at 4:35-57, with the main lead on the left and the echo on the right of the stereo image. The delay is long enough to clearly register the echo as an answer to the lead guitar's dry phrase.

> *The Edge has stated that he did not find his identity as a guitarist until he got hold of an echo unit. Echo is fundamental to the band's music.*

Echoed guitar solos dominate the music of U2. The Edge has stated that he did not find his identity as a guitarist until he got hold of an echo unit. Echo is fundamental to the band's music. One could cite the solos on 'In God's Country' or 'The Fly', where echo is combined with distortion and wah-wah; The Edge wanted to re-record the latter solo because he didn't think it was good enough, but fortunately was over-ruled.

One of the best-known extended solos with echo is that created by Brian May on Queen's 'Brighton Rock' (*Sheer Heart Attack*, 1974), which developed from May's experiments with an Echoplex tape echo. Having made multi-track guitar harmonies a signature of Queen's sound, May had the problem of how to emulate them onstage, and echo was a device that might help. May said, "I turned up the regeneration until it was giving me multiple repeats. I discovered you could do a lot with this: you could set up rhythms and play against them, or you could play a line and then play a harmony to it."

During the 'Brighton Rock' solo, each note has two echoes, so that triple lead harmonies result. To time the echoes right, he had to adapt the position of the tape head, and ended up with two personalised Echoplexes. He also achieved greater clarity when the two echoes were fed into separate amps, reducing the interference. The impact of the echo in this solo is heightened because apart from a few percussive stabs no other instruments are heard. For another Brian May solo using echo, see 'Tenement Funster' from the same album. This is a solo that benefits from a chord progression that swings from the song's key of E minor into a G-G♯m-Bm sequence that provides fertile ground for a lead solo.

Another memorable use of delay is the haunting last solo break on Led Zeppelin's 'Achilles Last Stand' (8:25-55), from *Presence*, which is the second peak solo of the track. Part of what makes it so effective is the hammering rhythm underneath from the drums and bass, sketching the Em-C chord change. This break has two or three guitars panned backwards and forwards. It's one of those few guitar solos where the instrument sonically transcends itself and is liberated from all the customary clichés.

Distortion, overdrive, and fuzz

More than any other single effect, distortion seems to belong with guitar solos. Originating in the natural response of overloaded valve amplifiers, it was distortion that helped thicken a single guitar note to the point where it had enough authority to feature as a solo line. There is a 'politics' of distortion, and effects-pedal manufacturers have objectified this by building pedals that offer a wide array of levels of distortion to suit various rock sub-genres. One way to approach overdrive is to add enough to make notes sparkle and sustain (a compressor also gives sustain). More distortion suits more aggressive styles. It begins with blues overdrive, into mainstream rock and into heavy rock, metal, thrash metal, etc, to the point where one pedal might not be enough.

Distortion provides more sustain to lead guitar. This in itself shapes the kind of solo you play if you have it. The longer the notes you hold because the sustain is there to do it, the fewer notes are played. Sustained notes, especially involving bends, create tension by making the listener anticipate their end. They can be further extended through finger vibrato. A sustained bend is a classic feature of a rock guitar solo, as illustrated in the second solo by Scott Gorham on the live version of Thin Lizzy's 'Still In Love With You' (*Live And Dangerous*, 1978, 5:25-7:03). It can be compared with the first solo, by Brian Robertson, on the same track (2:40-4:16), which has a longer echo and clearly distinguishable repeats. At this time Thin Lizzy were using the Watkins Copycat tape echo.

For the main solo on Fleetwood Mac's 'Go Your Own Way', Lindsey Buckingham plays only four phrases with gaps and a lot of sustain (1:48-2:10). This middle passage proceeds for several bars before he starts playing. His guitar is on the verge of feedback to get the sustain and his last note bleeds into the last chorus. His coda solo (2:39 to end) on two lead guitars is double-tracked but occasionally the two guitars deviate. This could have originated as take one and take two of a single solo with both takes incorporated, which would explain the clashing pitches heard at 3:06-07, and why one ends before the other, dipping down at 3:15, while the other, much more rocky and designed to intensify the song, goes on to 3:21, staying at a high pitch. This solo becomes the song's climax.

Fuzz is a more 'blurred' type of distortion from the 1960s and associated with Jimi

Hendrix and psychedelic rock. Fuzz encourages the striking of fewer notes to let the fuzz tone come through. It has sometimes been combined with other effects, as in the fuzz-wah solo. To hear how outrageous a sound that can create (causing notes to bleed into one another) listen to Marc Bolan's fuzz-wah solo on 'Jewel' (*T. Rex*, 1970). If Jonny Greenwood of Radiohead had grown up two decades earlier and acquired the blues-rock lead style of 1970 this is surely what he would have sounded like. Another wild example is the sustained fuzz solo on Blur's 'Coffee & TV' (2:52-3:25) where the notes are sustained and at times very slowly bent into pitch, with some tremolo arm wobbling as well.

Wah-wah pedal

A wah-wah pedal applies an active EQ boost moving through the high-mid frequency (500-3kHz) range. It is usually positioned after the distortion in the signal chain. The original Vox Clyde McCoy model in 1967 was named after a trumpeter known for producing crying noises with a trumpet mute. At one time it came with a certain amount of rock history baggage, namely its association with late 1960s psychedelia and blues-rock, courtesy of the playing of Eric Clapton on Cream's 'Tales Of Brave Ulysses' and Blind Faith's 'Presence Of The Lord' (also using a Leslie cabinet), David Gilmour on Pink Floyd's live version of 'Astronomy Domine', and Jimi Hendrix on tracks like 'Voodoo Chile (Slight Return)', 'Up From The Skies', and 'Burning Of The Midnight Lamp'. Hendrix's use of the pedal on the intro of 'Still Raining, Still Dreaming' results in an astonishingly vocal phrase. Mick Ronson combined the pedal with bending and rapid picking to create a macabre mocking laugh for the dark theatre of David Bowie's 'Time' (2:15-28).

Aware of this history, Peter Buck put a first-take wah-wah solo on R.E.M.'s 'Stand' almost as a joke, having decided the song didn't need a bridge. The wah-wah on Bread's 'Guitar Man' functions as a sonic symbol of the archetypal guitar man of the title, a tribute to the way that Clapton and Hendrix had both popularised the pedal. It also has associations with soul music and film soundtracks (notably Isaac Hayes's 'Theme From *Shaft*') from the 1970s. Motown had guitarists who added wah-wah to songs like 'Papa Was A Rolling Stone' and 'Up The Ladder To The Roof', and it crops up even on a later Motown song like Marvin Gaye's 'Let's Get It On'.

Other good examples include the lead guitar solo on Hawkwind's 'Silver Machine' from 1:44, played with fairly constant pentatonic minor eighth-note movement through a wah-wah. The Rattles' 'The Witch' has wah-wah fills throughout the verse, keeping the tone clean and using reverb. Marc Bolan made excellent use of the pedal for playing lead on Tyrannosaurus Rex's 'By The Light Of A Magical Moon', and T. Rex's 'Root Of Star' and 'Monolith'. Deep Purple's early single 'Amoretta' has wah-wah throughout and a wah-wah solo. Wah and distortion were used for guitar solos on The Stooges' '1969'; the last minute of the song is given up to this wah-wah soloing. Thin Lizzy's 'Don't Believe A Word' has a fine lead solo that begins with the effective device of the rapid picking of a single bend with the pedal moving slowly back and forth.

The wah-wah pedal has also coloured solos by being switched on but not rocked with the foot. Switched on in the down (closed) position and passive, it acts as a treble booster. If you only have a guitar with double-coil pickups and need to approximate the sound of single-coils, this is one way to do it. The high register solos on Led Zeppelin's 'Communication Breakdown' and 'Whole Lotta Love', ending the instrumental 'electric cloud' freak-out section (3:06-22), were recorded this way, giving what Page described as "a really raucous sound". For 'Rusty Cage', Soundgarden's Kim Thayil ran a Les Paul through a wah-wah that was a quarter of the way depressed.

Johnny Marr had a wah-wah pedal slightly open for some guitar breaks on The Smiths' 'Shoplifters Of The World'. He said that he approached it like a tone-pot. The same point was made by Ultravox's Midge Ure to *Guitarist* in November 1991: "It makes different harmonics jump out as well, which is quite nice. It gives it an almost voice-box type sound but with a much wider range. It gives more expression, makes it almost talk, which I really like." Joey Santiago of The Pixies used it as a tone box on songs like 'Subba Culture'.

Mick Ronson often played with a pedal wedged in the up position, both with David Bowie and on Lou Reed's *Transformer* album. Dire Straits' 'Money For Nothing' also did this. On 'Fade To Black', from Metallica's *Ride the Lightning* (1984), Kirk Hammett combined the neck pickup on a Gibson Flying V with a wah-wah in its maximum open position. Marty Willson-Piper plays a great solo on 'Freeze', from All About Eve's album *Ultraviolet* (1992), mixing wah-wah with echo and volume-swell effects.

Leslie rotary speaker

This effect was popularised with the 1968-70 period in rock. The rotary speaker creates a swirling effect and is particularly effective on arpeggio ideas. The Beatles' 'While My Guitar Gently Weeps' features a 16-bar verse sequence solo using a Leslie speaker effect and plenty of vibrato. The pitch wobble in this song has an extra-musical meaning because of the weeping mentioned in the lyric. Likewise, 'Old Brown Shoe' has a 16-bar solo (1:25-52), the first half on slide, the second half on picked lead through a Leslie speaker. The solo using C pentatonic major on 'Let It Be' is also played through this effect (2:00-26). There's a thick Leslie-treated guitar playing a double-stop solo on 'Yer Blues', before a second much higher-pitch solo that has also been treated.

The guitar part and solo on Jimi Hendrix's 'Little Wing' (*Axis: Bold As Love*, 1968) was fed through a miniature Leslie-type unit that had an eight-inch speaker. According to producer Bob Ezrin, David Gilmour's classic guitar solo on 'Comfortably Numb' from Pink Floyd's *The Wall* (1979) was recorded with Yamaha rotating speaker cabinets. The solo on Led Zeppelin's 'Good Times Bad Times' and 'Black Dog', Free's 'On My Way', and on the arpeggio riff on the bridge of Cream's 'Badge', also have rotary speaker effect added.

Tremolo

Not to be confused with the tremolo arm, this is an amplifier effect included in many multi-fx units, which causes notes to shimmer by rapidly gating and releasing the signal. It is associated with late 1950s and early 1960s guitar, including Duane Eddy and the surf guitar genre, and some of the pop ballads of the time, in which it stands for heartbreak (imminent or actual), as on Sandie Shaw's 'Always Something There

SOLOS, GUITARS, AND GUITAR EFFECTS

To Remind Me'. It is usually more effective on chords, which it turns into shards of broken glass, than single notes. The Hollies 'I'm Alive' has a 12-string solo (1:31-46) played through a tremolo unit, and there is a tremolo guitar melody at the beginning of The Four Pennies' 1964 hit 'Juliet'.

The low-pitched Duane Eddy-style solo featured as the coda to Glen Campbell's 'Galveston' and 'Wichita Lineman' (1:49-2:08), and on many Bruce Springsteen songs such as 'Thunder Road', 'Darkness On The Edge Of Town', 'Man's Job', 'Tougher Than The Rest', 'Out On The Streets', and 'The Wish'. It was a sound revived in the 90s by bands like Portishead, whose guitarist Adrian Utley said he liked 'spy guitar' and 1960s soundtracks. It is an influence on the solo in Anna Calvi's 'Love Won't Be Leaving'. Fairground Attraction's 'Perfect' has a 12-bar guitar solo (1:53-2:20) drawing on various 1950s solo ideas including Duane Eddy twang, country double-stops, thirds, and tremolo arm vibrato. It is worth saying that a solo based on a vocal melody is likely to have slower movement, to have fewer big jumps in it, and to be less obviously based on a finger-pattern, though it may be scale-derived. Sheryl Crow's 'If It Makes You Happy' has a tremolo guitar break at 3:07-24 that provides a strong contrast to the Stones-like rhythm riff of the verse.

The Pretenders' 'Kid' revives the historical associations of the tremolo by starting with a short solo using sixths, a tremolo tone, and a low-pitched Duane Eddy melody. This returns in edited form as a link from the first chorus to the second verse. A new guitar solo occurs after the second chorus and bridge at 1:30 and is arpeggio-dominated with a few bends; there is a key change for it. The song starts in C major, the bridge plays with A-G-F, and the solo comes in on E major. A tremolo effect is prominent throughout The Clientele's *Strange Geometry* (2005) album. The pentatonic major solo in 'Riot Van' by The Arctic Monkeys (1:33-50) also uses tremolo.

Chorus, phasing, and flanging

These effects offer another way of colouring a solo. Chorus is the subtlest of the three, thickening the tone, smoothing the treble edge of the notes, and adding sustain, especially to chords and arpeggio ideas. It suits situations where the musical dynamic is on the quieter side and the solo isn't fast.

Phasing creates a wind-tunnel sweeping sound that can be combined with distortion, as on 'Who's That Lady' and 'Summer Breeze' by The Isley Brothers, Suede's 'Animal Nitrate' (1:45-2:05), and on the coda solos of 'House Burning Down' and 'Bold As Love' by Jimi Hendrix. Ace's 'How Long' has a phased solo after the first chorus (1:35-2:05). Phasing became popular in 1970s soul and funk. David Bowie's guitarist Carlos Alomar used it on *Station To Station* (1975). You can hear it lending sustain to the chords in the intro and first verse of Deniece Williams's 'Free'.

Flanging is a more extreme effect, suitable for a solo that may depend as much on sound-effects as the melodic and harmonic value of the notes. The solo on Smashing Pumpkins' 'Cherub Rock' has flanging generated by using two tape machines, the analogue method for creating it. A good example of flanging in a solo can be heard played by John McGeoch on Siouxsie & The Banshees' epic 'Nightshift' (*Ju-Ju*, 1981), where it is coupled with echo and sustain. This solo owes nothing at all to scales. Instead, McGeoch picks high Am and A♭ chords and allows the effects to turn his arpeggios into a screeching cloud of powdered black glass.

Harmonizer

In the early days of rock guitar, if a player wanted to harmonise a lead line they had to multi-track a solo or share the task with another player. But by the mid-1960s gadgets were created that would add an octave above the note played. As the decades passed, these effects became more sophisticated, giving consecutive thirds with out-of-key notes; and then came 'intelligent' harmonizers and pitch-shifters that corrected the intervals so parallel lines would always be in key. (Consecutive thirds derived from the major or minor scale will always be a mixture of major thirds and minor thirds, not all the same.) These were handy for single guitarists to re-create studio multi-tracking in concert, but soon players fiddled with them to get unorthodox ideas. Pitch-shifting can now be triggered by a pedal, giving solos of wild, unpredictable notes.

One player who did some of this experimentation was Billy Corgan with The Smashing Pumpkins. The cybergrunge of the solo on 'Siamese Dream' (3:10-32) is an anarchic and fragmentary rock solo with pitch-shifting applied to the bends. 'Quiet' has a similar solo at 2:03-38, the first part of which is free and the second half a repeated harmonised phrase. 'Soma' (3:10-22) has a quiet guitar solo played with a muted tone, the main guitar ghosted by at least one other. There's a second solo at 4:28, full of slow bends, rapid runs, and distortion. 'Mayonaise' has a phased solo, with a highly processed sound. Corgan also used an Electro-Harmonix Micro-Synth for extra distortion on some tracks.

The use of harmonizers means it is no longer always easy to tell if octaves in a solo are actually played or generated digitally – as in the solo of Teenage Fanclub's 'Neil Jung'.

Feedback

"Because 'Sweetness Follows' and 'Try Not To Breathe' are so quiet, you want to add an air of tension rather than solo over them. You take this distorted, deranged feedback sound and layer it underneath the song – it's kind of subliminal." (Peter Buck, December 1992.)

A feature of live performance, and at first considered a nuisance, feedback can be an expressive device in a solo. It enhances the guitar's sustain, giving notes that do not drop in volume, and adds a creatively dangerous instability because of its tendency to boost overtones so they get louder than the initial pitch. To explain this point, any note – such as the guitar's open sixth string E – actually comprises many higher pitched notes that climb beyond human hearing as they get fainter. These overtones are the richness of any individual note. If the fundamental is the sixth string E:

- the first overtone is the E one octave higher
- the second overtone is the B one octave and one fifth higher
- the third overtone is the E two octaves above
- the fourth overtone is a G-sharp two octaves and a major third above.

When feedback decays, one of these will overwhelm the fundamental, and a higher-pitched wail occurs. You can hear this in the version of 'Since I've Been Loving You' from Led Zeppelin's remastered soundtrack album *The Song Remains The Same* (2007), where at 0:28 a G flips up an octave. Another example occurs during the guitar solo by Dan Ar Bras on Alan Stivell's 'Spered Hollvedel' at 2:42-46 (*A Dublin*, 1975).

There are three basic approaches to using feedback in a solo: the anarchic, the sustained, and the harmonised. Early solos featuring feedback tended to use it in a self-consciously rebellious and anarchic manner. The Who's 'Anyway, Anyhow, Anywhere' has feedback during its solo, modified by flicking a toggle switch – the 'morse-code' effect. Pete Townshend told *Guitar World* in October 1994: "The toggle switch thing was literally to make the guitar sound like a machine gun ... when it was feeding back. And when I bought my first Rickenbacker, I packed it with paper and found I could actually produce feedback on select harmonics, which was quite extraordinary." The feedback in The Jam's 'In The Crowd' coda solo is modelled on this Who track. Toggle-switch feedback can be heard on the end of David Bowie's 'John I'm Only Dancing' and in 'Bull On Parade' by Tom Morello of Rage Against The Machine on *Evil Empire* (1996).

The second solo break on The Who's 'My Generation' is a feedback freak-out solo (2:23-49) over two chords with over-dubbed guitar, toggle switch effects, and pick slides until the vocal hook returns at 2:49. The Beatles started 'I Feel Fine' with a feedback note, as did Hendrix on 'Foxy Lady' and The Stooges on 'I Wanna Be Your Dog'. The same band's 'No Fun' uses feedback in its minimal opening minor pentatonic solo, along with tremolo arm and fuzz. This solo takes over from the vocals for the last two minutes of the 5:15 track.

The sustained feedback solo has fewer notes than other types, the point being to show off the held notes. The challenge is to keep the fundamental note from decaying too soon into a higher overtone, except at the end of the solo for a dramatic climax. This approach was favoured by Carlos Santana. The sustained feedback solo also lends itself to unorthodox solos, as typified by Andy Summers' anti-solo solo on The Police's 'Bring On The Night', where a high E feeds back, changes to a high A briefly, before returning to the E and repeatedly struck fourths. This was a bold, imaginative choice for the solo because the underlying chords would have lent themselves to a standard scale-based rock solo. Feedback also assists Mick Ronson to play sustained notes on the coda solo to David Bowie's 'Moonage Daydream'.

The sustained feedback solo has fewer notes than other types, the point being to show off the held notes. The challenge is to keep the fundamental note from decaying too soon into a higher overtone.

The Jam's 'Strange Town' shows how feedback can be controlled to some degree in a mini-choir guitar arrangement. After the initial guitar solo (1:26-39) and succeeding vocal bridge (1:39-55), a descending guitar riff enters at 2:00. Three lead guitars enter one after the other in harmony, the final notes of their phrases allowed to feed back, ending when the last verse starts at 2:20. There is a similar instance in 'When You're Young' (2:15-32).

Feedback can also link one section with another in a song. This is effective if it links the end of the guitar solo into the next chorus or verse. An example is The Darkness's 'Out Of My Hands' where at 2:45 one of the guitar solo notes feeds back into the following chorus by another eight seconds. Blue Oyster Cult's 'Don't Fear The Reaper' has a full guitar solo (2:43-3:19) where the last note feeds back into the last verse and is audible in that verse until 3:46. This feedback G links across a song section where there is a change of key. The earlier chord change was Fm-G, the pause is on G and then the main riff starts again on the song's main sequence of Am-G-F-G. These uses of feedback remain under-exploited in rock music.

The E-bow device gives a similar sustain to feedback but in a more controlled way. It works by creating a moving conductor in a magnetic field. There are E-bow solos on The Smashing Pumpkins' 'Soma', The Mission's 'Butterfly On A Wheel', and R.E.M.'s 'E-Bow The Letter' (from *New Adventures in Hi-Fi*, 1996).

Miscellaneous effects

"What I discovered I loved to do was to make the guitar sound like things. I began with things that were around me in the air, like car horns and seagulls. The first thing was to work out how to do sounds like that on the guitar – and even sounds no-one ever heard on the guitar – and secondly, how to work that into music." (Adrian Belew, *Guitarist* July 1990.)

The search for strange guitar sounds goes back a long way. On Black Sabbath's 'Paranoid' (1:22-44), listen carefully and on the right channel it sounds as though some of the signal has been fed through a ring modulator. Eddie Philips used a violin bow on The Creation's 'Making Time' (1966) before Jimmy Page made it a trademark on Led Zeppelin's 'Dazed And Confused' (*Led Zeppelin*, 1969). The Creation solo starts at 1:29-2:04 with a lead guitar playing as well. The bow is then used to play the chords in the following verse, which is less effective.

The talk box is perhaps a guitar effect too unhip to be resurrected now, but at one time was marketed as the Hell Talk Box, Electro-Harmonix's 'Golden Throat', or Dean Markley's Voice Box. A comparable tone could probably be created by putting a lead guitar through an Auto-Tune unit. Among the first people to use it were Joe Walsh on 'Rocky Mountain Way' and Pete Drake on 'Forever', and then it was forgotten until Peter Frampton asked Walsh how to use it. Frampton then showcased it on two hits, 'Show Me The Way' (0:15-29), and 'Baby I Love Your Way'. It was later heard on Bon Jovi's 'Livin' On A Prayer' (solos at 1:20-26, 2:25-53).

PRODUCTION AND MIXING TECHNIQUES

Once a solo is recorded its sound can be further modified and developed. At this stage stereo and other types of echo can be applied. Reverb can be applied to the entire mix but also increased for a solo to give extra body to high notes if they are at risk of thinning out (another way to tackle this is to have the solo line doubled either by itself or by another instrument). Interest can be added to a solo by panning it from left to right and back, as happens on Jimi Hendrix's 'If 6 Was 9' (*Axis: Bold As Love*, 1968). It could also be double-tracked. During the recording of *Blizzard of Oz* (1981),

SECTION 5

Randy Rhoads would record a solo in two or three takes. For the solo on 'Crazy Train', Rhoads triple-tracked the solo. The best one was centred in the middle; the other two were panned hard left and right and reduced slightly in volume by engineer Max Norman. The guitar solo on Ted Nugent's 'Cat Scratch Fever' (1:40-2:07), using A pentatonic minor, is double-tracked fairly closely.

Backward guitar solos

Backward guitar was developed in the 1960s by reversing tape reels and recording a solo starting where the solo was due to end and ending where the solo should start. When the tape was threaded back the right way the solo would be in the correct place but the notes would sound backwards. (Now it can be done digitally in simpler ways.) This is a compelling effect, partly because it is never heard in nature. Except through technology, we cannot hear a sound reversed in time. The character of a backward sound depends on the instrument. The way in which an instrument's sound is produced affects what is heard when the solo is reversed. On the guitar, notes are at maximum volume as soon as they are struck and then fade. Backward guitar notes crescendo rapidly from a quiet note and then suddenly are gone. Backward piano gives good results because of its long sustain – an effect used by the creators of The Beatles' *Love* (2006) when they reversed the long E major piano chord from the end of 'A Day In The Life' and put it at the start of 'Get Back'.

Tomorrow's hit 'My White Bicycle' has backward guitar solos three times after a vocal line. This entire section lasts 12 bars, two bars per phrase, and the idea is used twice.

Other examples are include The Who's 'Armenia City In The Sky' (*The Who Sell Out*, 1967), and The Jam's 'Start!', where the Beatlesque six-bar solo has an overdubbed backward guitar phrase, and 'In The Crowd' with backward guitar on the freak-out coda. Blur's 'Sing' from the album *Leisure* has some backward guitar. The Beatles' 'I'm Only Sleeping' (*Revolver*, 1966) has a five-bar solo (1:33-44) using two backward guitars, which illustrates the dream-world of the lyric. They play out the song when everything else has finished. See also the coda solo on T. Rex's 'Cosmic Dancer' (*Electric Warrior*, 1971), where two guitars play lead phrases on the left and right of the stereo mix (3:10-4:28), and the coda of 'Chariot Choogle' (*The Slider*, 1972). This fits the other-worldly lyric about reincarnation. Duran Duran's cover of Led Zeppelin's 'Thank You' has a backward guitar solo. There is backward solo guitar on many tracks by The Jimi Hendrix Experience, including 'You Got Me Floatin'' and 'Castles Made Of Sand' (1:31-48), and on The Verve's 'Judas' (4:33-53).

The 'wailing choir' solo

If you finally have three, four, or five solos and no single one is quite what you want, you could either use the two best as a stereo pair and live with the slight deviations in phrasing between them (if they're supposed to be the same) or have them as a duo with marked differences. On Love's 'A House Is Not A Motel' the coda has two lead solos playing against each other. You could also do this with three takes, panned left, centre, and right. This creates a type of solo that I call the 'wailing choir'.

This solo approach was made possible by advances in recording technology in the late 1960s and 1970s. When popular music was captured in two, four, eight or even

16-track, there often wasn't room for the soloist to have more than part of one track or one dedicated track or possibly two. Irish guitarist Rory Gallagher told *Guitarist* (June 1987) about recording in one take on 16-track: "You haven't got a million tracks and you can't be laying down four guitar solos to pick one from later – just putting off the dreaded moment ... the first few albums we did, most of the tracks I sang live as well, and played the solos live and maybe overdubbed the rhythm guitar." As track numbers increased, this changed. It then became possible for a guitarist to solo maybe five or six times, hoping to get a single brilliant pass, but retaining each take in case it proved impossible to do better. This could be used to experiment with guitar tones rather than the notes. On the *Metallica* album, Kirk Hamett recorded one of the solos 15 times with 15 different guitars, and then listened to them one at a time and chose the one that had the best tone – regardless of which guitar it was.

In earlier days of recording, if the first solo wasn't good enough it would be recorded over. The opportunity to postpone decisions about what to keep and what to erase or exclude has increased with developments in multi-track recording technology, first in analogue and then digital. It was only natural curiosity to wonder what it might be like to hear all the takes of a lead guitar break at once: hence the 'wailing choir' solo, which can be a superb effect. T. Rex's 'Ballrooms Of Mars' (*The Slider*, 1972) is a fine example. Marc Bolan and producer Tony Visconti thought that, having recorded a number of passes, why not push all the faders on those guitar takes up at once? All the lead guitars start on the same couple of notes, worrying away at D and E before spiralling into different lines, some at a higher octave, and then all coming together for the final bend. The effect is otherworldly, in keeping with the imaginative lyric. Something of a T. Rex feel informs Grant Lee Buffalo's 'Fuzzy', which has a guitar solo at 2:25-48 using the first electric heard on the track, with many slow bends and a fuzzy tone. The guitar breaks into two leads, playing freely from 2:38. The solo repeats from 4:05 to the fade, where the deviation between the two leads is more obvious.

There are multiple lead guitars on The Clash's 'London Calling'. A 16-bar solo section comes after the second chorus, with feedback at 1:51-2:05 and then the backward guitars that can be heard from 2:09 to 2:20. The guitar solo thus perfectly complements the apocalyptic scenario of the lyric. Other examples include Python Lee Jackson's (ie, Rod Stewart's) 'In A Broken Dream' where the chorus initially has the lead guitar playing the vocal melody with the voice. A fuzzy high-pitched guitar solo returns at 2:35-3.00 and there's a second solo that partially overlaps and then carries through the last chorus. By the record's end there are three leads, panned central, left, and right.

There are two guitar solos recorded as alternate takes and then both used at the same time on Wishbone Ash's 'Throw Down The Sword' (*Argus*, 1972). The give-away is the presence of several consecutive seconds at one point, which would be certainly avoided if two leads were planned to work together, and the way the solos come together for certain key phrases which were obviously markers in the overall shape of the solo. You can hear a double-tracked guitar solo where the parts are not quite exact, and therefore suggest different takes being kept, on The Libertines' 'Time For Heroes'.

SECTION 5

SOLOS, SCALES, AND HARMONY

The quickest way to find the notes for a solo is to know which scales will fit your chord sequence.

SOLOS, SCALES, AND HARMONY

In this section it is time to look at scales and their relationship to keys and harmony. When most players think of solos, the first source material that comes to mind are scales. Regardless of the instrument, solos tend to be associated with scales. The scale is the group of notes that enables an effective melody, or set of melodic phrases, to be created over any given chord progression in a key. But a scale is only the raw material for a solo, and the correct scale alone won't magically create a memorable solo. All it does is minimise the risk of playing notes that sound wrong in context. But a knowledge of which scales fit which groups of chords is certainly important when constructing solos, especially if some of the chords over which the solo is to be played are not in key.

This section describes the most useful scales, their musical characteristics, and which chords they work with. Finger-patterns are provided for guitarists to practise them. Before that, some cautionary points. First, it is possible to play a decent solo in a song without knowing much about scales, if you have a good ear; that will guide you to the right notes for the progression, as long as the chords are not complicated. Second, much information about scales and lead soloing is over-complicated and sometimes misleading. Third, some of what is taught about lead guitar scales has little practical value in the context of playing solos in songs; many exotic scales are irrelevant to mainstream songwriting, which is what *Songs And Solos* is about, rather than progressive rock instrumentals or jazz improvising.

FEAR OF A FALSE NOTE

Anxiety when soloing comes down to fear of playing a wrong note. Knowledge of scales and chords is sought to reduce the playing of wrong notes. From a simple perspective, a note is wrong if it sounds out of place, which it might do if it is not in key and clashes with the underlying harmony. This could be the background chord in a given bar and/or the overall key of the solo section. The key is a musical 'field' generated by a specific scale and the chords derived from it. In this case, a wrong note could be described as musically ungrammatical.

But a wrong note could actually be a 'right' note. If the soloist deliberately wants to clash with the harmony, it would no longer be a wrong note from a creative perspective. This shows that in a broader way the impression that a note is wrong is partly subjective. In 'I Want You', Elvis Costello plays a two-note guitar solo in the key of E minor on the notes B♭ and E (single version, 2:29-36) over a turnaround of Em-G-C-B7. The 'wrong' note is B♭, which in those seven seconds clashes with the B-natural in Em, G, and B7, and implies an out-of-key C7 with the C chord. The dissonance is intentional, embodying the negative emotion of the lyric. It may be theoretically wrong, but artistically it is dead right. The same applies to the freakish solo by Robert Fripp on David Bowie's 'Fashion', and to parts of Richard Thompson's solo on 'Hard On Me' (*Mock Tudor*, 1999). In some situations deliberately playing wrong notes can be an effective musical statement, and the stricter the musical context the more powerful it can be. In a song with limited harmony there are many opportunities for wrong notes; in free jazz very few.

There are aspects of rock/pop harmony that are in themselves ungrammatical, judged by the rules of traditional harmony, but they are now part of its harmonic style and not heard as incorrect by its audience. There are thousands of 12-bar blues-derived songs whose three chords are all dominant sevenths: in the key of E major: E7, A7, B7. By traditional theory two of those chords (E7 and A7) do not belong to the key of E major; a major key can only have one dominant seventh – on the dominant (ie, the fifth) note of the scale, which in E major is B. But now everyone accepts that these three chords sound together in blues-influenced songs without wrecking the sense of key.

So what sounds right or wrong is partly dependent on genre and how your audience relates to genre. A note could be ungrammatical by genre, because most songs in that genre don't include those pitches. Your listeners partly decide what is a wrong note with reference to what they're accustomed to. A solo in a jazz song, with many chromatic (out-of-key) notes, might be accepted by a jazz audience but not an easy listening crowd. By contrast, in a mainstream pop song, exactly the same solo might sound wrong to its audience because it doesn't match their expectations. In any style where rebellion and a certain level of dissonance is tolerated, a soloist has a freer rein to play as they wish.

Some players take a more relaxed attitude to the idea of playing 'wrong' notes. Slash told *Guitar World* in February 1992: "The most important thing is to play the way you feel. Just go with whatever emotion and music come to you. If you hear more notes, play more notes; if you hear fewer notes, play less. If you hear some 'out notes' in the song, fit them in – they may just be the magic notes! A producer might say, 'That's out of key!' It may just be out of key – or in the key of Z somewhere – but if it's in the emotion, go with it."

This book is not a theoretical encyclopaedia of scales, but a songwriter's guide to using them in a solo. Our approach to scales begins where the songwriter starts: with songwriting chords. We want to know which scales fit over which chords and groups of chords, and how to do this with as few scales as possible. Scales can be considered

"There are conscious decisions being made while improvising, but I never think, 'Now I'm going to play a diminished scale, or now I'm going to play a pentatonic scale and then finish with some chromatic displacement.' It's more a free play between the conscious and the subconscious."

Vernon Reid of Living Colour, Guitar World, *April 1993.*

as covering a whole key or a chord type. The approach taken here is to describe how a scale could cover a whole group of chords, and then how to find those chords that might need another scale.

Note: in this section a distinction is made between 'scale' and 'pattern':

- 'Scale' describes the theoretical set of notes that defines each scale type, regardless of the instrument on which it is played.
- 'Pattern' describes a position (of which there are many) where that scale is found on the guitar fretboard.

In this section a number of patterns are provided for each type of scale. These do not include open strings, so that the patterns can be transposed to any desired key or chord. The patterns include two-octave scales whose root notes are located on the sixth and fifth strings, as well as shorter patterns located on the upper strings. Higher notes are more useful in solos than lower ones.

HOW TO WORK OUT SONG-CHORDS FOR A MAJOR KEY

The first step is to work out which chords a songwriter uses in any major key. This is described in detail in *How To Write Songs On Guitar*, where there is also a table giving songwriting chords for every major key. Some combination of these will be what the solo is played over. Here is a method for doing this, with examples of how it is worked out.

1 Choose the key note: C (for C major).
2 Construct a major scale from that note by writing seven letters alphabetically from the one selected (from A B C D E F G): C D E F G A B C.
3 Make the intervals match the pattern 2-2-1-2-2-2-1, where 2 is a tone/whole-step and 1 is a semitone/half-step, remembering that, of the natural notes, E-F and B-C are separated by a semitone but all the others by a tone. This gives a scale of C-D-E-F-G-A-B-C. The two semitones line up in exactly the right place.
4 Turn these notes into chords (you don't need the theory of how). The first, fourth, and fifth notes give a major chord; two, three, and six are minor, and seven is a diminished.
5 Write them out like this with the addition of Roman numerals:

I	II	III	IV	V	VI	VII
C	Dm	Em	F	G	Am	Bdim

These are the seven chords of C major. In songwriting, chords I-VI are more important than VII, which, in its simple diminished form, is not very useful (though it does have an interesting seventh mentioned further on). The sequence of the seven chords – major-minor-minor-major-major-minor-diminished – is the same for every major key, regardless of the note you start on. However, if you construct a major scale on any other note than C, sharps or flats (a major scale never includes both) have to

SECTION 6 |

be added to make the interval gaps fit the 2-2-1-2-2-2-1 pattern. Here are two more examples:

Sharp key
1 Choose the key note: A (for A major).
2 Construct a major scale from that note by writing seven letters alphabetically from the selected one: A B C D E F G A.
3 These notes have the pattern 2-1-2-2-1-2-2. Three sharps are needed to make the intervals match the pattern 2-2-1-2-2-2-1. This gives a scale of A-B-C♯-D-E-F♯-G♯-A.
4 Turn these notes into chords:

I	II	III	IV	V	VI	VII
A	Bm	C♯m	D	E	F♯m	G♯dim

Flat key
1 Choose the key note: E♭ (for E♭ major).
2 Construct a major scale from that note by writing seven letters alphabetically from the selected one: E♭ F G A B C D E♭.
3 These notes have the pattern 2-2-2-2-1-2-1. Two more flats are needed to make the intervals match the pattern 2-2-1-2-2-2-1. This gives a scale of E♭-F-G-A♭-B♭-C-D-E♭.
4 Turn these notes into chords:

I	II	III	IV	V	VI	VII
E♭	Fm	Gm	A♭	B♭	Cm	Ddim

There are seven flat keys, seven sharp keys, and C major, which has no sharps or flats. This brings us to the first scale type, illustrated in the three prior examples.

USING THE ESSENTIAL SCALES IN SOLOS

The major scale: C-D-E-F-G-A-B-C   2212221

This seven-note scale has been the foundation of Western music for about five centuries. It can be played over any of the seven chords in a major key. Since those chords are made only of notes taken from this scale, there can be no wrong notes, although some notes sound smoother against certain chords than others, especially at the start or finish of a phrase. When soloing over a major key progression which uses only some mix of chords I-VII, no other scale is strictly necessary, though there are several whose patterns on the guitar provide desirable effects (especially with string-bending).

In lead solos, the major scale might be used where the vocal melody was being imitated. It does not generate any blues effects, so it is not always tough-enough sounding for rock. Examples of solos that use the major scale include Boston's 'More Than A Feeling' (*Boston*, 1976), Bebop Deluxe's 'Adventures In A Yorkshire

C major, sixth-string root, two octaves

C major, fifth-string root, two octaves

C major, third-string root, one octave

C major, fourth-string root, one octave

Landscape' (*Axe Victim*, 1974), where they fit over the underlying major seventh chords, and Thin Lizzy's 'Downtown Sundown' (*Bad Reputation*, 1977). Nik Kershaw's hit 'Wouldn't It Be Good' has a major-scale solo with guitar and synth brass. Norah Jones's 'Come Away With Me' is a quiet, jazzy ballad that has guitar using a placid major scale and a clean tone (1:44-2:31); its first idea is an ascending scale, from the fifth (G) to the third (E) in C major. The two solos in Dinosaur Jnr's 'Get Me' draw heavily on the major scale despite their distortion.

Europe's pop-metal 'Superstitious' (1988) has a 16-bar solo (2:34-3:17) in a song lasting 4:33. The solo uses the F major scale over the chorus progression. It is both pointedly melodic and in places very fast. The first two phrases show the variant of

SECTION 6

inverting the end of the phrase (up rather than down). An intervallic leap is then repeated to reach a higher position. The second half of the solo repeats the first two phrases an octave higher.

The Stones Roses' 'Ten Storey Love Song' (*The Second Coming*, 1995) has a ten-bar solo from 3:10-34 on D major. The lead guitar plays counterpoint to much of the song, showing use of the guitar as a melodic accompaniment rather than playing chords, so the solo is a spin-off from that. During the solo the guitar is doubled at the octave for the last two phrases. The major scale in the main part of the song contrasts with the instrumental intro, where the guitar plays the mixolydian mode (discussed further on) up and down the string to emulate a 1960s psychedelic sound.

The pentatonic major: C-D-E-G-A-C   22323

This is an abbreviated major scale, in which two notes – the fourth and seventh – have been omitted. It has an uncomplicated, upbeat, and melodic character. It is easier to finger and bend on the fingerboard than the full major scale, and many players find it more adaptable. It suits rock and blues more than the major, partly because it omits the leading note (the seventh) of the major scale. It provides positive contrast to the pentatonic minor (see below) when used in a major key-12-bar or similar sequence. It is probably more common than the full major.

Every pentatonic major scale has a relative pentatonic minor, on the note three semitones below:

- C pentatonic major (CDEGA) = A pentatonic minor (ACDEG)
- F pentatonic major (FGACD) = D pentatonic minor (DFGAC)
- G pentatonic major (GABDE) = E pentatonic minor (EGABD)

These are expressed by the chord pairs I-VI (C-Am), IV-II (F-Dm), and V-III (G-Em).

One way of relating these by pattern is to understand that form or pattern 5 of the pentatonic major (for C: ACDEG) is equivalent to form 1 of the relative pentatonic minor (Am: ACDEG).

Knowing a couple of patterns for each scale and how to transpose them to the right position enables you to solo over most common progressions in songs. Know one pattern where the relevant root note is positioned on the sixth string, and one where it is on the fifth. This automatically places you in different areas of the fingerboard. Moving these patterns up or down 12 frets (where possible) gives the same scale at a higher or lower octave. The other option for certain keys is to know the right notes in first position to take advantage of open strings – but open strings cannot be bent nor treated with vibrato.

Songs that have pentatonic major solos include Graham Parker & The Rumour's 'Pourin' It All Out' (*Heat Treatment*, 1976), which has two guitar solos. The first, after the second chorus (1:57-2:16), uses E pentatonic major and lasts ten bars (eight bars with a two-bar build-up) with marked 'inverted arch' phrasing (ie, high-low-high). The second solo takes place in the coda (2:50-3:06, with the song finishing at 3:14). George Harrison's C pentatonic major solo in The Beatles' 'Let It Be' comes like a consoling ray of sunlight into the song's atmosphere of gloomy resignation. The lead fills on Mountain's 'Pride and Passion' illustrate the lyrical quality this scale can have.

C pentatonic major, sixth-string root, two-and-a-half octaves

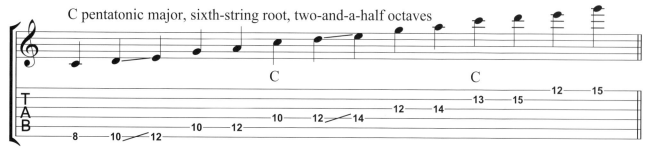

C pentatonic major, fifth-string root, two octaves

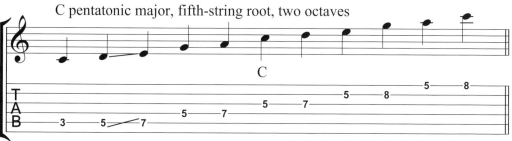

C pentatonic major, third-string root, one octave

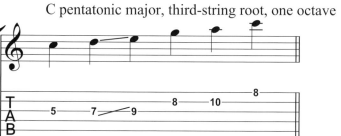

C pentatonic major, fourth-string root, one octave

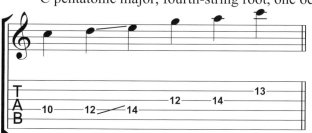

'Living Loving Maid' (*Led Zeppelin II*, 1969) has a brief four-phrase solo (1:27-42 in a track 2:38 long) played mostly on the pentatonic major, with a chromatic climb to finish. As the chromatic run ascends, the amount of reverb and echo increases, adding depth to the notes. The solos in T. Rex's 'Jeepster' and 'Mambo Sun' (*Electric Warrior*, 1971), and Oasis's 'Live Forever' (first solo) are based on the pentatonic major. The first lead break in The Who's 'Behind Blue Eyes' (2:18-26) brings in the pentatonic major just as the song changes key from E minor to E major; the scale emphasises the key-change. Notice that the next lead fill uses the pentatonic minor for contrast (2:40-44) and the third uses both scales (2:58-3:05). The pentatonic major in E is also heard in Ricky Byrd's solo on Joan Jett & The Blackhearts' 'I Love Rock'n'Roll', where there is a very effective sixth-string bend close to the start of the solo.

There are two other pentatonic major scales that could be played in a major key, taking chords IV and V as their root notes. In the key of C major chord IV is F major, whose pentatonic is F-G-A-C-D, and chord V is G major, whose pentatonic is G-A-B-D-E. Notice that these scales only use notes that are within the scale of C major. The major scale therefore always includes the pentatonic majors of I, IV and V. These other two pentatonics *as patterns* give slightly more emphasis to the notes of the chords of IV and V, as opposed to the effect of playing the full major scale.

The pentatonic minor: C-E♭-F-G-B♭-C   32232

The minor pentatonic can be thought of in two ways:

■ as an abbreviated form of the natural minor scale (see below)
■ as a lowering of important notes on the major scale, making them 'blue' notes.

Considered in the latter instance, the pentatonic minor has two notes that do not belong in the key of C major: E♭ and B♭, the lowered third and seventh of the scale. It might be asked, why introduce this minor scale into a major key context? Surely these are wrong notes? Well, if you play the C pentatonic minor over the three minor chords of the key (Dm, Em, Am – II, III and VI) or the diminished VII (Bdim) it won't sound that good. The tonic (key note) pentatonic minor can sound sour over these minor chords. But if played over the three major chords (C, F, G – I, IV, V) it sounds tough, assertive and bluesy. This is what happens in many blues, rock, and rhythm & blues songs that have solos.

Guitarists are often told to learn five patterns (or 'forms') for a pentatonic scale. In C minor, pattern 1 starts on C (C-E♭-F-G-A), pattern 2 on E♭ (E♭-F-G-B♭-C), and so on, continuing with F, G, and B♭. Personally, I think this is unnecessary. For every new pattern only one note is gained on the first string and one is lost on the sixth string, assuming the patterns go from sixth to first. All the notes added at the top of patterns 2-5 are available if pattern 1 is simply moved up an octave. Pattern 1 is given in two forms on the right, the second with an optional shift to an 'extension box', comprising the last six notes of the scale. If you want to add one other I would choose pattern 5, which has some nice bends laid out on the central strings.

The pentatonic minor sounds less upbeat and lyrical compared to the pentatonic major. It can create a delinquent effect outside of a blues, its flattened notes clashing awkwardly with major key harmony. This effect occurs on The Velvet Underground's

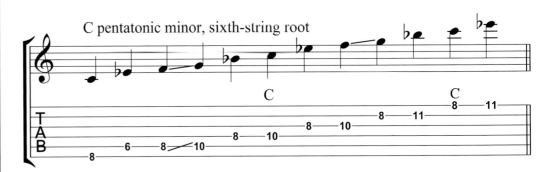

C pentatonic minor, sixth-string root

SECTION 6

C pentatonic minor, sixth-string root, two-and-a-half octaves

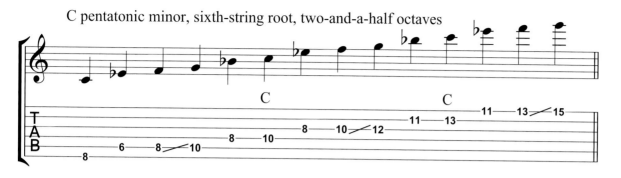

C pentatonic minor, fifth-string root, two octaves

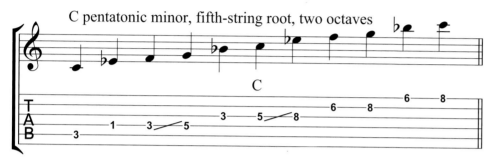

C pentatonic minor, third-string root, one octave

C pentatonic minor, fourth-string root, one octave

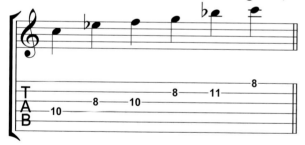

C pentatonic minor, pattern 5

SECTION 6

'Pale Blue Eyes' (2:51-3:46), where the guitar plays a pentatonic minor solo that has a delinquent sound (2:51-3:14) because of the major chords used until then and reinforced by the sixths. The solo changes back to the major scale and sixths after a few phrases.

Other examples include The Beatles' 'Can't Buy Me Love', which has a 12-bar solo that gives the music a harder edge compared to the minor-chord chorus that follows. Preceded by a rock'n'roll scream, the solo (1:12-28) is pentatonic minor with some chordal ideas. Another example would be Fleetwood Mac's 'Don't Stop' (*Rumours*, 1977) where a solo is reached after chorus two at 1:33-53. Initially, Lindsey Buckingham plays some bluesy pentatonic minor phrases that contrast with the major harmony, injecting a little toughness, and a dramatic conclusion working one high note. The Rolling Stones' 'Sway' concludes with a lengthy Mick Taylor solo that is largely C pentatonic minor over a C-B♭ (I-♭VII) chord change.

Pentatonic major and minor scales on the same key note can be used in the same solo if the harmony allows – this works for any progression using I-IV-V. The changes of scale can themselves be a call-and-answer idea. Mixing major and minor creates a mood change. T. Rex's 'Rabbit Fighter' (*The Slider*, 1972), which is in E major, contrasts E pentatonic major and E pentatonic minor. Wishbone Ash's 'Blowin' Free' has a middle solo (2:55-3:52) in D that uses both scales; this scale is given extra kick by the sudden increase in tempo and dynamic following a quiet, relaxed lyrical passage. The first eight-bar solo in Led Zeppelin's 'Celebration Day' is mostly A pentatonic major; the longer coda solo is mostly pentatonic minor.

Paul Kossoff's solo on Free's 'All Right Now' uses both A pentatonic major and minor. The backing progression is the verse riff, which is a common rock idea of ♭VII-IV-I. Brief as it is, the solo exhibits:

- repetition of phrases, also with small variants
- octave transposition
- slides of fretted notes against open strings
- contrasted major pentatonic phrases with an equivalent pentatonic minor
- a pitch climb from low to high
- a dynamic curve from soft to loud
- a climax bolstered by the insertion of an E chord in the harmony, the only time it appears in the song. Inserting an unexpected chord at a solo's end offers the possibility of a dramatic ending
- new backing instruments entering for the solo – here piano and subtle organ.

With careful string-bending, differentiating semitone bends from tone bends, it is possible to switch between pentatonic major and minor without changing position.

Each minor chord (II, III, VI) in a major key has its own pentatonic minor scale. In C major these chords are Dm, Em, and Am. A pentatonic minor is ACDEG; D pentatonic minor is DFGAC; and E pentatonic minor is EGABD. Notice these are also using notes on the C major scale but emphasise these minor chords. To counter this effect, play A pentatonic minor over an F chord, or E pentatonic minor over a C.

Here are the pentatonics that occur on the notes of the C major scale:

Chord I:	tonic pentatonic:	CDEGA	CDEFGAB
Chord II:	supertonic pentatonic:	DFGAC	DEFGAB♭C
Chord III:	submediant pentatonic:	EGABD	EF♯GABCD
Chord IV:	subdominant pentatonic:	FGACD	FGAB♭CDE
Chord V:	dominant pentatonic:	GABDE	GABCDEF♯
Chord VI:	mediant pentatonic:	ACDEG	ABCDEFG

Notice that none require a note that is not already in key. For comparison I have included the notes of the major scale or natural minor on notes 2, 3, 4, and 5, adding the necessary altered notes. No such note is needed with notes 1 and 6, but the others bring in either B♭ or F♯. In other words, the natural minor scales of D and E, and the majors of F and G cannot be used in the key of C, but their pentatonics can because they do not contain these altered notes.

To summarise: any pentatonic scale selected from the notes of the major scale will fit any of the chords of that key, though some are better than others. But note that these scales are only patterns, since whichever of these you play will still comprise the notes of a C major scale.

The major blues: C-D-E♭-E-G-A-C   211323

The tonic pentatonic scales can be extended into six-note scales with the insertion of a flattened 'blue' note minor third before the usual third. In this one, often called the 'major blues' an E♭ is placed between the second and third degrees of the scale. The sound is typical of rock'n'roll lead guitar breaks, and has a playful, almost jaunty quality. This flattened third can be bent to the normal major third or fretted. It is often heard in slide playing on the third string in standard tuning. Although this E♭ is a wrong note for the key, its collision with the underlying harmony is minimised because it tends to occur as a brief passing note in a run.

C major blues, sixth-string root, two octaves

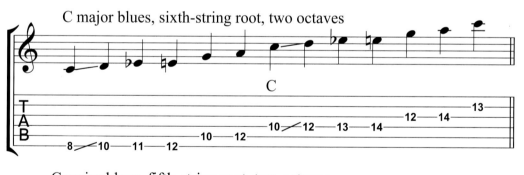

C major blues, fifth-string root, two octaves

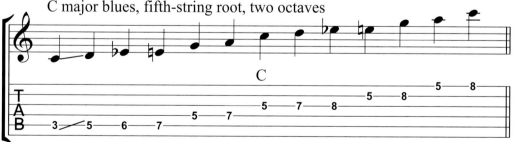

Continued over page

SECTION 6

C major blues, third-string root, one octave

C major blues, fourth-string root, one octave

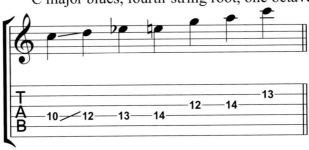

The minor blues: C-E♭-F-G♭-G-B♭-C   321132

This is an equivalent of the 'major blues', but based on the pentatonic minor with the insertion of a flattened fifth just before the usual fifth. This has a jagged, pungent effect, often heard in blues and hard rock solos. It can be achieved by bending the fourth note of the scale up a semitone, though the fretted flat fifth has its own tone, so use both. There are many in the lead breaks in Led Zeppelin songs such as 'Whole Lotta Love', 'Heartbreaker', 'The Ocean', 'Over The Hills And Far Away', and 'Sick Again'. Jimmy Page also exploited its dissonant quality for solos such as those in 'For Your Life' (4:16-27), 'Nobody's Fault But Mine' (5:00-03), and 'In The Evening' (4:08-16), in a manner which took the note beyond the blues-rock framework.

SECTION 6

C minor blues, sixth-string root, tw

C minor blues, fifth-string root, t

C minor blues, third-string root, one octave

C minor blues, fourth-string root, one octave

SECTION 6

Two other additions to the major scale worth mentioning are the bebop dominant and the bebop major:

The bebop dominant   C-D-E-F-G-A-B♭-B   22122111

This is an eight-note jazz scale, consisting of the major with a lowered seventh in addition to the usual leading note. This puts the last four notes of the scale each only a semitone apart. It facilitates chromatic runs that are major in feel but with a blue note (the flattened seventh). The name comes from the fact that the lowered seventh forms a dominant seventh chord on chord I.

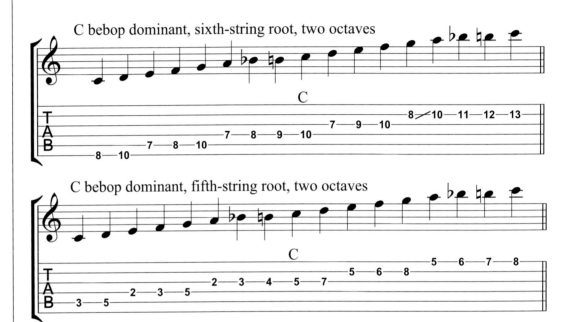

The bebop major   C-D-E-F-G-A♭-A-B   22121121

This is another eight-note jazz scale, consisting of the major with a lowered sixth as well as the usual sixth and leading note. This puts a three-semitone gap between notes six and seven. With both these bebop scales (and there are others), if a phrase starts on the first downbeat of a bar of 4/4 and the entire scale is played in eighth-notes the main chord tones fall on the beat.

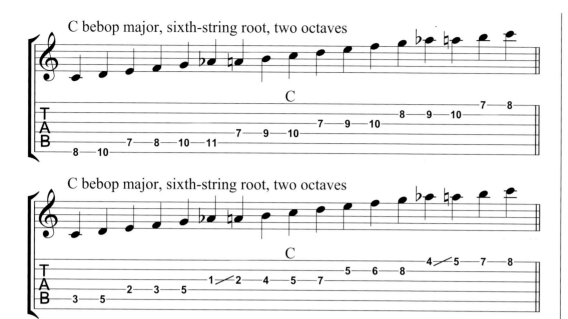

C bebop major, sixth-string root, two octaves

C bebop major, sixth-string root, two octaves

CHROMATIC NOTES

Scales (and lead guitar melodies) can also be extended by the inclusion of notes. A chromatic note is one that does not belong in the key. To any seven-note scale there are five additional chromatic notes. As passing notes, these often form a semitone step between two diatonic notes. Approached thus, their unsettling presence merely lends a certain pleasing surprise and twist to melodic phrases. Approached in a broader leap, they are more pointed. Duration is also a significant factor: the longer they last, the more they make their presence felt. Notes in scales with less than seven notes will only function as chromatic if they do not inadvertently convert that scale to the nearest major or minor. If a guitarist is soloing with the A pentatonic major scale (A-B-C♯-E-F♯), and decides to join the notes C♯ and E with a D, that note is not chromatic because it belongs to the scale of A major. A D♯ coming in between the D and the E would be chromatic because it belongs neither on the A pentatonic major nor the A major. Associated with jazz, chromatic notes often give a solo an air of sophistication. By contrast, in Royal Trux's 'Stevie' they help to give the solo its strange, wayward feel.

HOW TO WORK OUT SONG-CHORDS FOR A MINOR KEY SOLO

The process is similar to that for the major key, but minor keys are slightly more complicated because there are three main types of minor scale, where there was only one major. Here is a method for working out the minor-key chords, with an example working underneath each step.

SECTION 6

119

SOLOS, SCALES, AND HARMONY

1 Choose the key note: A (for A minor).
2 Construct a natural minor scale from that note by writing seven letters alphabetically from the one selected: A B C D E F G.
3 Make the intervals match the pattern 2-1-2-2-1-2-2, where 2 is a tone and 1 is a semitone. The semitones between E-F and B-C are in exactly the right place so no accidentals are needed.
4 Turn these notes into chords. The first, fourth and fifth notes are minor; three, six and seven are major; and two is a diminished.
5 Write them out with the addition of roman numerals:

I	II	III	V	V	VI	VII
Am	Bdim	C	Dm	Em	F	G

The natural minor or aeolian mode: C-D-E♭-F-G-A♭-B♭-C 2122122

In rock, blues and folk, this is the most common minor scale. For example, the A natural minor scale is A-B-C-D-E-F-G. Notice that it finishes with a tone between G and A. If you build a chord on the fifth note you get a chord V of E G B, which is E minor. In comparison to the pentatonic minor, the natural minor provides two additional notes – the second of the scale and the fourth. Both are very expressive and apt to give a solo a kind of introverted, wounded passion. The second is especially potent because against chord I in A minor it implies Am add9, which is an intensifier of the straight minor chord. It is a favourite note of both Slash (see 'November Rain') and Jimmy Page. Unlike the studio version of 'Stairway To Heaven', the longer live solo featured in Led Zeppelin's *The Song Remains The Same* has many phrases which hammer on and pull off around this note. The same is true of the centre solo in 'Achilles Last Stand' (the ninth is F♯ in the key of E minor). The first minute of the solo on Wishbone Ash's 'Phoenix' is a natural minor scale. Which minor scale fits in a minor key depends on which chords are selected. First, the

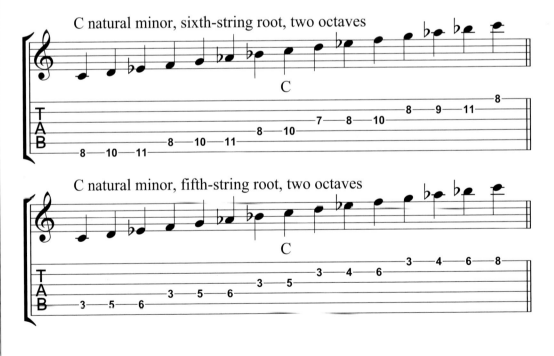

C natural minor, sixth-string root, two octaves

C natural minor, fifth-string root, two octaves

C natural minor, third-string root, one octave

C natural minor, fourth-string root, one octave

natural minor scale can play over any minor key chord progression that has the initial seven chords.

The pentatonic minor   C-E♭-F-G-B♭-C   32232   see also p112

These minor key chords can also be played with the pentatonic minor. When this scale was introduced on p112 it was stated that it had two derivations. The first viewed it as flattening the third and seventh of the major scale. It can also be seen as an edited version of the natural minor (A-C-D-E-G) in which the second and sixth notes (B and F) are omitted. As no alterations have been made by way of flattening, the pentatonic minor has no 'blue' notes when it is in a minor key. The minor blues scale (A-C-D-E♭-E-G) can also be used.

Two other types of minor scale affect which chords are available for a minor key song. These are the harmonic minor (A-B-C-D-E-F-G♯) and the melodic minor (A-B-C-D-E-F♯-G♯). There is more on these scales a bit further on. For the moment, observe that the additional notes of F♯ and G♯ on these A minor scales make it possible for chord IV to be D instead of Dm and for chord V to be E instead of Em. Minor-key chord progressions can therefore draw on the following nine chords:

I	♭II	III	IV	IV^	V	V^	VI	VII
Am	B♭	C	Dm	D	Em	E	F	G

The diminished chord II has been lowered by a semitone and turned into a major chord. (The symbol ^ is mine for indicating that a chord is major where it might be expected to be minor. The allocation of the Roman numerals is based on the assumption that the natural minor is the starting point, so the chord on the seventh degree is labelled VII, not ♭VII as it might be in a system where the minor chords were judged against the major scale that starts on the same note.)

SECTION 6

121

The harmonic minor: C-D-E♭-F-G-A♭-B-C 2122131

This sharpens the seventh note of the natural minor from G to G♯, giving ABCDEFG♯. Chord V becomes E G♯ B, which is E major. The presence of G♯ gives a more 'classical' sound. The harmonic minor does not sit easily with rock, being at odds with its roots in the blues, but it does work in progressive and neo-classical rock.

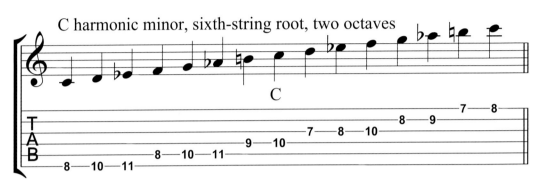

C harmonic minor, sixth-string root, two octaves

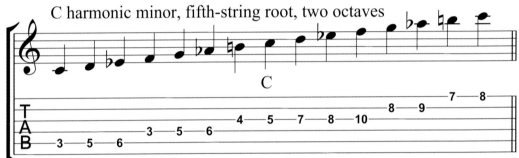

C harmonic minor, fifth-string root, two octaves

C harmonic minor, third-string root, one octave

C harmonic minor, fourth-string root, one octave

SECTION 6

Rainbow's 'I Surrender' (1981) is harmonic minor – hence its baroque feel. The solo starts at 2:10-32 and again at 2:55-3:55, going five times round the chorus sequence and fading on a sixth. There is no harmony on this one and Ritchie Blackmore gets to improvise, with the vocal supplying the odd phrase. It is indicative of Blackmore's stature that he could do this.

You can hear E harmonic minor on songs by Muse such as 'Knights Of Cydonia', 'Sunburn', and 'New Born', F♯ harmonic minor in 'Muscle Museum', and D harmonic minor in the solo on 'Micro Cuts' (2:42-3:06) and in 'Darkshines'. The band's chord sequences often imply the harmonic minor scale by having the major chord V in the minor key. 'Feeling Good' has the chords Gm-Gm/F-E♭-Dsus4-D, implying G harmonic minor. The solo on Queen's 'Killer Queen' has a harmonic minor flavour.

Some minor key songs may use Vm and V, and this requires a switch between the pentatonic/natural minor scales and the harmonic minor. The opening solo of Wishbone Ash's 'Persephone' is a good example. The chord sequence in E minor is Am-Bm-Am-B-C-Am-B-Am-Bm-Em, where Bm is Vm and B is V. 'Persephone' has a beautiful slowed-down E natural minor solo that is only about four bars long. The coda has a second solo that is more dramatic and extrovert and pitched higher.

If an additional chromatic note A is added to this scale, between the sixth and seventh notes, it gives the 'bebop harmonic minor'.

The melodic minor: C-D-E♭-F-G-A-B-C   2122221

This scale is sometimes called the 'jazz minor'. The first four notes (or 'tetrachord') are the same as the natural and harmonic minor, but the upper four notes are the same as the major scale. It can be used to play over the minor/major seventh chord with the same root note. It will also match a IV7♭5 in the same key (F7♭5 = F A C♭ E♭, in which C♭ = B). For any dominant 7th♭5 or 9♭5 use the melodic minor scale whose

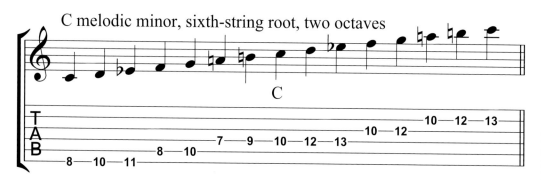

C melodic minor, sixth-string root, two octaves

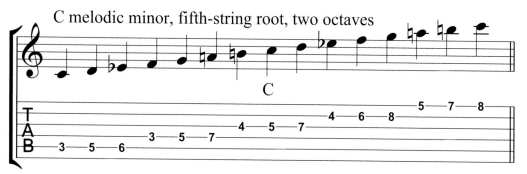

C melodic minor, fifth-string root, two octaves

Continued over page

SECTION 6

C melodic minor, third-string root, one octave

C melodic minor, fourth-string root, one octave

root is a fifth above the chord. For example, for G B Db F use D melodic minor (D-E-F-G-A-B-C#). If an additional chromatic note Gb is added to this scale between the fifth and sixth notes it gives the 'bebop melodic minor'.

As for dealing with the extra three chords:

- chord V^ (E in A minor) needs the A harmonic minor scale;
- chord IV^ (D in A minor) needs D pentatonic major, the melodic minor, or A dorian mode;
- chord bII (Bb in A minor) needs Bb pentatonic major or A phrygian mode.

At this point we need to explain what is meant by 'mode'.

MODES

A mode is simply another type of scale. There are seven main modes, and they are what you hear if you play up an octave from any white-key note (A, B, C, D, E, F, G) *using only natural notes*. Each has a different sequence of interval gaps. The modes have names that are Greek in origin:

- ionian   C-D-E-F-G-A-B   2212221   major scale from its first note
- dorian   D-E-F-G-A-B-C   2122212   major scale from its second note
- phrygian   E-F-G-A-B-C-D   1222122   major scale from its third note
- lydian   F-G-A-B-C-D-E   2221221   major scale from its fourth note
- mixolydian G-A-B-C-D-E-F   2212212   major scale from its fifth note
- aeolian   A-B-C-D-E-F-G   2122122   major scale from its sixth note
- locrian   B-C-D-E-F-G-A   1221222   major scale from its seventh note

Two of these modes have already been mentioned: the ionian mode is the major scale, and the natural minor is the aeolian mode. The dorian and phrygian are regarded as minor (chord I on both them is a minor). The lydian and mixolydian are closer to the major scale and both their chord Is are major. The locrian is odd man out, having a chord I that is diminished. All of these modes are theoretically contained within the C major scale. As the diagram explains, they can be played from each degree of the scale.

This creates another over-complication of lead-playing. Guitarists are sometimes instructed that when playing in C major they must change mode for each chord. They must play C ionian over chord I (C), F lydian over chord IV (F), G mixolydian over chord V (G) and A aeolian over chord VI (Am). In fact, these modes are purely theoretical in the key of C major because they are simply made of the seven notes of the major scale. How would anyone actually hear F lydian in the key of C major if it is the same notes as the major scale? The only way to stand a chance of this would be to emphasise the mode by starting and ending a phrase on the note F. But that would be audibly playing a scale and not an adequately independent phrase. This applies to all seven modes in the major key. Therefore, when in a major key (assuming chords I-VI) forget about matching modes to chords – just play the major scale or any of the others described a few pages back in the major key section.

Modes become audible when they are superimposed on a key against the harmony or allowed to also change the harmony to fit their own. Any of the modes can be transposed onto any note by preserving the sequence of interval gaps with the addition of any required flats or sharps. Here are the fingerboard patterns and the note sequences for the modes transposed onto the note C:

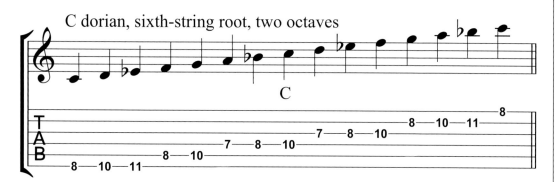

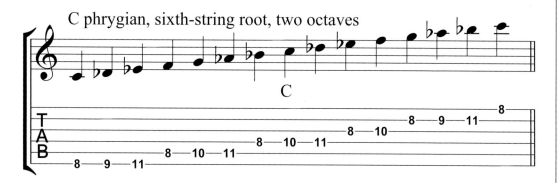

Continued over page

SECTION 6

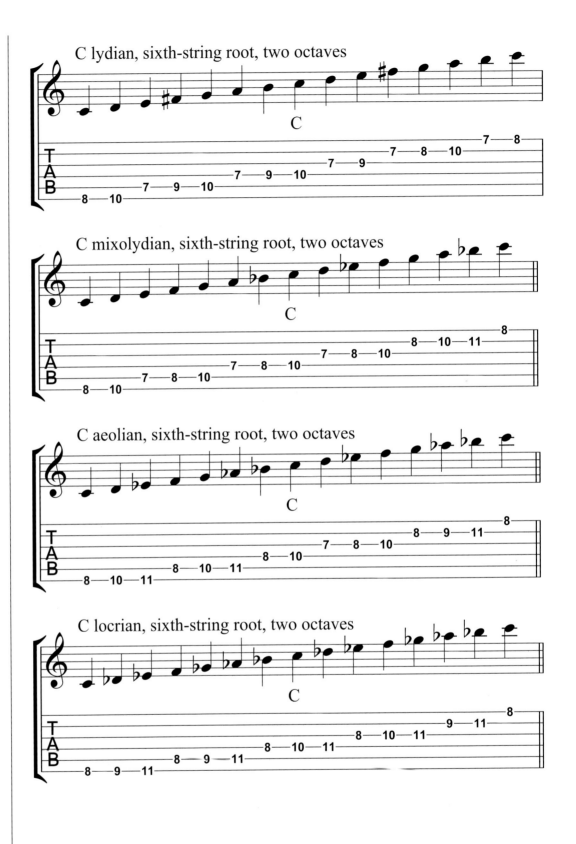

C lydian, sixth-string root, two octaves

C mixolydian, sixth-string root, two octaves

C aeolian, sixth-string root, two octaves

C locrian, sixth-string root, two octaves

SECTION 6

- dorian   C-D-E♭-F-G-A-B♭   2122212
- phrygian   C-D♭-E♭-F-G-A♭-B♭   1222122
- lydian   C-D-E-F♯-G-A-B   2221221
- mixolydian C-D-E-F-G-A-B♭   2212212
- aeolian   C-D-E♭-F-G-A♭-B♭   2122122
- locrian   C-D♭-E♭-F-G♭-A♭-B♭   1221222

(The ionian is discounted because it is identical to the major scale.) If a solo puts any of these modes (except the ionian) over C major harmony it will be obvious that the melody line is not on the major scale. There will be at least one note clashing with the harmony. The clashing notes are marked in bold. This effect is not often used in songs unless the harmony is changed so that these altered notes are also in the harmony and the clash is removed, as is discussed below.

The dorian mode: C-D-E♭-F-G-A-B♭-C   2122212

This scale is the natural minor with a raised sixth. It often features in the Latin American rock of Santana. This raised sixth can also be used to give a minor solo more edge than the natural minor. The typical progression over which it might be used is I-IV^ in a minor key. Santana's 'Evil Ways' (1969) has a I-IV dorian change of Gm-C. The organ takes a solo first, and the guitar plays a short solo on the fade-out. The solo on the live version of Led Zeppelin's 'No Quarter' (1973) has a pronounced dorian flavour (B-natural stressed in the key of D minor), as does the band's C minor blues-ballad 'Since I've Been Loving You', and the wah-wah solo in Wishbone Ash's 'The King Will Come' (3:15-4:24). If an additional chromatic note E is added to this scale between the third and fourth notes it gives the 'bebop dorian'.

C dorian, sixth-string root, two octaves

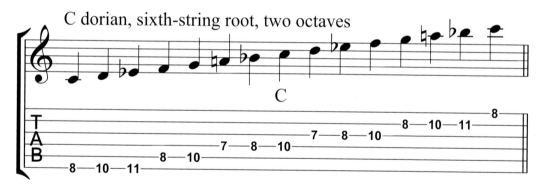

C dorian, fifth-string root, two octaves

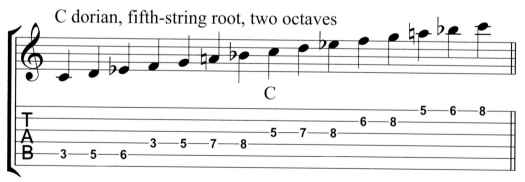

Continued over page

S E C T I O N   6

C dorian, third-string root, one octave

C dorian, fourth-string root, one octave

The phrygian mode   C-D♭-E♭-F-G-A♭-B♭-C   1222122

This scale is the natural minor with a lowered second. It has a marked Mediterranean/flamenco character and features in the stereotypical 'Spanish solo'. On All About Eve's 'Scarlet' (*Scarlet And Other Stories*, 1990) guitarist Tim Bricheno plays a phrygian solo full of Spanish-sounding phrases (main solo after the bridge at 2:05-22, reprised during the coda. Played on a steel-string acoustic, the guitar solo on 'Farewell Mr Sorrow' (*Touched By Jesus*, 1991) has a Spanish feel made more interesting as it comes over a sinister set of fifths (2:10-32). It is phrased in three sections – the first descending, the second rising, both using a triplet semiquaver plus quaver figure, moved up or down in pitch by steps. Jimmy Page's short break on 'Babe I'm Gonna Leave You' at 3:17-27 (*Led Zeppelin*, 1969) also conforms to type. Steve Harley's 'Make Me Smile (Come Up And See Me)' has a solo immediately after the second chorus and a moment of silence (1:50-2:20) that is in the same style.

Having explained the minor key, it is time to return to the major key and look at how songwriters extend its harmony.

SECTION 6

C phrygian, sixth-string root, two octaves

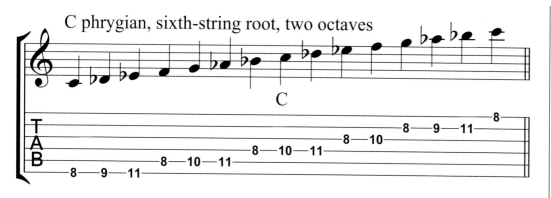

C phrygian, fifth-string root, two octaves

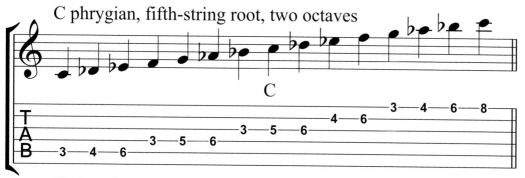

C phrygian, third-string root, one octave

C phrygian, fourth-string root, one octave

SECTION 6

EXTENDING THE SONGWRITING CHORDS

The most important chords for songwriting are I-VI. Chord VII, as a diminished triad, is not much use, unless it is turned into a half-diminished seventh (in C major, B D F A) and treated as a substitute for chord V (compare the notes of G9 – (G B D F A) – with B half-dim 7, also known as Bm7♭5). The C major scale will take care of this. But there are six other chords that are often dipped into to broaden the palette of the harmony. Let's return to the earlier account of finding the chords in a major key. Here are the chords of C major:

I	II	III	IV	V	VI	VII
C	Dm	Em	F	G	Am	Bdim

To find the three 'flat degree' chords, take chords III, VI, and VII, lower them by a semitone and turn them into major chords: ♭III = E♭, ♭VI = A♭, and ♭VII = B♭. If we check which notes are in these chords we find that E♭ (E♭ G B♭) and A♭ (A♭ C E♭) have two notes off-scale, and B♭ (B♭ D F) has one note that is off-scale.

To find the three 'reverse polarity' chords, take chords II, III, and IV, and turn them into their opposites, minor into major and vice versa: II (Dm) becomes II^ (D), III (Em) becomes III^ (E), and IV (F) becomes IVm (Fm). If we check which notes are in these chords we find that each introduces one note which is off-scale: D (D F♯ A), E (E G♯ B) and Fm (F A♭ C).

This gives the 12 most likely chords for a song in a major key:

I	II	III	IV	V	VI	♭VII	♭III	♭VI	II^	III^	IVm
C	Dm	Em	F	G	Am	B♭	E♭	A♭	D	E	Fm

(The '^' symbol indicates a 'reverse polarity' minor chord turned into a major. If a major becomes minor an 'm' is added). If any of these additional six chords feature in the chord progression over which the solo is played the chord can potentially clash with the major scale. So it may be necessary to find another scale. Here are some options using only the scale types already discussed:

- For ♭VII: use the home key pentatonic major.
- For ♭VII, ♭III, ♭VI: use the home key pentatonic minor.
- For ♭VII, ♭III, ♭VI, II^, III^: use the chord's pentatonic major or full major.
- For ♭VII, ♭III, ♭VI, II^, III^: use the chord's pentatonic minor for a blues sound.
- For II^: use the chord's mixolydian or pentatonic major.
- For III^: use the chord's pentatonic major or the home key's VI harmonic minor.
- For IVm: use the chord's dorian or pentatonic minor.
- For VI^: use the chord's pentatonic major or IV's pentatonic minor.

The critical point is how many bars are occupied by any of these additional chords. The more bars, the more important it will be to get the right new scale. The fewer bars, the easier it is to hack it, using these techniques:

- playing an arpeggio on that chord;
- bending from a note on the major scale into the new chord;
- hitting and sustaining its root note;
- playing a one-octave scale pattern.

The Arctic Monkeys' 'Mardy Bum' has a solo (2:09-26) based on the progression D-F♯-G-F♯m-Em. The challenge here is that the second chord is III^ (F♯ in key of D major) which has an A♯ in it. But within a few beats F♯ has been replaced by F♯m, so there is not enough time to change scale. This is handled by avoiding the note A♯; instead the solo hits C♯ which is both in that chord and on the major scale.

The mixolydian mode: C-D-E-F-G-A-B♭-C   2212212

This is the major scale with a lowered leading note. It is often more suited to solos than the major scale, because it fits progressions that have the ♭VII chord. It is also associated with dominant seventh chords and their extended forms. In the key of C major the lowered leading note means that a seventh chord built on C will turn out as C7 not Cmaj7. It creates a conspicuous blue note against chords V and III (G and Em, which have B-natural) but its B♭ sounds smooth against chords IV and II. With the additional inclusion of a flattened third the scale becomes the classic rock'n'roll scale heard on a Chuck Berry song such as 'Johnny B. Goode'. The usual seventh can be placed as a passing note between the flat 7 and the tonic, as happens in the swing coda solo that finishes Led Zeppelin's 'The Ocean'.

In its pure form it is used for the 'raga-rock' solo, a style of lead break that imitates the Indian sitar in psychedelic tracks. It moves up and down a single string on this scale, sometimes with an open string above or below it, ornamenting the scale with hammer-ons, pull-offs, and slides. It features in the repertoire of bands such as The Beatles, The Byrds, and Buffalo Springfield. Roy Wood with The Move used a

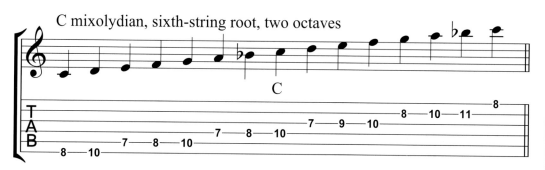

C mixolydian, sixth-string root, two octaves

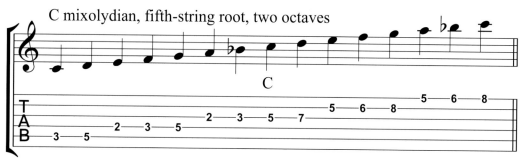

C mixolydian, fifth-string root, two octaves

Continued over page

SECTION 6

C mixolydian, third-string root, one octave

C mixolydian, fourth-string root, one octave

Strat with three of the bass strings tuned down to D so it sounded like a sitar on 'I Can Hear The Grass Grow'. The Beatles' 'Good Morning Good Morning' has a four-bar guitar solo that contributes to the deranged feel at 1:16-27: this is a typical descending mixolydian raga solo. The Beatles' 'Taxman' has a solo of eight bars after the bridge and another on the fade out. This uses a descending mixolydian played to simulate sitar (1:12-24).

It can be heard on the intro to Vanilla Fudge's 'You Keep Me Hanging On', and at 2:35-50 on The Clientele's 'E.M.P.T.Y', with a rapid descending mixolydian phrase clearly influenced by the 1960s. The solo on The Moody Blues' 'Ride My See-Saw' uses the mixolydian scale, and Thin Lizzy's 'Whiskey In The Jar' contrasts it with the major during the central solo. The guitar solo on Fleet Foxes' 'Sun It Rises' begins on D pentatonic major (1:39-2:00) before bringing in the note C (2:01-18), which implies a D mixolydian.

The lydian mode   C-D-E-F♯-G-A-B-C   2221221
This scale is the major scale with a raised fourth. It can be used to play over II^ (D in C major) especially if II^7 (D7) is the exact chord. The F♯ can also be treated as the ♯11 of the chord of C in an extended chord. The lydian dominant is a variation which lowers the seventh by a semitone.

C lydian, sixth-string root, two octaves

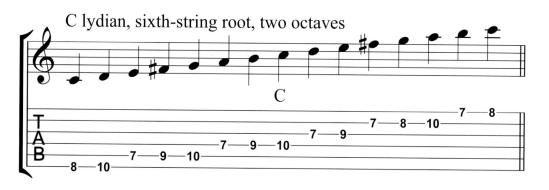

C lydian, fifth-string root, two octaves

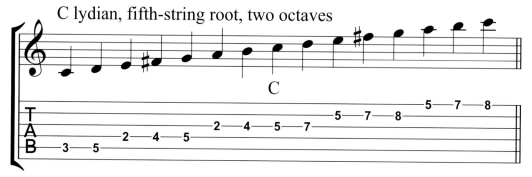

C lydian, third-string root, one octave

C lydian, fourth-string root, one octave

SECTION 6

The locrian mode   C-D♭-E♭-F-G♭-A♭-B♭-C   1221222

This scale is unusual in that is it the only one of the seven classic modes whose chord I makes a diminished triad rather than a major or minor. It is also known as the half-diminished scale and is effective over a half-diminished chord (VII in a major key, II in a minor) or a minor 7♭5 that has the same root note: note that they are the same chord, but different names are used in different contexts. Chord VII7 in C major is B D F A; this is also Bm7♭5, and B locrian is B-C-D-E-F-G-A.

C locrian, sixth-string root, two octaves

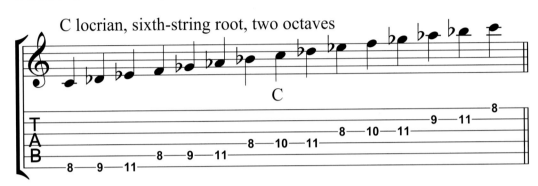

C locrian, fifth-string root, two octaves

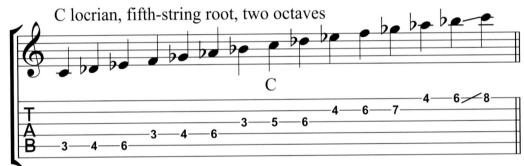

C locrian, third-string root, one octave

C locrian, fourth-string root, one octave

SECTION 6

The super-locrian mode   C-D-E♭-F-G♭-A♭-B♭-C   2121222

This scale can be thought of as a natural minor with a flattened fifth, or as a locrian mode with a raised second. The super-locrian on the supertonic (second step) of a major key gives the notes for II7♭5 and V7♭9. In the key of C major, D-E-F-G-A♭-B♭-C covers D F A♭ C and G B D F A♭ (though the third of the V7♭9 chord, B-natural, contrasts with the B♭ of the scale).

C super-locrian, sixth-string root, two octaves

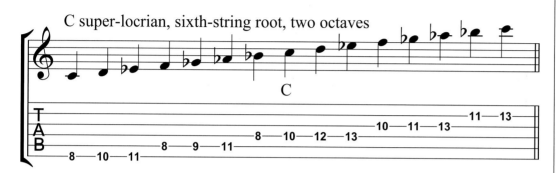

C super-locrian, fifth-string root, two octaves

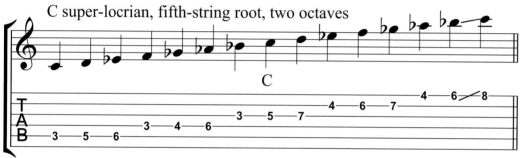

C super-locrian, third-string root, one octave

C super-locrian, fourth-string root, one octave

The wholetone scale   C D E F♯ G♯ A♯ C   222222

The wholetone scale has no semitones in it. This means it divides the octave into six equal steps in contrast to the uneven mixture of steps that characterise major, minor and pentatonic scales. Accordingly it does not correspond to a key. Its use is for playing over the augmented chord. It is also a rootless scale in that any note can be the root note; if you play from any note the sequence will still be 222222, only some of the notes will change their spelling enharmonically from sharps to flats or vice versa. It has two forms: C-D-E-F♯-G♯-A♯ and C♯-D♯-E♯-G-A-B. It includes the root, third, and flattened seventh of a dominant seventh chord, all four notes of a 7♭5 and 7♯5, and can be played over versions of the dominant chord such as the 7♭5, 9♯5, and 9♯11 that have an altered note.

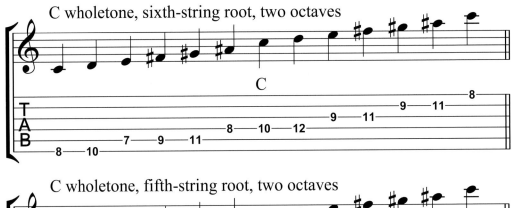

C wholetone, sixth-string root, two octaves

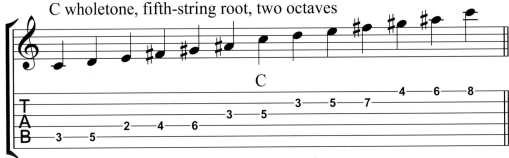

C wholetone, fifth-string root, two octaves

The diminished scale   C D E♭ F G♭ A♭ B♭♭ B C   21212121

This is an eight-note scale moving in alternating tones and semitones (whole-steps/half-steps). It is also known as the 'octatonic'. It includes the four notes of a diminished seventh starting on any note, which cannot be created from the major scale without the addition of an accidental (only the half-diminished scale is possible on the major scale – the super-locrian). It can be reversed as semitone/tone (12121212): C D♭ E♭ F♭ G♭ A♭ A B C. There are only three scales of each, starting on C, D, and E, the others being merely transpositions of these. This example will make it clear. Here is the first octatonic (21212121) on C, D, and E and then F:

C D E♭ F G♭ A♭ B♭♭ B
D E F G A♭ B♭ B C♯
E F♯ G A B♭ C C♯ D♯
F G A♭ B♭ C♭ D♭ D E

SECTION 6

It can be seen that the scale beginning on F is only repeating the scale on D starting on its third note. The 1, 3, 5, and 7 notes are equivalent roots (as for the diminished seventh chord). The 2, 4, 6, and 8 are equivalent roots for the 12121212 octatonic. These scales are played over diminished sevenths. The second octatonic is also called the 'altered dominant' and can be played over any dominant seventh or ninth with an altered note as long as it isn't the raised fifth: C7♭5, C7♭9, C7♯9, C7♭9♯11, C7♭9♯11, C13♭9, C13♯11.

SUMMARY

When faced with a chord progression to solo over, work out if there are any out-of-key chords. These contain notes that are not on the underlying major or minor scale. These will include three 'flat degree' chords, three 'reverse polarity' chords (II^, III^, IVm), any augmented chords or diminished sevenths, and any chords with altered notes (such as a ♭5, ♭9). The same analysis would have to be applied to any section of the song that changes key.

In most blues-derived 12-bar sequences the music will be a progression using I, IV, and V in the major or minor key. Beyond this, mostly the guitar solo section will probably use chords I-VI in the major key and I, III-VII in the minor. Extended versions of these chords will not affect the choice of notes unless they have an altered note (such as a flattened or raised fifth). If any of these chords are turned into augmented triads or diminished sevenths, or if VII appears as a diminished triad, extra notes will have to be found in the lead part. The same is true if flat degree chords (♭III, ♭VI, ♭VII) or reverse polarity chords (II^, III^, IVm) appear in the major key. In the minor key the correct scale is often determined by whether IV and V are major or minor.

The phrases that make up a solo can be scale-based in two senses:

- A phrase draws on the notes of the scale.
- A phrase replicates the order of the notes in the scale.

Although doing the second is sometimes musically effective, it risks sounding insufficiently melodic and too literal (it is a common fault to play solos that move up and down scales by step replicating the note-order.) To avoid giving this impression, remember that a scale is only the raw material of a solo. Runs that replicate note-order (especially if they start on the root note) should be used selectively and combined with other soloing ideas like chords, arpeggios, intervals, and bent notes. These are surveyed in Section Seven. But since it has a powerful sense of direction a scale-phrase can make an effective end or beginning to a solo. Robbie Blunt plays an effective rising two-octave G major scale for the solo to Robert Plant's 'Like I've Never Been Gone' (*Pictures At Eleven*, 1981), even throwing in a few chromatic notes toward the end to delay arriving at the last note and chord change.

THE SOLO AS VOICE

Ideally, a guitarist playing a solo doesn't allow the scale-pattern to dictate what is played, but rather the imagined melody. As Slash once explained, "The most important thing is to be able to hear it in your head and apply it through your fingers to your neck in a split second. Instead of playing patterns, hear the melody you're going for. I'm still learning this: it's something that very few guitar players of my generation ever paid attention to ..." (*Guitar Techniques*, September 2002). A good test of whether a solo meets this melody test is whether you can easily remember it or sing it.

Richie Sambora told UK *Guitar* magazine in December 1994 that he could sing the solos on records by Page, Clapton, and The Beatles.

When Kirk Hammett was trying to come up with a guitar solo for the Metallica song 'Of Wolf And Man' he was initially blocked by the difficulty of trying to find notes that would fit the E-B♭ change. He solved the problem by singing phrases and then finding them on the guitar. His conclusion was that singing phrases during solo composition helped circumvent the limits of finger-patterns and assumptions about scales.

Some lead guitarists see their soloing very much as the expression of a voice. When I interviewed him in September 1992 Carlos Santana said, "I'm trying to sing through my guitar. I want my guitar to be more like a voice. People are interested in listening to the guitar that way … I went to see Ry Cooder open up for Eric Clapton. People were walking around, getting a beer, taking a piss, whatever. When Ry Cooder put his finger on the guitar to play a solo, everybody stopped, and I mean froze. They all turned around and looked at him. When he finished they all went back to doing what they were doing. That, to me, is a voice." In January 1990, Johnny Marr told *Guitar Player* that he was pleased that the first proper solo on a Smiths record ('Paint A Vulgar Picture') was singable.

Ultimately, you learn technique and theory to forget it in the moment of creativity. It operates at an unconscious level, or is consciously recalled when needed to solve a problem. Frank Zappa stated in 1982 that he looked for unlikely things in a solo – because fundamentally he wanted to play what was on his mind. If all you have on your mind is C pentatonic minor or E dorian then you're not playing from a good place.

SECTION 6

OTHER SOLO TECHNIQUES

A solo can consist of much more than simply phrases that use just scales and single notes.

SECTION 7
OTHER SOLO TECHNIQUES

Important as scales are to soloing, they are not the whole picture. There are other musical devices and techniques on which a soloist can draw, including some specific to the guitar, and these are described in this section. They include using chords – full, partial, or arpeggiated – mixing open strings with fretted strings, string-bends, working with intervals, double-stops, pull-offs, hammer-ons, slides, and harmonics.

USING INTERVALS

After scales, a soloist should be aware of how intervals can be incorporated in a solo. The two notes in an interval can be played together or sequentially. In faster, more complex phrases they could be distributed between two guitar tracks by over-dubbing, or with two players. Harmonizers will digitally put the interval of your choice over each note in a phrase. Depending on whether the pitch is low enough, a 12-string guitar also offers this option. For harmonized guitar solos see below. Using wider intervals such as sixths, sevenths, octaves, and more melodically, stops a solo relying too much on step-movement. The intervals that work best in solos are:

- octaves
- thirds
- sixths
- fourths.

Thirds and sixths (and, to a lesser degree, fourths) can also have the effect of emphasising the harmony in a solo. This is useful if the backing has only a minimal statement of the chords, or none at all (as in a power trio with only bass and drums as the backing). Some double-stop licks will achieve other effects if they are played over the non-conventional chord choice.

Octaves are the most straightforward interval for soloing. On guitar they must be played either muting the string(s) between the octave or played by the plucking hand with pick and finger. They are tricky at any speed, but speed would defeat their point, since octaves lend body and emphasis to a melodic line. Playing a melody in octaves is like having two players on the same line. They have been favoured more by jazz players than rock guitarists, though Jimi Hendrix made use of them, especially in some of his later songs. John Squire of The Stone Roses and Billy Corgan of Smashing Pumpkins have also favoured lead lines in octaves.

On guitar, octaves are sometimes combined with an open string. The solo on Soundgarden's 'Fell On Black Days' consists of octaves plus a high phrase over a drone D open string (2:19-45), the main phrase played three times. At 3:13-35 a wave

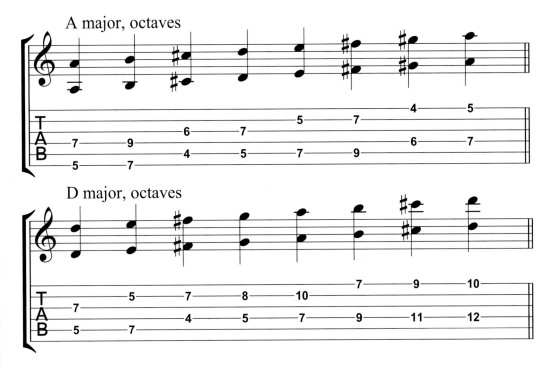

A major, octaves

D major, octaves

of wah-wah brings in a second solo with the wah as a filter. Other octave solos include Wheatus's 'A Little Respect' which has a short solo after the second chorus (2:06-15) in octaves. The Beatles' 'The Night Before' has an eight-bar solo (1:32-42) made up of a four-bar idea, with the guitars in octaves, played twice. The Who's 'Slip Kid' (*The Who By Numbers*, 1975) has a double solo section: a first half of the solo gets new ideas out of a blues lead because of the underlying harmony and ends with a sequence of octaves (2:04-34); the second half of the solo is approached by feedback and then chords played with a volume pedal (2:47-3:10). The coda features octaves and a second lead guitar. Thin Lizzy's 'Dancing In The Moonlight' includes a single but effective octave phrase (2:17-21). There are distorted octaves rapidly strummed on the solo in Nirvana's 'Breed'. Radiohead's 'Just' uses an ascending octave phrase as part of the intro.

Examples of solos played through an octave-splitter (an unstable prototype harmonizer) would include Hendrix's 'Purple Haze' and T. Rex's 'Life's A Gas' which has an octave-splitter for the short solo. Early analogue octave splitters couldn't always track the note properly, which gave them an additional tone-colour.

Thirds and **sixths** occur in two forms, major and minor, which makes their fingering on the guitar less straightforward than octaves:

- A minor third is two notes, three semitones apart.
- A major third is two notes, four semitones apart.
- A minor sixth is two notes, eight semitones apart.
- A major sixth is two notes, nine semitones apart.

When a major or minor scale is harmonised in thirds or sixths it will naturally result in a sequence that comprises a mixture of minor and major intervals. For this reason,

S E C T I O N 7

thirds and sixths carry more harmonic information than single notes or octaves. Both are clearer when sounded on the higher three or four strings. Here are some typical patterns of thirds. If a sequence is notated 1/3 below it means the sequence begins with the first and third notes of the scale; if it is shown as 3/5 it begins with the third and fifth notes of the scale. If a pattern is 1/3 the root note is the lower of the pair; if 3/5 the third is the lower. Knowing these helps you transpose the sequence to whichever key is needed.

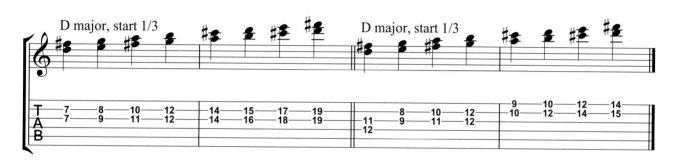

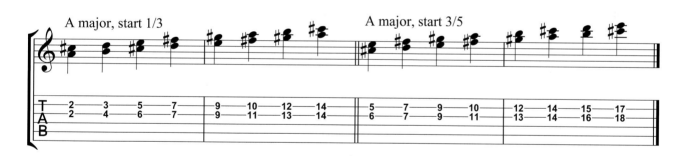

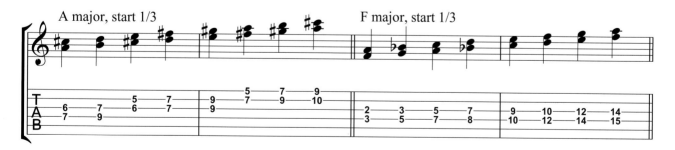

Continued over page

SECTION 7

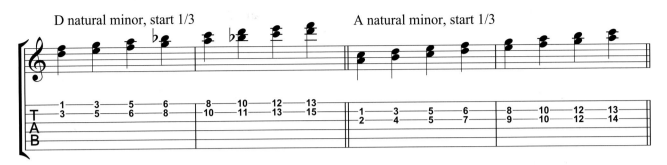

D natural minor, start 1/3   A natural minor, start 1/3

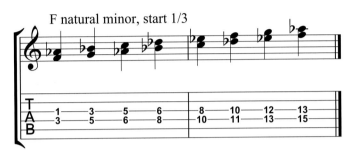

F natural minor, start 1/3

Thirds have a sweet, appealing sound and often harmonise a melodic line in a solo (as they do in vocal harmonising). They are often heard in pop and indie rock. They dominate The Smiths' 'This Charming Man'. Robert Smith finishes off a clean chiming guitar solo on The Cure's 'It's Friday, I'm In Love' with a series of ascending thirds. The fuzz solo on Aimee Mann's 'Choice In The Matter' (1:36-55) ends with a run of thirds. Most of the solo on Them's 'Here Comes The Night' is played in thirds (1:42-2:01) and Van Morrison's 'Brown-Eyed Girl' opens with a run of high thirds. There's a clean guitar solo, mostly in thirds, in King Harvest's cover of Toploader's 'Dancing In The Moonlight' (1:33-46), with electric piano as the main backing, played over the chorus progression.

For more aggressive thirds in a solo, listen to the distorted break in The Beatles' 'Hey Bulldog'; and The Swinging Blue Jeans' 'Hippy Hippy Shake' has a Chuck Berry-derived solo in thirds. Pete Townshend uses distorted thirds in the guitar solo on The Who's 'Relay' and in 'Won't Get Fooled Again'. For instances of thirds used as fills, see The Eagles' 'Lyin' Eyes', at the end of the guitar link passage, and there is a passage of thirds used as a link to the second verse of Them's 'Gloria' (1:09-20); the same thirds are repeated at the end of the song.

Thirds can also be generated through a delay effect. Thin Lizzy's 'That Woman's Gonna Break Your Heart' (*Bad Reputation*, 1977) has a two-part solo where the second part (2:22-50) uses an echo that produces descending thirds from a single descending run.

Opposite are some typical patterns of **sixths**. If the pattern is 3/1, the third note in the scale is the lower of the pair; if 5/3 the fifth is the lower.

Sixths are used as fills throughout Cat Stevens's 'Lady D'Arbanville' and 'The Boy With A Moon And Star On His Head', in the verses of Velvet Underground's 'Pale Blue Eyes', and The Beatles' 'The Ballad Of John And Yoko'. The first short eight-bar solo on Led Zeppelin's 'Celebration Day' finishes off with sixths. Sixths are heard

F major, start 3/1   D major, start 5/3

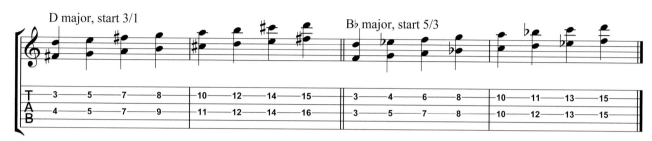

D major, start 3/1   B♭ major, start 5/3

A major, start 3/1   F major, start 5/3

F harmonic minor, start 3/1   D harmonic minor, start 5/3

F dorian, start 3/1   A dorian, start 5/3

Continued over page

SECTION 7

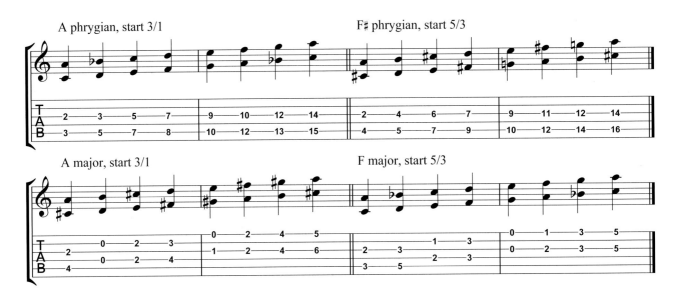

during the bridge of Percy Sledge's 'When A Man Loves A Woman' as fills and on the intro of Sam & Dave's 'Soul Man', reprised toward the end before the final hooks. Led Zeppelin's 'The Lemon Song' and Jimi Hendrix's cover of 'Rock Me Baby' use similar 12-bar related ideas in sixths. Sixths provide an important turnaround fill in the chorus of Eric Clapton's 'Bell-Bottom Blues'.

The solo in The Beatles' 'She's A Woman' is mostly comprised of descending sixths (1:53-2:09). The sixths are transposed depending on the chord, and the style is adapted from 1950s rock'n'roll. Sixths finish off the verse of 'Yer Blues'. 'Dig A Pony' (*Let It Be*, 1970) has a 13-bar solo (2:12-31) with some sixths at its climax and many sixth-based fills in the verses. Sixths provide fills in 'While My Guitar Gently Weeps'. The solo on Sheryl Crow's 'I Know Why' (*Wildflower*, 2005) climaxes with a descending sequence of sixths in D. Eclection's 'Nevertheless' has an eight-bar solo with sixths and broken chord ideas played over the chorus. The Verve's 'Sit And Wonder' has a run of sixths in the guitar lead from 4:08-20.

Fourths are harder to use than thirds or sixths, because moving them consecutively with either the top note or the lower on the key scale results in one chromatic false note that has to be altered. Here are consecutive fourths above and below a C major scale:

Perfect fourths, C major lower

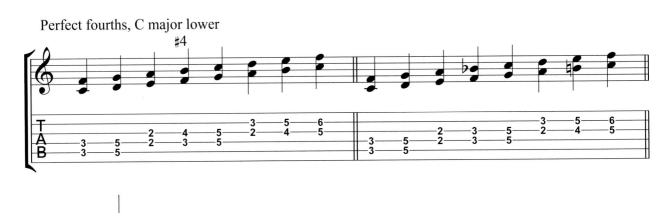

Perfect fourths, C major upper

On each scale an augmented fourth is created involving the notes F and B. Unlike thirds and sixths, there is no sequence of continuous fourths on the major scale; the finger shape has to be altered to remove this note. But changing this interval means adding an off-scale note, namely B♭. This would be okay for C mixolydian but not C major. It is easier to edit the scale to a pentatonic major, where this problem disappears. Here are examples for C major, G major, A minor, and E minor:

Perfect fourths, C pentatonic major upper

Perfect fourths, G pentatonic major upper

Perfect fourths, A pentatonic minor upper

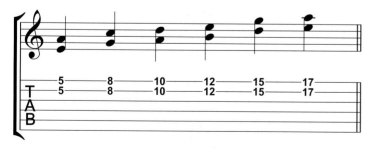

Continued over page

SECTION 7

Perfect fourths, E pentatonic minor upper

When playing fourths you can either play up and down a pair of strings or across the fretboard.

Fourths have a bare, assertive sound, and give a solo phrase an exotic, at times oriental quality (think of the opening riff of Television's 'Marquee Moon'). Blue Oyster Cult's 'Don't Fear The Reaper' has a fill in fourths at 1:33-37 in verse two. Fourths are part of the accompaniment figure on Sting's 'Fortress Around Your Heart', transposed onto various pitches. The Eagles' 'Tequila Sunrise' has an eight-bar solo after verse two (1:42-2:01) which begins with thirds strummed on acoustic and ends with a couple of fourths. It could be argued that the pungent quality of fourths makes them effective as a final gesture in a solo.

Andy Summers climaxed the solo in The Police's 'Bring On The Night' with two sixths after repeatedly playing a repeated fourth on D. Blondie's 'One Way Or Another' has a guitar solo (1:50-2:01) that repeats a suspended fourth idea over an F♯-A-C♯ chord change, then goes into thirds (2:02) and fourths (2:08) for the climax at 2:14. Wings' 'Band On The Run' has an opening solo in fourths, and the second solo in Led Zeppelin's 'Ten Years Gone' has several phrases playing fourths on the top two strings.

A notable use of the perfect fourth is when it resolves into a chord by turning into a third, either by fretting or bending – what could be termed a '4-3 double-stop'. An example would be to play the top two strings at the third fret and by hammering on the third string you imply a C or Em chord. Here are some useful patterns for this technique that can be applied to any chord sequence. The '+' symbol indicates where the direction is onto the chord (ie, a fourth to a third); the others are travelling off the chord (from a third to a fourth or a second).

To be able to move these around the fretboard it is vital to memorise the location of the root note. These are mostly the last eighth note in a group of four, and are marked with a 'R'; the others are the upper half-notes. These patterns have a different effect depending on how quickly the initial hammer-on is played.

The approach to the chorus of Bob Dylan's 'Like A Rolling Stone' has an example of the double-stop played by Michael Bloomfield, as does the coda solo of Fleetwood Mac's 'Over And Over'. There are many by Ron Wood throughout The Faces' 'Debris'. The 30-second guitar solo that introduces Gene's 'We Could Be Kings' (*Drawn To The Deep End*, 1997) has many double-stops combined with slides. The Eagles' 'Take It Easy' has a country-style guitar solo with bends and double-stops, etc (1:43- 2:10), after the second chorus. Markedly close to the chord changes, it suggests

SECTION 7

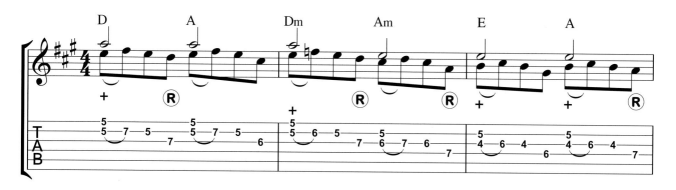

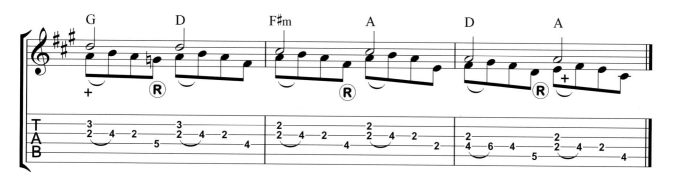

a way of soloing where the solo is abstracted from the chord tones. This can be done via triads or '4-3 double-stop'. You can hear this on the coda solo in Sheryl Crow's 'If It Makes You Happy'. There are 4-3 fills on the chorus of 'Sitting On The Dock Of The Bay' by Otis Redding and in Eddie Floyd's 'Knock On Wood'. The classic Chuck Berry rock solo uses double-stops comprising fourths and thirds, single-note mixolydian runs, and unison bends.

The first solo on Tears For Fears' 'Everybody Wants To Rule The World' (2:31-48) combines thirds and fourths in an inventive way and has a pointed sense of rhythm (sometimes the notes you play are no more important than the rhythm in which you play them). The coda solo (3:35-fade) and the solo on 'Broken' (1:09-42), both played by Neil Taylor, are fine examples. They have unpredictable interval leaps and rhythms, and their manic energy fits the tortured psychodrama of both songs.

The intro solo on The Who's 'Dreaming From The Waist' makes effective use of leaping a perfect fourth from E to A, then playing a repeat lick based on an A chord, the last note of which is allowed to feed back, before the run is finished with a bent phrase.

OPEN STRINGS

On p150 are some examples of running a scale up one string whilst playing an adjacent string as a drone note. The open E-string is treated as the root of a major scale (E), the natural minor (E minor), the third of a major (C), the third of a harmonic minor (C minor), the fifth of a major (A), and the fifth of a harmonic minor (A minor). The root note of the key is marked 'R' where it appears as a fretted note.

SECTION 7

Intervals can also be a resource if they arise from a mix of fretted notes and open-string drones. To do this, choose an open-string note that fits the key – usually the first or fifth of the scale – and fret the scale or phrase on the adjacent string. The result is a melody with a constant pitch running through it. U2's The Edge is fond of this technique, using it in the solo on 'Sunday Bloody Sunday', where both the top E-string and the G-string serve as the drone at varying moments. 'Pride In The Name Of Love' is another U2 example, where the same one-bar phrase is played eight times (1:40-58) using the open B-string as the lower drone support.

The value of open strings in soloing lies in their resonance and hammer-on/pull-off figures. But they cannot be bent (except with a tremolo bar) and cannot have slides or vibrato (ditto).

SECTION 7

SOLOS THAT USE CHORDS

In addition to scale-based phrases or intervals, a solo can also include chord-based ideas – one note at a time (arpeggio) or with triads and full chords. Either are useful when the soloist wants to spell out the underlying harmony. An arpeggio can create an impression of rapid ascent or descent by leaps. Major, minor, major/dominant sevenths, minor sevenths, and suspended fourth chords are probably the most popular for arpeggios in solos. The sevenths offer the chance to finish the arpeggio with an ear-catching bend from the seventh up to the root note. This idea occurs frequently in Dire Straits' 'Brothers In Arms'. Arpeggios can also facilitate a change of position.

Solos that use **arpeggio** ideas include Led Zeppelin's 'Achilles Last Stand', where for the first phrase Jimmy Page plays a Bm arpeggio over the E minor backing. Bryan Adams' 'Run To You' has a guitar break where two guitars harmonise on sus4

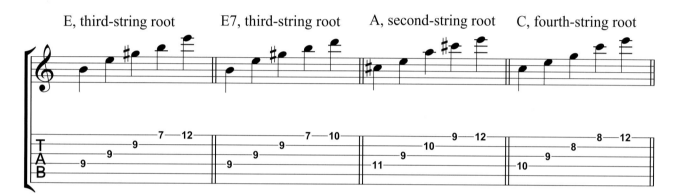

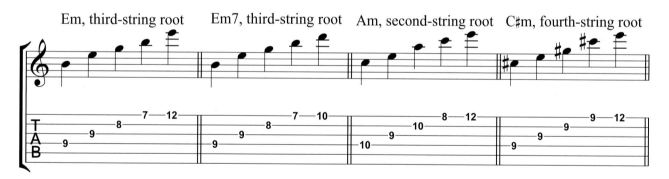

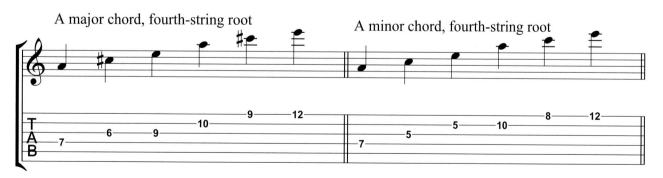

Continued over page

SECTION 7

E major chord, fifth-string root   E major chord, fifth-string root

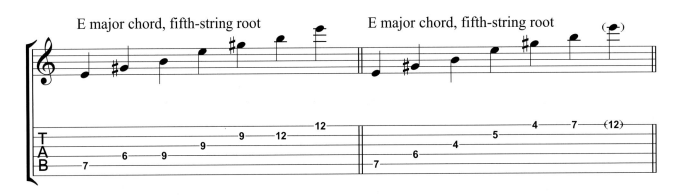

E minor chord, fifth-string root   A7 chord, fourth-string root

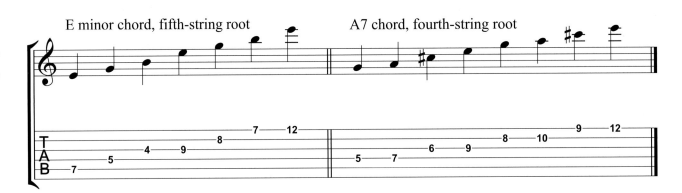

arpeggios (2:05-35 in a track of 3:36). From 0:48-1:04, The Beatles' 'Nowhere Man' has a chordal solo based on the verse progression probably double-tracked and ending with a glissando on the bottom E and a single harmonic. Mastodon's 'Seabeast' has an angular intro with raised fourths in A and C chords that allows the lead guitar to play some unusual Am arpeggio phrases across two octaves. The quiet first solo on Wishbone Ash's 'Blowin' Free' (2:29-55) starts with a rising and falling D major arpeggio that moves through an octave and a third. Mott the Hoople's 'All The Young Dudes' opens with several arpeggio-based lead ideas.

Blondie's 'Picture This' (1:38-2:00) has a solo with a descending pull-off phrase played three times and then picked chords, arpeggio-style. Ash's 'Goldfinger' has a guitar solo with the same arpeggio played four times over a single chord change, not used elsewhere in the song (2:35-58 in a track of 4:30). The radio edit is 3:59 with the solo starting at 2:20-31 and losing two phrases. Nick Lowe's 'Cruel To Be Kind' has a solo after the second chorus with three chordal phrases and then a single-note arpeggio descending with increasing rapidity. The Beatles' 'What Goes On' has a picked dominant chord-based solo at 1:38-54 which refers back to the soloing of 1950s players such as Scotty Moore. The solo on Buddy Holly's 'Peggy Sue' is chord-based.

Chordal solos are more likely to occur on keyboards, because keyboards facilitate them by way of their layout. The Doors' 'Love Her Madly' has a 16-bar solo based on chords (1:32-44) with a Farfisa organ sound. At 2:30-56 the electric guitar takes a solo based on the vocal melody developing a two-note motif.

SECTION 7

HARMONISED GUITAR SOLOS

The harmonised or twin-lead solo has sequences of thirds or sixths with one note distributed to each player. This permits the intervals to be coloured by string-bending and vibrato, which might be difficult when one player is holding down both notes, and means the lower and upper lines can be contrasted through the tone of different pick-ups, guitars, or effects. With twin-lead or triple-lead, the solo parts (along with bass guitar) effectively voice a chord progression without the arrangement needing any harmony instruments. At phrase endings one of the two lines may create a fourth or fifth instead of a third if coming to rest on the notes of a chord. An additional guitar can also be effective if it appears at the end of a solo to double the last few phrases, as happens with Bebop Deluxe's 'Adventures In A Yorkshire Landscape'.

An early example of a harmonised guitar solo is on The Beatles' 'And Your Bird Can Sing', during the intro and at 0:51-1:05, moving in thirds. On The Eagles' 'Hotel California', the guitar twin lead, played by Don Felder and Joe Walsh, takes over a lengthy coda (4:19-6:28), which is a third of the song. The precision of the coda's arrangement is perhaps more fitting, given the lyric's theme of being trapped, than free-flowing jamming solos would have been. Ram Jam's 'Black Betty' has many harmonised lead guitar passages, including high trills. The Vapors' 'Turning Japanese' has harmonised guitar breaks and unison bends to lead to a climax. Bad Company's 'Can't Get Enough' has a harmonised twin lead solo at 1:47-2:20 after the second chorus. 'Feel Like Makin' Love' (2:40-3:02) has a triple lead break of four bars (repeated), introducing a minorish harmony that contrasts with the song's mixolydian three-chord trick (D-C-G-C). Deep Purple's 'Highway Star' has an extended harmonised guitar solo before the last verse.

The first guitar break on 'Standing In The Road' by Blackfoot Sue has a harmonising melody with the main theme; a second solo uses the same strategy but goes higher. In the middle section of Golden Earring's 'Radar Love', the guitar harmonises in thirds with a synth brass line. Other examples are the coda solo of 'Friday Night' by The Darkness, and Queen's 'You're My Best Friend' and 'Killer Queen'. The coda of Jam's 'Down In The Tube Station At Midnight' has an effective twin-lead part. For a more minimal approach take the harmonised break on Supergrass's 'Grace' at 1:56-2:10, near the end of the song. Both parts are oscillating either a tone or a semitone. Another unconventional break occurs at 1:07-22 of Garbage's 'Only Happy When It Rains' with one or two harmonised phrases on treated guitars, with an additional lead over the top, over the same sequence of I-V-♭VI-♭VII, which colours the repeated phrase.

The planned character of a harmonised guitar solo can make it sound stilted, and the more notes there are the stronger this impression becomes. But such solos do not have to have lots of notes. In Led Zeppelin's 'Ramble On', after verse two at 1:47-2:04, there is a simple harmonised guitar part with sustain, giving an almost flute or horn effect. It comprises a single phrase played four times, harmonised in thirds, the guitars panned hard right and left. Since the lyric is an imaginative play on Tolkein's *Lord Of The Rings*, the slightly unearthly sound fits the song. A second harmonised guitar break, with a quicker set of notes, occurs before the last verse at 2:25-36, straight after the second chorus.

SECTION 7

Harmonising only the last few phrases of a solo is another possibility. In Marillion's 'Kayleigh', the solo (1:41-2:08) repeats its first phrase with a slight variation, then plays single notes in time with the chords, and ends with a harmonised phrase. Toto's 'Hold The Line' has an example of a fast high-pitched virtuoso solo that comes in after the second chorus and is played over the main riff. Its last phrase (2:25-30) is harmonised to create a climax, because it would be harder otherwise for a single lead to have a dynamic ending as it has already played fast, high, and bent notes: several ways of finishing are already used.

A prominent, repeated twin-lead idea may replace the need for a solo altogether. There is no single guitar solo in Thin Lizzy's 'The Boys Are Back In Town', primarily because the eight-bar twin lead passage that follows each chorus makes it redundant. Their 'Wild One' has a triple harmonised lead break in the middle, while the intro of 'Waiting For An Alibi' has twin lead in sixths, and a central solo which has a fast twin-lead cascade run. Twin lead can be used to introduce a single guitar solo. Their 'Downtown Sundown' has a brilliant solo prepared for by a few bars of twin lead. This makes the lead solo sound like it has broken free from constraints. This solo's timing has many rhythmic twists and turns. It also includes an example of a momentary muting of notes – this is good for making the latter part of a phrase seem brighter. And 'Bad Reputation' has a harmonised guitar break immediately followed by two lead guitar solos. Meanwhile, the solo on 'Reelin' In The Years' by Steely Dan is introduced by a passage of harmonised lead.

SOLO TECHNIQUES

Tremolo picking

Part of the guitar's expressiveness as a solo instrument is the fact that even a single note can be articulated in many ways. It can be:

- fretted in more than one place on various strings
- bent up to from a note one, two, or three frets lower
- approached from above or below by a slide
- hammered-on or pulled-off
- trilled
- given vibrato or muting.

For example, tremolo picking is a way to accentuate a phrase in a solo. This is where the notes are scrubbed by the pick moving quickly back and forth, instead of being played with a single down or up pick. Use a hard plectrum and hold it tightly. Examples can be heard on U2's 'In God's Country' and 'The Fly', where it is enhanced with echo; on Bruce Springsteen's 'Adam Raised A Cain', The Who's 'I Can See For Miles', Catatonia's 'I Am The Mob', and Pantera's '5 Minutes Alone'. The solo on Ozzy Osbourne's 'Shot In The Dark' ends with fierce tremolo picking to create a dramatic conclusion. Brian Robertson starts his solo on Thin Lizzy's 'Don't Believe A Word' with a tremolo-picked bend from D up to E and down again through a wah-wah pedal. It is also used during the instrumental break in Nirvana's 'Drain

You' at about 1:41-2:33 where it is applied to a whole chord, building to a crescendo back into the riff. The Strokes' 'The Modern Age' solo (1:49-2:15) starts with minimal notes and then has some rapid picking.

String-bending

Most electric guitar solos feature some degree of string-bending. The subtleties of pitch variation and vibrato generated through pitch-bending mean it came to imitate the pitch-shifting of a singer. One of the most idiomatic techniques for the instrument, it developed when players strung their guitars with lighter strings. Pete Townshend of The Who told *Guitar World* in October 1994 that James Burton was the first player he heard make a normal guitar sound like a pedal steel by bending notes. In the early 1960s there were no light gauge strings, so bending was difficult; Burton solved the problem by using two second strings instead of a second and a third.

The most-used bends travel a semitone or whole tone, though wider bends as far as two-and-a-half tones are possible. The smaller quarter-tone bend, which is like smudging the pitch, is used in blues. A multiple bend can reach several pitches without moving position. Always try to support the finger executing the bend by putting other fingers on the string behind it, then push with all three. On strings 1-3 bends usually go upwards toward you; on strings 4-6 they go downwards, away from you.

A player can also silently bend a note – the pre-bend – before striking it and letting it drop, which is less expected and good with echo. A pre-bend is often surprising because we're not used to notes dropping in pitch. The effect of a bend rests on many factors, including the relationship of the notes to the underlying harmony. The musical meaning of a single bend changes if you change the chord underneath it. Even the most familiar bend or lick can sound fresh over a different chord to the usual one that invites it, as long as there is some harmonic relationship between the bent note and the chord. Bends can be grouped into those that go into a chord or out of a chord. A bent note can be played off against a fretted note that is static. A single bent note played with two fretted notes can create a complete major or minor triad. Bending can also imitate slide and pedal steel guitar, as the outstanding solo by Amos Garrett on Maria Muldaur's hit 'Midnight At The Oasis' demonstrates.

Speed is another factor. Fast bends reduce the initial fretted note to a grace-note decoration to the destination note; slower bends give more or equal weight to both and extend the gradual change of pitch involved in moving from one to the other. A note can return from a bend without being re-struck.

As Richard Thompson commented to *Making Music* in June 1991, "In a sense, the best guitar players are the ones who don't play many notes at all. B.B. King is a classic example of someone who can make one note sound really fantastic, lots of vibrato, great tone, full of emotion. Hubert Sumlin was the greatest man for making one note sound unbelievable on the guitar. A note isn't just a note – it's all these micro-sounds, and if you bend it slightly, different things will happen."

Bruce Springsteen uses wide bends in the solos on 'Roulette', 'Restless Night', and 'Incident On 57th Street'. The solo on 'Kitty's Back' at 2:47-3:10 pits two guitars against each other, left and right, and includes harmonised bends. The Beatles' 'You're Gonna Lose That Girl' has an eight-bar solo, after two choruses, two verses and a short bridge, with a single four-bar phrase repeated. At 1:08 it starts with a

Chuck Berry-ish bend which sounds different because of the verse sequence it is played over: I-III^-II-V (E-G♯-F♯m-B). The Queens Of The Stone Age's 'Leg Of Lamb' (2:23-31) is a short, ironic solo with repeated strikes of a bend, and something similar can be heard on the intro of 'Auto Pilot'. This track has the guitar playing a lead counter-melody to the vocal on the chorus. It also has many quasi-vocal wailing bends.

Unison bends

One special type of bend is the unison bend, when a fretted note is combined with a lower note that is bent upward to match it. It is a useful tool in a solo because it:

- thickens the sound, especially if the notes are struck together
- creates emphasis
- creates a quasi-vocal effect, especially when 'staggered'
- works well in a first phrase or a last phrase.

Unison bends often occur at the beginning of a solo, especially in blues. To play a unison bend, hold a note on the first string and a note three frets higher on the second. Strike them together and bend the second string up until the notes are roughly in tune. On strings two and three, the lower note on the third string is only two frets further up. Try this somewhere above the seventh fret until you get the feel of it; it is more difficult closer to the nut. Support the finger that is bending the lower string in both cases, by fretting with the second and third fingers.

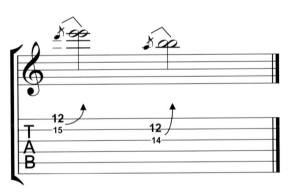

The short solo on Alice Cooper's 'School's Out' (1:27-41) opens with several unison bends, as does Portishead's 'Glory Box'. The guitar solo of Led Zeppelin's 'Dazed And Confused' starts with a sequence of unison bends whose vocal quality is amplified by Robert Plant singing with them (3:40-52). The Manic Street Preachers' 'Found That Soul' solo (1:58-2:24) enters in a blaze of unisons and about half the solo is done with them. The Stranglers' 'No More Heroes' ends with a coda of unison bends ascending on guitar (3:08-25), each answering the bass riff up to the end. In The Darkness's 'Get Your Hands Off My Woman' the solo ends with a sequence of rising unisons for the climax at 2:15-19. Gene's 'We Could Be Kings' has a short four-phrase guitar solo with several unisons at 3:15-24.

Queens Of The Stone Age's 'The Lost Art Of Keeping A Secret' has a solo at 2:32-48 with almost all unison bends, which are allowed to go out of tune to fit the demented character of the track, in contrast to the cool, sardonic vocal. The coda guitar solo on 'Stairway To Heaven' (7:25-45) is mostly unisons. Listen to the intro of Rainbow's 'I Surrender', which has a three-note unison phrase played twice in the first six seconds. Wishbone Ash's 'Lady Whiskey' has unison bends at 3:57-4:08.

Repeat licks

Though they have gained something of a bad reputation, the repeat lick has been a part of many classic rock solos. They sound energetic and dramatic, making them good for solo introductions or conclusions. For the songwriter considering a solo to fit a song, they risk the impression of self-conscious virtuosity, the quality that causes a song to collapse from '3D' to '2D'. They often involve between three to six short notes, with the hand able to fret these without moving position. A repeat lick has additional colour if it is played with hammer-ons and pull-offs, or whilst slowly opening and closing a wah-wah pedal. To create a repeat lick choose three, four, or five notes of a scale or chord and group them in any way that allows them to be played within a single beat or most of a beat. The notes must be in a close bunch on the fretboard to be playable.

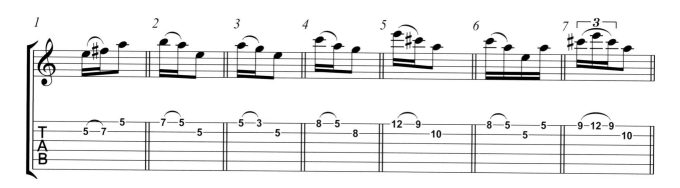

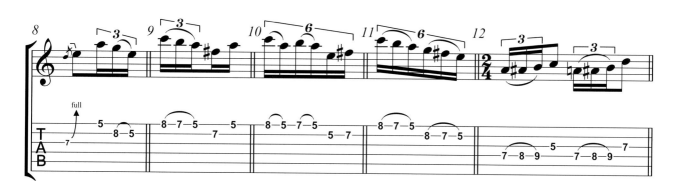

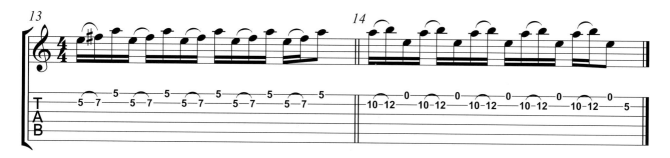

Examples 1-5 put three notes on the beat. Example 6 divides the beat into four equal notes. Examples 7-8 use a 16th-note triplet to get four notes on the beat. Example 9 uses a 16th-note triplet and two 16th-notes to get five notes on the beat. Examples 10-11 use a 16th-note sextuplet to get six notes on the beat. Example 12 shows that a repeat lick can include a variation – the last note in the group alternates. Example 13 shows a three-note repeat lick cycling across the four beats of the bar, displacing itself by one 16th-note at a time until it gets back on the beat. Example 14 shows how an open string might be worked into a repeat lick.

Examples of repeat licks include Dire Straits' 'Sultans of Swing' (5:08-11, 5:18-30 on three different triads), and at the end of the solo in 'Lady Writer' (at 2:07-10) and during the coda solo at 3:09-20. Wishbone Ash's 'Error Of My Ways' has repeat licks at 4:09-21 and a faster one at 5:04-12. You find them also in Led Zeppelin's 'Communication Breakdown' (1:25-29), 'Black Dog' (4:14-18), 'Heartbreaker' (2:24-30), and 'Stairway To Heaven' (6:14-20, and the last phrase). The guitar solo of 'Dazed And Confused' features two repeat licks in succession at 3:52-57, with others further on.

A chromatic repeat-lick – where the finger-pattern is moved up one fret at a time but the melodic and rhythmic shape stays the same – is a way of shifting position. This is how Jimmy Page uses the chromatic repeat lick at 1:56-59 of the solo in 'Rock And Roll', matching the chord change from A to D (he ends the solo with a standard repeat lick at 2:13-15).

The cascade run

One way of using a scale in a lead guitar solo is to map out a 'cascade run'. This involves moving up or down the scale three or four notes and then starting another run from one note higher or lower than the first. This makes the downward or

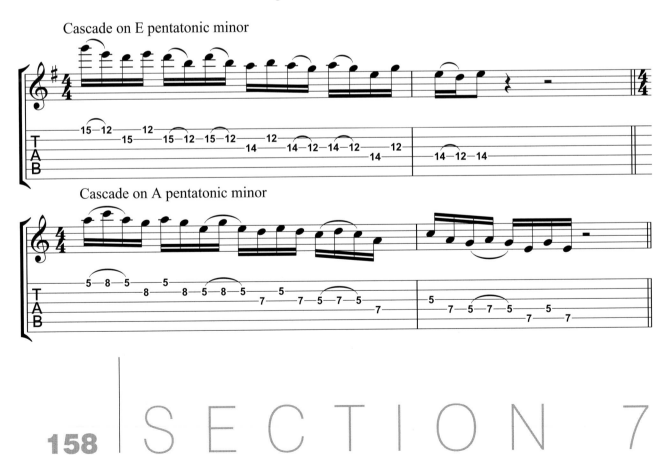

Cascade on E pentatonic minor

Cascade on A pentatonic minor

upward run last longer, which is useful at speed. Dire Straits' 'Lady Writer' has several (see 1:15-19). Led Zeppelin's 'Good Times Bad Times' has one at the end of the last chorus (2:03-09). Thin Lizzy's 'Waiting For An Alibi' has cascade runs with single lead and also harmonised lead during the main solo. Aztec Camera's 'Somewhere In My Heart' has a lead solo that starts with cascade phrases. It comes in to illustrate the lyric, which talks about the closest thing to heaven being rock'n'roll.

Harmonics

These light, high-pitched notes are good for decorative touches in solos but need a sparse texture. Echo, distortion, chorus, flanging, phasing, and a wah-wah pedal all give them more body on electric guitar. A tremolo arm will also sustain them. The harmonics at positions XII, VII, V, and IV (the 12th, seventh, fifth, and fourth frets) are the easiest harmonics to produce. They rise in pitch as they get nearer the nut. In relation to the open string:

- the XII position harmonic is one octave above
- the VII position harmonic is one octave and a fifth above
- the V position harmonic is two octaves above
- the IV position harmonic is two octaves and a major third above.

The top three strings produce a minor chord in harmonics – Em at XII and V, Bm at VII and G♯m at IV. Strings two-three-four produce a major chord in harmonics – G at XII and V, D at VII and B at IV.

To play a harmonic, touch the string right over the metal fret (don't press the string on to the fretboard), strike it, and lift your finger away so the string can resonate.

Harmonics sometimes appear as the final notes of a solo, as was the case with The Beatles' 'Nowhere Man'. With distortion, and by angling the pick, artificial harmonics can be created ('pinch harmonics'); they were popular in heavy rock solos during the 1980s. They can be heard in a more delicate form on the solo on Eric Clapton's 'Bell Bottom Blues'.

The solo on The Smiths' 'Shoplifters Of The World' has some harmonics.

THE SOLO'S HARMONIC CONTEXT: WHAT CHORDS ARE YOU PLAYING OVER?

"Soloing over standard changes is as boring as hell to me."

(Jeff Buckley, Guitarist, September 2004)

In Section Six we looked at the harmony over which a solo is played from the angle of finding the right scale for the chord or the key. Another way of looking at this is to see the chords as providing an opportunity for the soloist rather than an obstacle

SECTION 7

course. A solo depends on everything about its context: where it happens and what is going on at that point. The most important element to the context, which will colour whatever you do with the lead, is the chord sequence over which you're playing.

Some solos are played over a single chord, especially if they are short. Even solos that have more than one chord may have a number of bars on a single chord. It may seem that the 'single-chord solo' offers a great freedom to the soloist: if there are no chord *changes* it is harder to play a wrong note. But the soloist has less to play against and must work harder to generate melodic interest. I would always prefer to be soloing over a sequence of chords than a single chord. The musical value of the notes of a solo is strongly influenced by the chords you play over. Play a pentatonic major solo over chords I, IV, and V (all majors), and it will have one effect; play it over chords II, III, and VI (all minors) and it will have quite another – yet it consists of the same five notes.

There's a clean but muted eight-bar solo on The Beatles' 'Michelle', played on a front pickup with the tone wound off. This is over a more shifting harmony than was typical of a Beatles song. It is heard at 1:26-38 and then again on the coda. The harmony provided an opportunity for the solo. Kings of Leon's 'Pyro' has, at 2:31-47, an eight-bar solo with guitar, or possibly guitar and a keyboard sound, which is essentially one phrase repeated. The song introduces chords III and II to contrast this section from the rest of the song, which is I, VI, and IV.

SOLOS AND KEY-CHANGES

Similar potential arises when a solo involves a key-change. Transposing a solo section from one key to another, or changing key during it, can make a big difference to the solo. Does the new key allow for open strings? Does it place you at a certain point in the neck? Compare how soloing in E♭m would work as opposed to Em in first position.

The solo section will contrast with the rest of the song if it is in another key. If this key-change occurs immediately the solo starts, the effect can be powerful. There is a pronounced feeling of contrast, because not only the harmony but the melodic solo are likely to use different notes. Red Hot Chili Peppers' 'Californication' is in the key of A minor, but for the solo there is a key change to F♯ minor. Aretha Franklin's 'Respect' has a saxophone solo paired with a key change (1:11-28). The song starts in C major and changes to F♯ minor, then slips back via G major. The Who's 'Relay' has a solo which initially pits E pentatonic minor ideas against the E major chord backing (1:17-26) but shifts up a tone changing key to F♯ major (1:27-47) before dropping back to E.

Bryan Adams' 'Can't Stop This Thing We Started' has a 16-bar solo (3:05-22) preceded by a middle-eight that shifts key at 2:48 from A major to F major. The guitar solo coincides with a return to the home key of A major. Thin Lizzy's 'That Woman's Gonna Break Your Heart' has a verse in B♭ and a chorus in G minor. After the second chorus, the song plunges from a G minor chord to an E minor chord (and key change), at which point the lead guitar plays a short but intense solo that starts with a D to E bend at the 15th fret on the B-string. This is one of the most used bends in rock, yet here it sounds fresh because of the key change. This solo is followed by another, with a different character, in B♭ major. The same band's 'Sweet

S E C T I O N   7

Marie' has a solo that contrasts an A major first half with an A minor second half.

Catatonia's 'Londinium' uses the chorus progression I-VI-II-V in B major for the solo. It is preceded by a quiet passage at 2:44 where the chorus melody is heard. The chorus sequence is heard with a key change to C♯ major, and the solo is derived from the chorus melody (3:04-24). The key change makes it soar – a good example of how the power of a solo depends partly on the backing and harmony. Supergrass's 'Alright' has a two-part key-change solo. The first part (1:38-53) is a manic G pentatonic minor solo over what sounds like a I-♭VII change in G. The second part (1:54-) is a repeated bent phrase in D major, which is harmonised.

Turin Brakes' 'Underdog' has a solo initially playing in a minor key over the verse progression. The solo becomes more bluesy half-way through, turning into something more blues-influenced as it continues over the chorus progression, and then the song ends at 3:30. This is an interesting example of a solo that covers the verse and the chorus, which replaces the vocal last chorus, and which changes scale and style to fit both sections.

SECTION 7

HOW TO SOLO IN A MAJOR KEY

Here are some ideas for finding your way round a solo in the upbeat major key.

SECTION 8
HOW TO SOLO IN A MAJOR KEY

Songs And Solos has a CD with 42 musical examples to provide some ideas and concepts about how to play a solo. Sections Eight to Eleven of the book provide a commentary on these solos, describing their significant musical features. Each example has been designed to be multi-faceted, illustrating finger patterns, bends, scale-types, phrasing, and more. Each example has a certain chord progression, which in turn requires a certain scale or pattern. Keys, style, tempo, and time signature are varied. From these solos you can learn about phrasing and developing a solo. They cannot provide exactly the same experience as hearing a solo in the context of a whole song, but the many famous tracks mentioned in the text can help you with that. Each solo is present on the CD with lead guitar (odd-numbers) and without (even-numbers). The backing tracks without lead can be used to invent your own solos and try different approaches.

The emphasis is very much on musicality (melody, choice of notes, and phrasing), not on showing off technique. The solos do not feature many rapid passages of notes. Nevertheless, there are plenty of challenges among them because they do not stick to simple pentatonic patterns. The intention is to be able to hear the effect of notes and scales against the underlying harmony. This would be obscured if the notes were too quick. The chord progressions stay within what might be expected in song material rather than purely instrumental music. In addition to a central solo passage, usually in eight or 12 bars, or two eight-bars, some of the tracks have an intro of two or four bars – which could be thought of as a link *into* the solo – and an outro, as if a link out of the solo and into the next section of the song. The examples are often more explicit in their use of scale patterns than I would choose in a real solo; this is to make the illustration clearer.

In this section we begin by devising some solos for chord progressions that sit within the major key. Remember that in addition to the full major scale for the key, chords I, IV, and V can be soloed over on their own pentatonic majors because these scales do not have any notes foreign to the home key. The examples are presented mostly in keys that are guitar-friendly, ie, which permit the use of open strings: A, C, D, E, G, Am, Bm, Dm, Em, and F♯m.

CD TRACKS 1+2

Key / Key chords   A major: I (A), IV (D), V (E)
Additional chords   -
Solo structure   4+12+4
Bars   1-4 intro / 5-16 main solo / 17-20 outro
Scales used   A pentatonic major (A-B-C♯-E-F♯ / 1-2-3-5-6)

Comments

CD 1 is modelled on the famous 12-bar progression used in much blues and rock. The major pentatonic scale against these chords creates a positive, upbeat feeling. Only bar 10 presents a small challenge, a Dsus4 that decorates the D chord for two beats. This can be handled by bending off the pentatonic major from F♯ to G. Watch how certain rhythmic patterns are repeated and how the scale builds through three positions (second, ninth, 14th) towards its highest note. The strange thing about using the pentatonic major in this way is that the root note of chord IV (D) is never played (as it would be if the full major scale were used). Notice:

1-4: The aaab phrasing.
5: The triad arpeggio on A.
9: The third string slide shift of position.
13: The second half of the solo starts with a high bend.
13-16: Uses the 14th position.
17-20: Uses a rhythm pattern derived from the intro but played an octave higher.

SECTION 8

CD TRACKS 3+4

Key / Key chords   C major: I (C), IV (F), V (G)
Additional chords -
Solo structure   4+12+4
Scales used   C pentatonic major (C-D-E-G-A / 1-2-3-5-6)
                       F pentatonic major (F-G-A-C-D / 1-2-3-5-6)
Bars   1-4 intro / 5-16 main solo / 17-20 outro

Comments

The solo lasts 12 bars but the chords do not follow the bar allocation and sequence of a 12-bar blues. The solo's intro takes advantage of the spaces left by the rhythm part to insert ascending and descending G7 arpeggios. The solo starts high.

5, 7, and 9: These use a similar phrase and provide varying answer phrases.
11-12:   There is a characteristic figure with a unison bend at the fifth fret.
13-14:   Open strings create a different sound and facilitate a change of position.
15-16:   There is an F major pentatonic pattern (F G A C D) for the chord of F.
15-16:   Place the solo very low for the first time.
17-21:   The outro of the solo takes a two-bar phrase and repeats it.

CD TRACKS 5+6 (OVER PAGE)

Key / Key chords   D major: I (D), IV (G), V (A)
Additional chords -
Solo structure   4+8+8+4
Scales used   D mixolydian   D-E-F♯-G-A-B-C / 1-2-3-4-5-6-♭7
                       D major blues   D-E-F-F♯-A-B / 1-2-♭3-3-5-6
                       G major blues   G-A-B♭-B-D-E / 1-2-♭3-3-5-6
                       A major blues   A-B-C-C♯-E-F♯ / 1-2-♭3-3-5-6
Bars   1-4 intro / 5-12 solo part one / 13-20 solo part two / 21-24 outro

Comments

This 16-bar solo in D major has a strong blues feel because of the dominant seventh chords (D7, G7, A7) and the time signature of 12/8. There are four beats in a bar but each divides into three, giving a swing feel.

1-4:   The intro is based on a single chord of A.
5-11: Use the major blues scale on D, G, and A.
13-20: The second half of the solo sees the mixolydian scale appear.
21-22: The outro uses an ascending turn-around figure based on sixths and with a pull-off to the open E-string.

SECTION 8 | **167**

CD TRACKS 7+8 (OVER PAGE)

Key / Key chords E major: I (E), IV (A), V (B)
Additional chords -
Solo structure   4+8+8+4
Bars   1-4 intro / 5-12 solo part one / 13-20 solo part two / 21-24 outro
Scales used   E major   E-F♯-G♯-A-B-C♯-D♯ / 1-2-3-4-5-6-7
                       B pentatonic minor   B-D-E-F♯-A / 1-♭3-4-5-♭7

Comments

CD7+8 is also in 12/8. With a country blues feel, it makes extensive use of sixths, thirds and fourths rather than scales.

1-4:   Intro leads into the solo with a downward cascade run on E major, starting on the note B.

5-12:   Shows the use of consecutive sixths primarily drawn from the scale. Notice that bar five and bar seven are the same notes but fingered differently.

9:   D-natural gives a bluesier inflection.

12:   Notice the perfect fifth on the last beat.

SECTION 8

13-20: There is a double-stop hammer-on figure that emphasises the harmony. This idea is good if there is no rhythm guitar or keyboard.

20: Bare fourths lead up to the outro.

21-24: The outro has a blues flavour because of the pentatonic minor on B over a B7 chord.

SECTION 8

SECTION 8 | **171**

CD TRACKS 9+10

Key / Key chords G major: I (G), II (Am), IV (C), V (D), VI (Em)
Additional chords -
Solo structure 4+12+4
Bars 1-4 intro / 5-16 main solo / 17-20 outro
Scales used G major G-A-B-C-D-E-F♯ / 1-2-3-4-5-6-7

Comments

This is a relaxed break in the key of G major.

1-2: An ascending phrase in octaves (in contrary motion to the descending bass-line).

3-4: A descending set of thirds.

5-8: Initial lead phrases use the G major scale and an arch shape, rising and falling.

9: Compare with bar 5 – it is not an exact repeat.

10-11: Show how to phrase on an arpeggio of Em7 and Cmaj7. Arpeggios contrast well with scale movement.

13: When an Am chord first appears, there is a shift of position to the 12th fret.

15: A slight variation on bar 13 and each has its own answering phrase.

16: The solo ends on a high third for the chord of D.

17-20: Outro uses a sixth that straddles the open G-string, which is resonant and nicely puts the pitch of the strings no longer in order (an option when high on the fretboard and bringing in an open string). The last beats of 17 and 19 feature a different pair of notes.

CD TRACKS 11+12

Key / Key chords A major / F♯ minor: I (A), II (Bm), III (C♯m), IV (D), V (E), VI (F♯m)
Additional chords -
Solo structure 2+8+8+4
Bars 1-2 intro / 3-10 solo part one / 11-20 solo part two / 21-24 outro
Scales used A major A-B-C♯-D-E-F♯-G♯ / 1-2-3-4-5-6-7
F♯ natural minor F♯-G♯-A-B-C♯-D-E / 1-2-♭3-4-5-♭6-♭7

Comments
This progression is in A major but with an F♯ minor feel.

3-10: A two-bar phrase repeats with variations (including being displaced by another eighth-note) and a two-bar phrase answers.
3: A cascade run repeated in bars 7 and 9 in truncated form.
8: Has some sixths.
11-20: Double-stops appear and gradually work up the neck to a 14th-position scale, the highest notes saved until the end.
17: Notice the C♯ (the seventh of Dmaj7 and the root of C♯m) worked in from a bend.
21-24: The outro is a variation on the intro idea transposed up an octave.

SECTION 8

SECTION 8 | 175

CD TRACKS 13+14

Key / Key chords	C major: I (C), IV (F), V (G)
Additional chords	-
Solo structure	2+8+8+4
Bars	1-2 intro / 3-10 solo part one / 11-18 solo part two / 19-22 outro
Scales used	C pentatonic major
	A pentatonic minor
	A natural minor

C pentatonic major	C-D-E-G-A / 1-2-3-5-6
A pentatonic minor	A-C-D-E-G / 1-♭3-4-5-♭7
A natural minor	A-B-C-D-E-F-G / 1-2-♭3-4-5-♭6-♭7

Comments

1-2: The solo begins with a two-bar arpeggio idea.

3-10: Makes maximum use of a single position at the eighth fret, restricting the movement.

10: Notice how bars 6 and 10 copy the backing.

11: The Am has a pentatonic minor phrase often heard in blues lead. Here it has a different effect because this is not a blues.

15: The same phrase is repeated over the next Am chord, but with a small shift in pitch upward on the last few notes using the A natural minor scale.

18: Uses a three-semiquaver repeat lick that syncopates the rhythm, displacing itself repeatedly until returning to its original position.

19-22: The outro features a variation on the intro idea transposed up an octave.

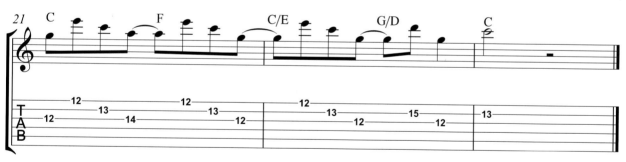

CD TRACKS 15+16

Key / Key chords	D major: I (D), II (Em), III (F♯m), IV (G), V (A), VI (Bm)	
Additional chords	-	
Solo structure	2+8+8+4	
Bars	1-2 intro / 3-18 main solo / 19-22 outro	
Scales used	D major	D-E-F♯-G-A-B-C♯ / 1-2-3-4-5-6-7
	D pentatonic major	D-E-F♯-A-B / 1-2-3-5-6
	A pentatonic minor	A-C-D-E-G / 1-♭3-4-5-♭7

Comments

1-2: The intro uses A pentatonic minor to give a harder sound to a solo that mostly has a strong major feel.

3-10: The first eight bars of the solo divide into two four-bar phrases, which start in a similar way.

10: Brings this section to a close with arpeggios on Bm and G making the transition to a 14th position start of the second half at bar 11.

11-18: The second half of the solo is dominated by thirds.

19-22: A high position D pentatonic major idea is used on the outro.

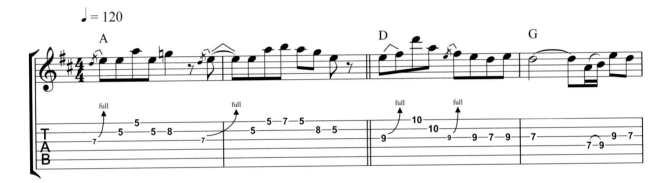

SECTION 8

SECTION 8

CD TRACKS 17+18

Key / Key chords	E major: I (E), IV (A), V (B), VI (C♯m)	
Additional chords	-	
Solo structure	4+16+4	
Bars	1-4 intro / 5-20 main solo / 21-24 outro	
Scales used	E mixolydian	E-F♯-G♯-A-B-C♯-D / 1-2-3-4-5-6-♭7
	E pentatonic major	E-F♯-G♯-B-C♯ / 1-2-3-5-6
	A mixolydian	A-B-C♯-D-E-F♯-G / 1-2-3-4-5-6-♭7

Comments

1-4: A mixolydian phrase with a blues third followed by a usual third.

5-16: The main part of the solo is made up of four phrases, making increasing use of a rock'n'roll double-stop idea that can be traced back to Chuck Berry. Despite its lineage, it can be refreshed by applying a non-standard approach beyond a 12-bar three-chord context. In this instance it is the C♯m chord (VI) that makes the change.

5-6 / 9-10: Answered by variant phrases.

12: A descending phrase that has the open E-string as a drone.

10: A standard blues bend is made to sound different by playing it over the C♯m chord.

16: An example of the use of the A mixolydian scale over chord IV.

19-20: The main solo ends with a rising idea based on a single A major chord.

21-24: The outro is based on parts of the intro moved up an octave.

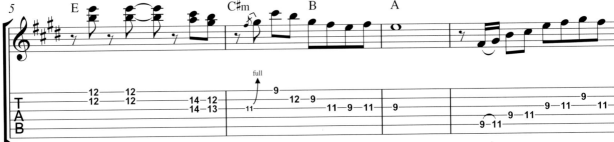

180 SECTION 8

SECTION 8 |

CD TRACKS 19+20

Key / Key chords   G major: I (G), III (Bm), IV (C), V (D), VI (Em)
Additional chords   -
Solo structure   2+16+4
Bars   1-2 intro / 3-18 main solo / 19-22 outro
Scales used   G major   G-A-B-C-D-E-F♯ / 1-2-3-4-5-6-7

Comments

This solo draws on all the notes of G major and has many scale-like runs, clear repetition of rhythm patterns, and brings another minor chord (III) into the progression. The presence of half-notes (minims), some of which are tied to an eighth-note, show this melody is designed not to move around too quickly.

1-2:   The intro uses an upward cascade idea, phrased aaab – three ascending, one descending.

3-10:   The melody has arpeggio figures in bars 3, 5, and 7, spelling out the chords for those bars.

9-10:   Notice the use of an open E-string (and in bars 17-18), and that the last two quarter-notes in these bars are varied, the second time rising rather than falling. These bars have a syncopated rhythm.

19-22:   The outro uses a higher two-bar phrase repeated with a variant ending.

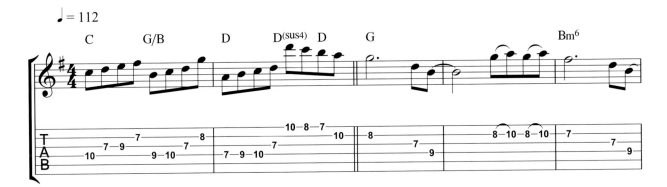

SECTION 8

SECTION 8

183

CD TRACKS 21+22

Key / Key chords	A major: I (A), II (Bm), IV (D), V (E)
Additional chords	-
Solo structure	2+15+4
Bars	1-2 intro / 3-17 main solo / 18-21 outro
Scales used	A pentatonic major A-B-C♯-E-F♯ / 1-2-3-5-6
	A major A-B-C♯-D-E-F♯-G♯ / 1-2-3-5-6-7

Comments

Soloists in songs are accustomed to play in symmetrical phrases, often four or eight bars long. This example is a challenge because the phrase-lengths are five bars (times three). Improvise with this backing track and you'll find how easy it is to be caught out by the fifth bar. Bars 3-7 and 8-12 are played mostly with the A pentatonic major scale in second position, although the note D is added to match the D chord; in bars 13-17 the scale shifts to the 10th and 14th positions.

1-2: The intro features an arpeggio idea based on the E7sus4 chord.

3-7: Notice how this solo interacts with the rhythm of the chords by playing on beats three and four of the bar when the chords are sustained, as if answering them.

7: This phrase is in rhythm with the accented backing idea (also in bars 12 and 17).

13-17: Notice the bent held minims in this third phrase.

18-21: The major scale provides the descending phrase of the last four bars, decorated by slides.

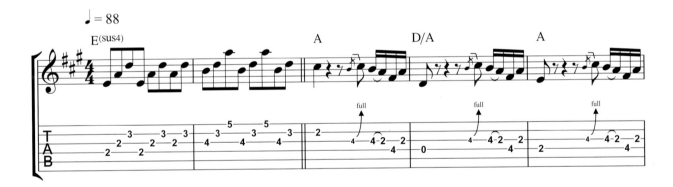

SECTION 8

SECTION 8

CD TRACKS 23+24

Key / Key chords	C major: I (C), IV (F), V (G), VI (Am), VII7 (Bm7♭5)
Additional chords	-
Solo structure	2+8+8+4
Bars	1-2 intro / 3-10 solo part one / 11-18 solo part two / 19-22 outro
Scales used	C major C-D-E-F-G-A-B / 1-2-3-4-5-6-7

Comments

This solo includes the most unusual chord of the harmony so far, a Bm7♭5 (VII7) in the key of C major. VII is the only flat fifth chord in a major key that does not require a change of scale since it draws only on notes from the major scale (B-D-F-A). (Compare it with Bm7, which needs an F♯.) As the lead part is often sounding two notes at a time, some of the solo could be re-arranged or re-fingered for two guitars (the twin-lead approach), with each interval divided between the players (or tracks, if overdubbing).

1-2:   Uses the notes of F pentatonic major.

3-10:   Uses thirds, with some other intervals for additional colour based on the chords underneath. There is a fourth in bars six and seven.

11-18:   Switches to octaves based on the C major scale.

19-22:   The solo concludes with its highest phrases, still on C major, around the 10th fret.

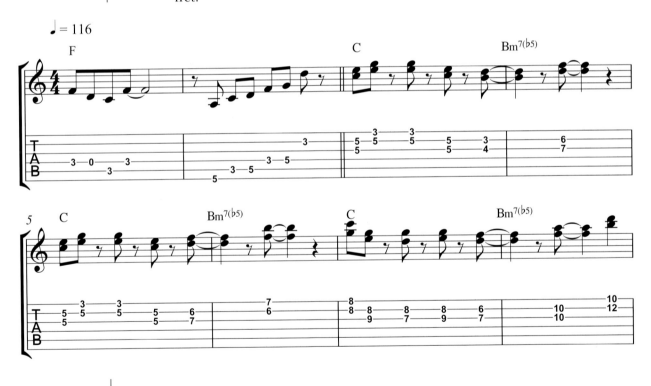

SECTION 8

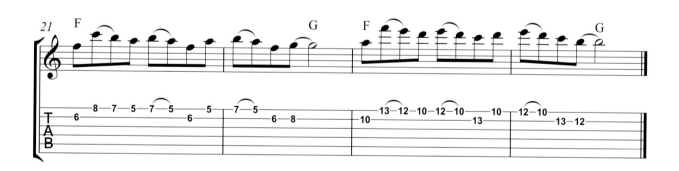

HOW TO SOLO IN A MINOR KEY

SECTION 9
HOW TO SOLO IN A MINOR KEY

The examples in this section look at handling the variations in minor chord harmony that stem from the fact that there is no single minor scale that is an equivalent of the single major scale.

CD TRACKS 25+26 (OVER PAGE)

Key / Key chords	A minor: I (Am), IV (Dm), V (Em), VI (F), VII (G)
Additional chords	-
Solo structure	4+8+8+4
Bars	1-4 intro / 5-12 solo part one / 13-20 solo part two / 21-24 outro
Scales used	A pentatonic minor A-C-D-E-G / 1-♭3-4-5-♭7
	A natural minor A-B-C-D-E-F-G / 1-2-♭3-4-5-♭6-♭7

Comments

The first of the minor key solos uses only chords derived from the A natural minor scale (Aeolian mode), so no sharps are needed. Almost all of the solo is played on the pentatonic minor, which here does not sound bluesy in the way it would in a major key because none of its notes are functioning as 'blue notes'. That is to say, they are on the scale and the harmony already includes them. The natural minor scale is felt wherever the note F is played (bars 11, 16, 22, 24) over the F or Dm chord, or the note B (bar 18). These are the two notes omitted when the natural minor becomes a pentatonic minor.

1-4: Notice the held note in bars one and three. Don't feel you have to keep playing notes; sustain is good. If a note has musical value, why rush to 'spend' it?

5-12: Much of the first half of the solo is focused around the eighth-fret position. It is good soloing discipline to see how much can be extracted from one such five-note position.

13-20: The second half shifts to the 12th position and then the 17th.

SECTION 9

CD TRACKS 27+28

Key / Key chords	B minor: I (Bm), IV (Em), V^ (F♯), VI (G), VII (A)
Additional chords	-
Solo structure	2+10+2
Bars	1-2 intro / 3-12 main solo / 13-14 outro
Scales used	B harmonic minor B-C♯-D-E-F♯-G-A♯ / 1-2-♭3-4-5-♭6-7
	B natural minor B-C♯-D-E-F♯-G-A / 1-2-♭3-4-5-♭6-♭7

Comments

This mildly jazzy solo is shaped by three factors: the skipping 12/8 rhythm, the almost constant flow of notes, and the inclusion of a major form of chord V (F♯ instead of F♯m). The presence of V^ in a minor key indicates the need for the harmonic or melodic minor scale. This makes itself felt through the A♯ note that occurs throughout, giving the solo a different character to the modal natural minor heard in track 25+26. On any other chord than the F♯ it is not necessary to play A♯ and therefore B natural minor could be used. There is a difference in tone between the two scales that can be drawn on for a minor key solo.

1-2:   The intro has arpeggio figures on G and F♯.

3-4:   The melody consists of two-bar phrases that generally make an arch.

5:   There is an A instead of A♯; this invites B natural minor (see 12 and 14 also).

16:   The last bar has an upward B natural minor run.

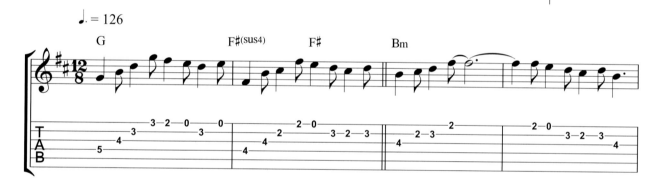

Continued over page

SECTION 9

CD TRACKS 29+30

Key / Key chords	D minor: I (Dm), III (F), IV (Gm), V (Am), V (A), VII (C)
	E minor: I, (Em), III (G), IV (Am), V^ (B), VI (C)
Additional chords	-
Solo structure	2+8+8+4
Bars	1-2 intro / 3-10 solo part one / 11-18 solo part two / 19-22 outro
Scales used	D pentatonic major A-B-C♯-E-F♯ / 1-2-3-5-6

Comments

This minor progression presents a two-fold challenge. First, it changes key halfway through: from D minor to E minor. Notice the 16th-note triplet hammer-on/pull-off figure throughout, which is moved up the neck to fit various chords.

1-2: Two implied chords create the intro, the first in bar one having an unusual semitone bend.

3-10: The first half is in D minor using D natural minor.

10: The change from chord V to V^ requires a C♯ instead of C.

11-18: The second half is in E minor, with V^ (B) consistently, so E harmonic or melodic minor will work in any bar with a B chord underlying.

11-12: The melodic idea from 3-4 is repeated transposed in the new key. Such exact or close transposition of a lead idea emphasises the key-change.

17: Notice the arpeggio on Am.

19-22: A series of fast hammer-on/pull-off ideas end the solo.

SECTION 9

SECTION 9 | **193**

CD TRACKS 31+32

Key / Key chords   E minor: I (Em), III (G), IV (Am), IV^ (A), V (Bm), V^ (B), VI (C), VII (D)

Additional chords   -

Solo structure   1+12

Bars   1 intro / 2-13 main solo

Scales used

E natural minor	E-F♯-G-A-B-C-D / 1-2-♭3-4-5-♭6-♭7
E pentatonic minor	E-G-A-B-D / 1-♭3-4-5-♭7
E dorian	E-F♯-G-A-B-C♯-D / 1-2-♭3-4-5-6-♭7
E harmonic minor	E-F♯-G-A-B-C-D♯ / 1-2-♭3-4-5-♭6-7

Comments

This slow minor key blues in 12/8 demonstrates the use of spaces and sustain. The approach is to keep the playing minimal. The scales are mainly E natural or pentatonic minor, but with some dorian phrases. It shows that a change of scale can be achieved sometimes merely by changing a semitone bend into a full bend (as here the difference between C and C♯). The slow tempo means the guitar may need some extra sustain.

1:   The intro is a rising 16th-note cascade on E natural minor

2:   Notice the beat rest before the first bent note.

2-7:   The first six bars have chords only from the natural minor scale, except for a chromatic B♭m7 inserted as a brief passing chord between Bm7 and Am7.

8:   Compare this full bend with the half bend in bar seven – each is correct for the chord.

8-9:   A two-bar progression with an A major chord (IV^), which implies the dorian mode; a C♯ is needed for this chord.

11:   When the 8-9 phrase repeats it concludes with a B major chord, which requires a D♯ (implying the harmonic minor.)

12-13: The cascade runs allude to the opening of the solo.

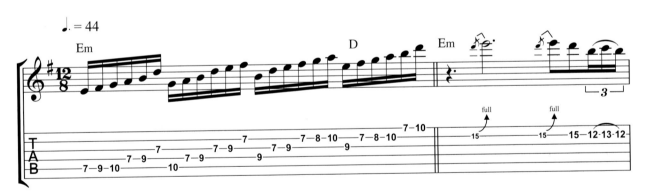

SECTION 9

SECTION 9

CD TRACKS 33+34

Key / Key chords	A minor: I (Am), III (C), IV ^ (D), V (Em), VII (G)
Additional chords	-
Solo structure	4+8+8
Bars	1-4 intro / 5-12 solo part one / 13-20 solo part two
Scales used	A dorian E-F♯-G-A-B-C♯-D / 1-2-♭3-4-5-6-♭7
	A natural minor E-F♯-G-A-B-C-D / 1-2-♭3-4-5-♭6-♭7
	A pentatonic minor E-G-A-B-D / 1-♭3-4-5-♭7

Comments

This solo gets some of its tone from a Strat pick-up in position two and the use of fingers rather than a pick to strike the notes. The absence of the chord of F (VI in A minor) and the presence of D major indicates the A dorian scale (where the sixth, F, is raised by a semitone to F♯). The dorian F♯ is stressed throughout. Some of the bends used are less common ideas.

1-2: The intro idea is played first as single notes and then harmonised as thirds.

5-12: Part one of the solo could be labelled a-a2-a3-b, in which a two-bar phrase is repeated with variations as it ascends.

11-12: A different idea comes in for the change of chords.

13-20: The second half of the solo has further variations on this two-bar idea, with the highest notes (with bends) saved to the end.

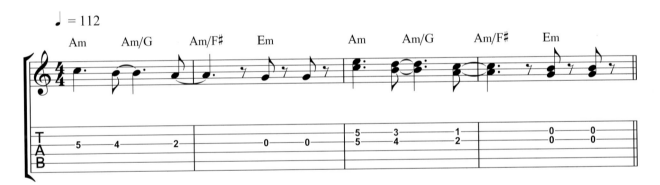

SECTION 9

SECTION 9

CD TRACKS 35+36

Key / Key chords   B phrygian: I (Bm), bII (C), VI (G), VIIm (Am)
Additional chords   V (F♯m7b5)
Solo structure   4+12
Bars   1-4 intro / 5-12 main solo
Scales used   B phrygian   B-C-D-E-F♯-G-A / 1-♭2-3-4-5-♭6-♭7

Comments

The key is broadly B minor, but with a twist, because the chords are derived from B phrygian and emphasise this mode's character. The intro has chord V – F♯m – in altered form as F♯m7♭5; the flattened fifth turns C♯ into C. The usual B minor scales would clash with this chord because they have C♯. The exception is the phrygian mode which has a flattened second (B C D E F♯ G A) and this altered chord as chord V belongs to this mode.

5-8:   The solo includes several arpeggio ideas with open strings. These spell out a chord effectively, and consequently the harmonic instruments can be reduced in presence in the mix if so desired.

5-12:   The chord progression moves from Bm to Cmaj7 and down to Am, outlining the distinct intervals of the phrygian mode: I-♭II-I-VII. This mode is associated with Spanish music.

9-12:   This flavour is strengthened with certain semitone bends (from B to C, for example).

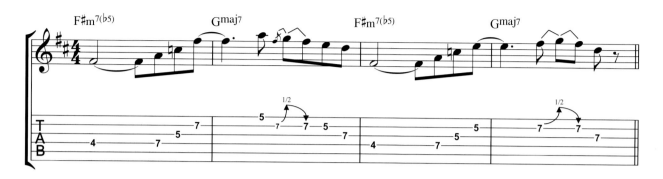

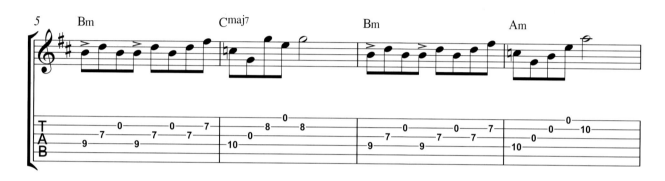

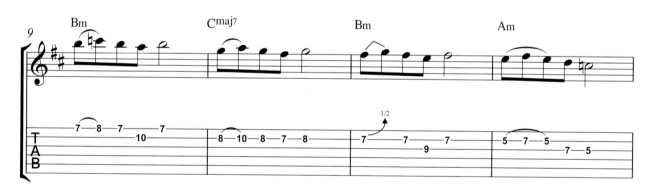

SECTION 9

CD TRACKS 37+38

Key / Key chords   D minor: I (Dm), III (F), IV^ (G), V (Am), V^ (A), VI (B♭), VII (C)

Additional chords   -

Solo structure   16

Bars   1-8 solo part one / 9-16 solo part two

Scales used   D natural minor   D-E-F-G-A-B♭-C / 1-2-♭3-4-5-♭6-♭7

                D melodic minor   D-E-F-G-A-B-C / 1-2-♭3-4-5-6-7

Comments

This progression is an eight-bar solo in D minor, repeated to make 16 bars. The first four bars have chords that imply a different scale to the next four bars. Notice the rhythmic identity of the first-bar idea and how that is repeated throughout with variations.

1-4:   Note that chord V is Am, implying the D natural minor scale.

3-4:   Bar one's idea is transposed down in bar three and up in bar five.

5-8:   Has a G chord (with a B-natural) instead of the expected Gm, and an A major chord (with C♯ instead of C). This requires the melodic minor scale with its raised sixth and seventh notes.

7:   Bar one's idea is altered to accommodate the B-naturals of the G chord.

9:   The idea is partially inverted.

11:   The idea is re-harmonised in bar 11 in its original form.

13-15:   The solo climaxes with runs of 16th-notes that break free of the rhythmic constraint of the opening.

16:   Notice the quarter-note triplet rhythm, floating across the beat.

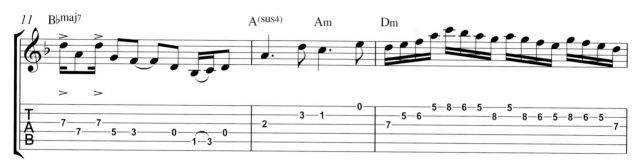

CD TRACKS 39+40 (OVER PAGE)

Key / Key chords	E minor: I (Em), III (G), IV (Am), V (Bm), V^ (B), VII (D)
	A major: I (A), II (Bm), IV (D), V (E), VI (F♯m)
Additional chords	-
Solo structure	4+8+4+8+4
Bars	1-4 intro / 5-12 first solo / 13-16 link / 17-24 second solo /
	25-28 outro
Scales used	E harmonic minor E-F♯-G-A-B-C-D♯ / 1-2-♭3-4-5-♭6-7
	E natural minor E-F♯-G-A-B-C-D / 1-2-♭3-4-5-♭6-♭7
	A major A-B-C♯-D-E-F♯-G♯ / 1-2-3-4-5-6-7
	F♯ natural minor F♯-G♯-A-B-C♯-D-E / 1-2-♭3-4-5-♭6-♭7

Comments

This progression requires planning to cope with a key change from E minor to A major half way through. This solo is dominated by wide-ranging syncopated figures that use open strings as drone notes. This is only possible in certain keys (because of the

SECTION 9

guitar's open-string pitches), so it is sometimes worth taking this approach, rather than playing a scale-based solo, if the key permits. Notice how the wide interval idea re-occurs in different forms; this type of repetition with variation gives a solo cohesion.

1-4: Has four bars on B7, chord V of E minor, and the two phrases use the E harmonic minor scale. Notice the gradual climb.

5-12: The first eight-bar solo in E minor has no chord V and can be played with the natural minor scale.

5-8: Use a wide interval idea.

9-12: Use single-note phrases.

13-16: During the four-bar link, the next B chord is a Bm, followed by E7, creating a key change into A major.

17-24: The new key requires the A major / F♯ natural minor scales.

17-20: Several sixths are heard.

25-28: The outro returns to the key of E minor and an E natural minor scale.

SECTION 9

HOW TO SOLO OVER OUT OF KEY CHORDS

Out of key chords can add spice to the context of a solo if you make them work for you.

SECTION 10
HOW TO SOLO OVER OUT OF KEY CHORDS

In this section we return to the major key but bringing in some of the additional chords that songwriters use. These are the chords that were called 'flat degree' chords and 'reverse polarity' chords in *How To Write Songs On Guitar*. They contain notes that are not in the key's major scale and require additional steps. These extra chords are tabulated under 'additional chords'.

CD TRACKS 41+42
Key / Key chords   A major I (A), IV (D), V (E)
Additional chords ♭VII (G)
Solo structure   2+12+8
Bars   1-2 intro / 3-14 main solo / 15-21 outro
Scales used   A mixolydian A-B-C♯-D-E-F♯-G / 1-2-3-4-5-6-♭7

Comments
This rock progression features the first of the 'flat degree' chords – the ♭VII. This requires the mixolydian scale rather than the major, although the major scale can be played over the other chords.

1-2:   The ♭VII chord is followed after only two beats by chord V with its normal seventh note (G♯). This is handled with a rock'n'roll double-stop, adjusting it to fit the E chord.

3-10: The main idea is an open-string pedal note – first on A and D, and then on G, with the fretted notes moving on the relevant scales up and down the adjacent string.

11:   The pedal note is replaced by mixolydian scale runs.

21:   The final bar provides a climax by shifting into shorter note values.

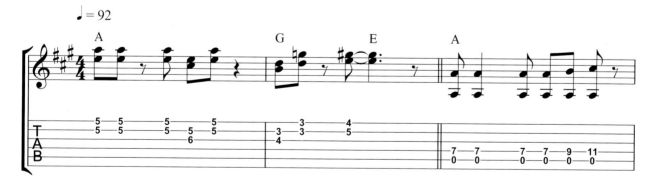

Continued over page

SECTION 10

SECTION 10

CD TRACKS 43+44

Key / Key chords C major: I (C), IV (F), V (G)
Additional chords Vm (Gm), ♭VII (B♭)
Solo structure 4+12+6
Bars 1-4 intro / 5-16 main solo / 17-22 outro
Scales used C mixolydian   C-D-E-F-G-A-B♭ / 1-2-3-4-5-6-♭7

Comments

This is another mixolydian chord sequence, this time in C. In addition to the ♭VII chord (B♭) there is the less frequent minor form of chord V (Gm) instead of G. Both chords require the scale to have a B♭ instead of B. This type of modal progression has to be handled carefully to prevent it sounding as though the music is really in F major.

1-4: The correct chord V (G) for C major is heard on the intro and outro.
5-12: A conscious exercise in playing fewer notes and allowing the changing chords to colour them differently.
5: This three note-phrase is repeated in bars seven, nine, and 11.
6, 8, 10, 12: Are different answers to bar five.
13-16: A four-bar contrast, with a sequence of linked scale phrases. In terms of fretboard patterns, these can be thought of as C pentatonic major, G natural minor, and F pentatonic major. But in fact the notes of these scales are all within C mixolydian.
17-22: The outro has variations that take the lead higher and higher, and bring in a B-natural to match the G chord.

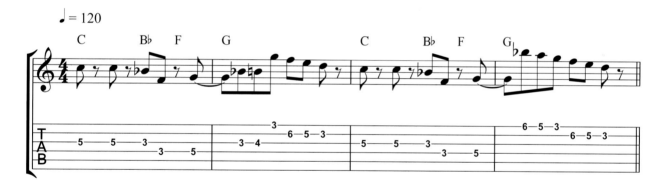

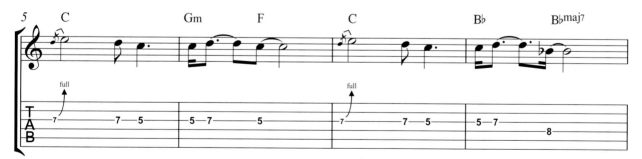

Continued over page

SECTION 10

207

SECTION 10

CD TRACKS 45+46

Key / Key chords D major: I (D), IV (G), V (A)
Additional chords ♭III (F)
Solo structure   4+8+8+4
Bars   1-4 intro / 5-12 solo part one / 13-20 solo part two / 21-24 outro
Scales used   D blues major   D-E-F-F♯-G-A-B-C / 1-2-♭3-3-4-5-6-♭7
                       D pentatonic minor D-F-G-A-C / 1-♭3-4-5-♭7
                       A blues major   A-B-C-C♯-D-E-F♯-G / 1-2-♭3-3-4-5-6-♭7

Comments

This piece is in 12/8 and brings in another of the flat degree chords, the ♭III. In the key of D major this is an F chord. The solo uses the D blues major scale and D pentatonic minor. The occurrence of the flattened blues third with the usual third in close proximity gives the solo a distinct bluesy character.

1-4:   The intro uses partial chords, emphasising the sevenths.
5-12:   The first half of the solo has falling and rising phrases in single notes.
13-20: The second time through, the solo switches to double-stops based on the chords.
19:   The solo resumes the scale-based runs.
21, 23: Listen for the flattened fifth (E♭) against the A7 chord.

Continued over page

SECTION 10

SECTION 10

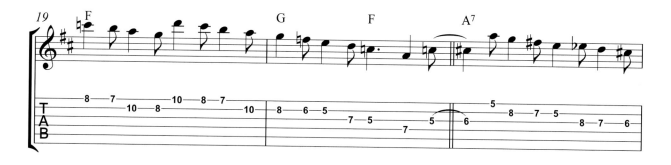

CD TRACKS 47+48 (OVER PAGE)

Key / Key chords	D major: I (D), V (A)
Additional chords	♭III (F), ♭VI (B♭), ♭VII (C)
Solo structure	4+8+8+4
Bars	1-4 intro / 5-12 solo part one / 13-20 solo part two / 21-24 outro
Scales used	D major D-E-F♯-G-A-B-C♯ / 1-2-3-4-5-6-7
	D natural minor D-E-F-G-A-B-C / 1-2-♭3-4-5-♭6-♭7

Comments

This ballad-like progression is, like the previous example, in 12/8 but asks for a different approach because it doesn't have any blues influence. You have worked with them individually, but now all three flat degree chords in the key of D major are present: F (♭III), B♭ (♭VI), and C (♭VII). These chords introduce the notes B♭, F, and C, which are not in the D major scale. Furthermore, each of the chords occurs as a major seventh, which also distances this use of flat degree chords from a blues idiom. They are, however, all on the D natural minor scale, which makes the D pentatonic minor scale also relevant.

1:   Shows how the rapid change of chord (two beats each) can be dealt with by using short scales that start on the root note of the chord (B♭ and F).

3-4:   This idea is repeated an octave higher.

5-12:   The first eight bars of the solo show how the D pentatonic minor can fit in this context. Over major seventh chords it creates the impression of jazzy sophistication.

SECTION 10

9-12: Shows a new phrase being repeated with small variations to make it fit the chord.

13-20: Begin with longer scale-based runs using D major and D natural minor.

17-20: Show a single phrase being repeated and altered to fit the changing chords.

21-24: A new idea closes the solo on a repeat of the intro bars' chord change.

SECTION 10

SECTION 10

CD TRACKS 49+50

Key / Key chords	E major: I (E), IV (A), V (B)
Additional chords	♭III (G)
Solo structure	4+12+4
Bars	1-4 intro / 5-12 main solo / 13-16 outro

Scales used		
E pentatonic minor	E-G-A-B-D / 1-♭3-4-5-♭7
E natural minor	E-F♯-G-A-B-C-D / 1-2-♭3-4-5-♭6-♭7
E pentatonic major	E-F♯-G♯-B-C♯ / 1-2-3-5-6
E natural minor	E-F♯-G-A-B-C-D / 1-2-♭3-4-5-♭6-♭7
E bebop major	E-F♯-G-G♯-A-B-C-D / 1-2-♭3-3-4-5-6-♭7

Comments

This rock progression includes the flat degree chords ♭III (G) and ♭VII (D) in the key of E major. The scales of E pentatonic and natural minor include these notes. E pentatonic major will also sound correct and upbeat over the E, A, and B chords; E pentatonic minor sounds tougher over the same chords.

1-4:	The intro has the bebop major, E mixolydian, with an additional flat third. The two-bar phrase ends differently in bar four to bar two.
4:	Open strings assist a change of position.
7-8:	The phrase is transposed down a tone in bars five to six to match the chord change (with a small variation).
9:	Repeats bar five but replaces the bent note with a fretted one.
11-12:	Moves up to a higher position.
13 and 15:	The solo uses a B pentatonic major pattern (but remember, these notes are contained within E major).
13-16:	The solo climaxes with 12th-fret unison bends and double-stop ideas.

CD TRACKS 51+52 (OVER PAGE)

Key / Key chords	G major: I (G), IV (C), V (D)
Additional chords	♭VI (E♭)
Solo structure	2+8+8+4
Bars	1-2 intro / 3-10 solo part one / 11-18 solo part two / 19-22 outro

Scales used		
G major	G-A-B-C-D-E-F♯ / 1-2-3-4-5-6-7
G pentatonic major	G-A-B-D-E / 1-2-3-5-6
G natural minor	G-A-B♭-C-D-E♭-F / 1-2-♭3-4-5-♭6-♭7
D pentatonic major	D-E-F♯-A-B / 1-2-3-5-6
E♭ pentatonic major	E♭-F-G-B♭-C / 1-2-3-5-6

Comments

This progression includes another of the flat degree chords, the ♭VI, which in G major is E♭. It brings in the off-scale notes E♭ and B♭, not in G major. The G natural minor scale (G A B♭ C D E♭ F) has these, as do E♭ major and pentatonic major. These can be played over the E♭ chord. G pentatonic minor (G-B♭-C-D-F) could be used over the I, IV, V if a bluesier sound were wanted.

Continued over page

SECTION 10 | **215**

2:   A D pentatonic major run that climbs through two octaves.

3:   G pentatonic major.

3-8:   A single rhythm dominates, the first half beat having a rest.

6:   For the ♭VI chord, bar three's phrase is transposed to E♭ pentatonic major. Watch for E instead of E♭ on the final beat to fit the C chord.

8:   Notice the triad on E♭ and the bend from A-B♭.

9-10: The first eight bars, which have drifted down in pitch, end with a change of rhythm to the quarter-note triplets, also based on a D chord.

11-12: Part two starts on the lowest G with pentatonic major phrases on G and then E♭.

13-14: The phrase is repeated with some blue-note bends.

15-18: The solo rises to the 12th position, ending with ideas based on D and C chords.

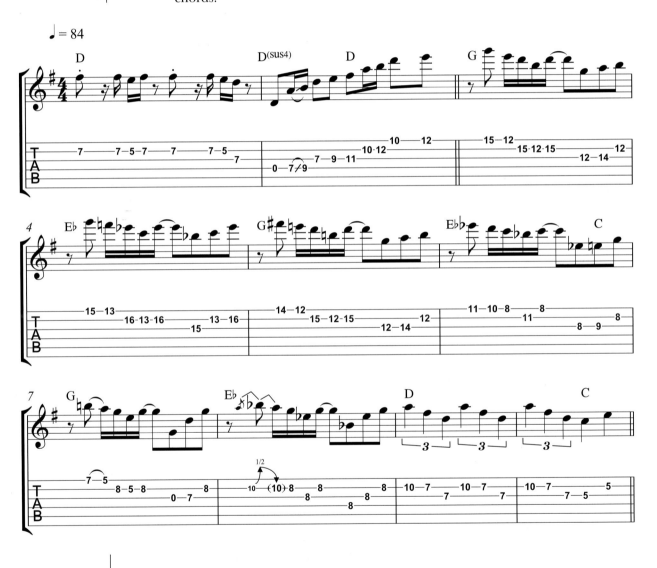

SECTION 10

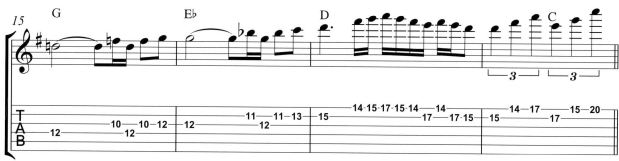

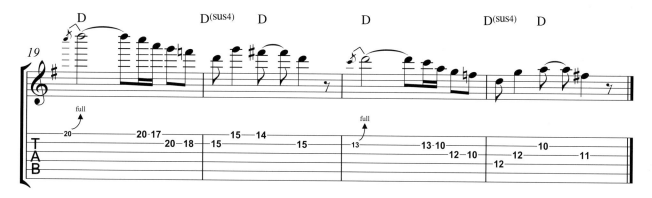

CD TRACKS 53+54 (OVER PAGE)

Key / Key chords	A major: I (A), IV (D), V (E)	
Additional chords	♭III (C), ♭VII (G)	
Solo structure	2+16+4	
Bars	1-2 intro / 3-18 main solo / 19-22 outro	
Scales used	A pentatonic major	A-B-C♯-E-F♯ / 1-2-3-5-6
	A pentatonic minor	A-C-D-E-G / 1-♭3-4-5-♭7
	C pentatonic minor	C-E♭-F-G-B♭ / 1-♭3-4-5-♭7
	D pentatonic minor	D-F-G-A-C / 1-♭3-4-5-♭7
	E pentatonic minor	E-G-A-B-D / 1-♭3-4-5-♭7
	A mixolydian	A-B-C♯-D-E-F♯-G / 1-2-3-4-5-6-♭7
	D mixolydian	D-E-F♯-G-A-B-C / 1-2-3-4-5-6-♭7

SECTION 10   217

Comments

This track draws on a harmony formula for writing hard rock songs: take chords I, IV, and V in a major key and add ♭III and ♭VII. In A major, this gives a progression using A, C, D, E, and G. (Notice the root notes of these five major chords make the pentatonic minor scale.) It shows what happens when scales change with the chords. This is not necessary – the entire chord progression could be played over with just A pentatonic minor. Compare the approaches: the first introduces more notes outside the scales of A major or pentatonic minor.

1-2: The intro phrase creates anticipation by raising its last note higher each time.

3-6: Each chord's pentatonic minor scale is used, with A at the fifth fret, C at the eighth fret, and D at the tenth.

6: The interval of a sixth provides contrast of idea and rhythm (see also 10).

7-10: Only A pentatonic minor is used over the same changes.

11-14: For the E chord, E pentatonic minor is used.

15-18: For the accented ending of the main solo, an idea based on pedal notes of A and D comes in, using A mixolydian and D mixolydian.

19-22: The coda is derived from the intro but pitched at a higher octave.

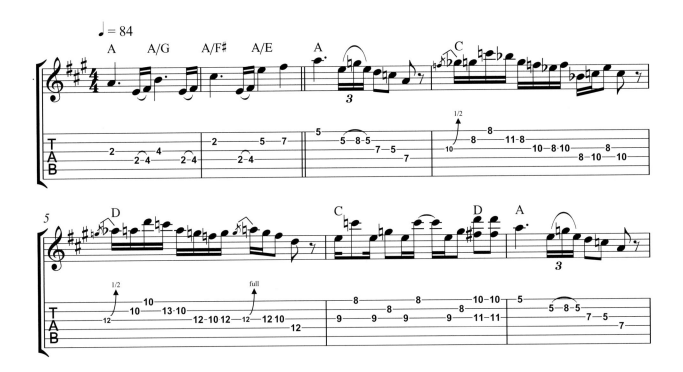

SECTION 10 | **219**

CD TRACKS 55+56

Key / Key chords	C major: I (C), IV (F), V (G)	
	D major: I (D), IV (G), V (A)	
Additional chords	II ^ (D) + II ^ (E)	
Solo structure	2+12+8	
Bars	1-2 intro / 3-14 main solo / 15-22 outro	
Scales used	C major	C-D-E-F-G-A-B / 1-2-3-4-5-6-7
	D major	D-E-F♯-G-A-B-C♯ / 1-2-3-4-5-6-7
	D pentatonic major	D-E-F♯-A-B / 1-2-3-5-6
	E pentatonic major	E-F♯-G♯-A-B / 1-2-3-5-6

Comments

Having looked at flat degree chords and how to play over them, let's consider another group of songwriting chords, those I call 'reverse polarity'. CD55 features chord II ^ in C major (D instead of Dm). Half way through this progression the music changes key to D major, and includes chord II ^ in the key of D major (E instead of Em). The solo's first half is dominated by arpeggio ideas.

1-2: The intro has two bars of descending thirds.

3-10: The solo in C major is designed around a static arpeggio idea at the third fret. This shape is repeated with only small changes of pitch to match the chords.

7-10: Change of position to fret seven.

11-14: The four-bar link prepares the key-change and is handled with an open E-string and fretted notes, the combination of which implies A7.

15-22: The second solo, in D major, contrasts with the first by changing to scale ideas.

15: D pentatonic major over D.

16: E pentatonic major over E, which brings in the G♯ needed to blend with the chord.

17: G pentatonic major over G.

18-20: Second time through, the patterns are not so obvious with fewer notes to a bar until the fast run in 22.

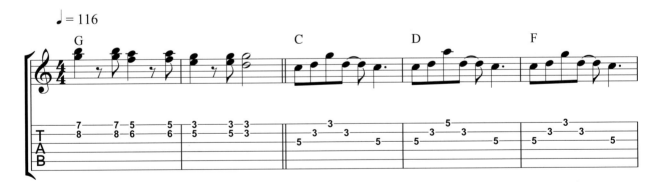

SECTION 10

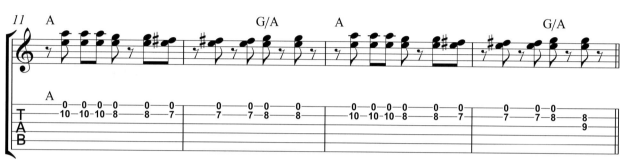

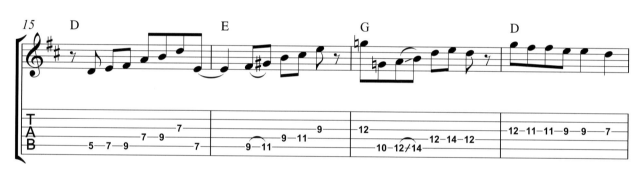

SECTION 10

CD TRACKS 57+58

Key / Key chords	D major: I (D), II (Em), IV (G), V (A), VI (Bm)
Additional chords	III ^ (F♯)
Solo structure	4+16+4
Bars	1-4 intro / 5-12 solo part one / 13-20 solo part two / 21-24 outro
Scales used	D major D-E-F♯-G-A-B-C♯ / 1-2-3-4-5-6-7

Comments

The next lead challenge is to solo over the reverse polarity chord III ^, which in D major is F♯ instead of F♯m. It includes one note off-scale to the key of D major, namely A♯. This note does occur in the scale of B harmonic minor (ie, the relative minor's harmonic form), and F♯ pentatonic major is another option. It is a good idea to build phrases on the additional chord that emphasise its harmonic novelty.

1-4: The intro idea is based on arpeggios.

5-7 and 9-11: Phrases created using sixths. Each is answered by a scale-like phrase (bars eight and 12) altered to fit the underlying chord (F♯, then A).

13-20: The second half of the solo is more scale-based, with D major dominating.

16: A B harmonic minor scale starting on C♯ appears for the F♯ chord.

21-24: The outro makes the solo end in its highest range.

SECTION 10

SECTION 10 | **223**

CD TRACKS 59+60

Key / Key chords	E major: I (E), IV (A), V (B)
Additional chords	IVm (Am)
Solo structure	2+12+4
Bars	1-2 intro / 3-10 solo part one / 11-18 solo part two / 19-22 outro
Scales used	E major E-F♯-G♯-A-B-C♯-D♯ / 1-2-3-4-5-6-7
	A natural minor A-B-C-D-E-F-G / 1-2-♭3-4-5-♭6-♭7

Comments

In this track the reverse polarity chord is IVm. The IVm chord has a pronounced romantic quality. In the key of E major this is Am instead of A. It introduces the note C in addition to the C♯ of the E major scale. This C is the note to emphasise to bring out the flavour of the IVm chord. The solo moves at an unhurried pace.

1-2:   The solo starts with a bend idea transposed up a tone with the chords.

3-10:   Bend effects dominate the first half of the solo, which is anchored on the keynote E.

4:   Notice the bend to G♯.

6:   The bend from bar four is adjusted to go only to G-natural.

11-18: The second half combines arpeggio ideas with open strings.

11:   The downward arpeggio on E balances the upward arpeggio on Am add9 in 10.

22:   The solo ends on its highest note.

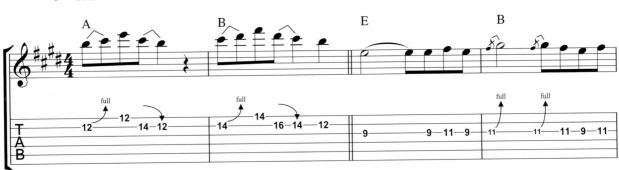

SECTION 10

CD TRACKS 61+62

Key / Key chords   A major: I (A), V (E)
Additional chords   IVm (Dm), ♭VI (A♭)
Solo structure   2+5+5+5+4
Bars   1-2 intro / 3-7 solo part one / 8-12 solo part two / 13-17 solo part three / 18-21 outro
Scales used

A major	A-B-C♯-D-E-F♯-G♯ / 1-2-3-4-5-6-7	
F major	F-G-A-B-C-D-E / 1-2-3-4-5-6-7	
D dorian	D-E-F-G-A-B-C / 1-2-♭3-4-5-6-♭7	

Comments

Developing the previous track, this example combines the IVm with a ♭VI (F and Dm in the key of A major). These chords introduce the notes F and C, instead of F♯ and C♯. For playing over them use F lydian / D dorian, or F pentatonic major / D pentatonic minor. F lydian and D dorian give B instead of B♭, which puts the scale closer to the home key of A major. The solo divides into three five-bar phrases, each using a different approach. There are many phrasing tips packed into this solo, such as changing direction, contrasting busyness with less movement, repeating ideas with a variant answering phrase, etc.

1-2:   The intro uses an idea based on sixths over chord V (E).
3-7:   The first part has ideas based on arpeggios.
8-12:   The second part uses scale runs.
13-17: The third part has fewer notes, sustains them, and has carefully pitched bends.
14:   Notice how B is bent only a semitone (C against the F chord) into the F.
18-21: The outro finishes with two short phrases that emphasise the Dm (IVm) chord in 19 and 21.

SECTION 10

SECTION 10 |

HOW TO SOLO OVER ALTERED

HOW TO SOLO OVER ALTERED CHORDS

Many of the chords you have played over in the previous examples were simple major or minor chords. What about sevenths, ninths, elevenths, etc? No off-scale notes are introduced by playing any standard extended chord, because these draw only from the scale. Chords such as sixths, suspended 2 and 4, add ninths, major sevenths, do not include off-scale notes. But in popular music other chords may be introduced.

ALTERED CHORDS AND OFF-SCALE NOTES

The dominant seventh chord includes notes outside the scale if it occurs on any other degree of the major scale than the fifth. In blues, chords I and IV often become dominant seventh chords. In C major, this chord on I and IV gives the result C7 = C E G B♭ and F7 = F A C E♭. To handle this, play either a mixolydian or pentatonic minor on C and F. C pentatonic minor sounds okay on both.

Chord types that include an off-scale note will be minor or major sevenths, augmented chords, diminished sevenths, and any chord with a lowered or raised fifth, ninth, 11th or 13th. Taking the first of these, in C major, there are three minor chords on Dm, Em, and Am. Their standard sevenths pose no problem. However, minor chords with a major seventh are different. Dm/maj7 = D F A C♯, Em/maj7 = E G B D♯, Am/maj7 = A C D E G♯. In each case, the off-scale note is in bold.

Remember that the easiest way to deal with a difficult chord is to find a bend that works or play part of the chord as an arpeggio.

CD TRACKS 63+64

Key / Key chords	C major: I (C), II (Dm), V (G), VI (Am)	
Additional chords	III ^ (E), ♭III (E♭), IVm (Fm), ♭VI (A♭)	
Solo structure	4+8+8+4	
Bars	1-4 intro / 5-12 solo part one / 13-20 solo part two / 21-24 outro	
Scales used	C major	C-D-E-F-G-A-B / 1-2-3-4-5-6-7
	F melodic minor (alt)	F-G-A♭-B-C-D-E / 1-2-♭3-♯4-5-6-7
	E pentatonic major	E-F♯-G♯-B-C♯ / 1-2-3-5-6
	E♭ pentatonic major	E♭-F-G-B♭-C / 1-2-3-5-6

Comments

This progression is one of the most challenging so far because of the chromatic movement of the chords. The intro has four bars on IVm in C major. Moreover, this Fm has been altered to Fm/maj7♯11 (F A♭ C E B) which rules out F natural minor (F-G-A♭-B♭-C-D♭-E♭) and pentatonic minor (F-A♭-B♭-C-E♭). In both, B♭ and E♭ would clash with the E and B (the major seventh and ♯11 in the Fm chord). One solution is F melodic minor: F-G-A♭-B-C-D-E with the fourth note raised by a semitone from B♭ to B. Or to put it another way, the C major scale with a flattened sixth. The main eight-bar sequence moves chromatically through I-III ^ -♭III-II, and then I-III ^ -♭III-♭VI-V. E♭ (♭III) and A♭ (♭VI) are related chords, so an E♭ major scale fits both. When it comes to the III ^ (E) no one scale covers the chords of E and E♭, so the easiest tactic is to use major pentatonics on each.

1-4: The intro ends with an exotic version of a repeat lick.

5-8: Judicious control of bent phrases can fit a chromatic sequence, with minimal movement.

9-12: Use variation by changing the last note of each phrase to fit the chord.

13-15: Each chord has its own pentatonic major.

16-19: Take the earlier bending idea and transpose it with variations up an octave.

21-24: The outro alludes back to the intro.

21 and 23: Notice the alternate fingering for the scale.

S E C T I O N   1 1

SECTION 11 231

CD TRACKS 65+66

Key / Key chords	D minor: I (Dm), IV (Gm)		
	D major: I (D), IV (G), V (A)		
Additional chords	Daug, Gaug, Aaug		
Solo structure	4+8+8+4		
Bars	1-4 intro / 5-12 solo part one / 13-20 solo part two / 21-24 outro		
Scales used	D natural minor	D-E-F-G-A-B-C / 1-2-♭3-4-5-♭6-♭7	
	D major	D-E-F♯-G-A-B-C♯ / 1-2-3-4-5-6-7	
	D aug pentatonic	D-E-F♯-A♯-B / 1-2-3-♯5-6	
	G aug pentatonic	G-A-B-D♯-E / 1-2-3-♯5-6	
	A aug pentatonic	A-B-C♯-E♯-F♯ / 1-2-3-♯5-6	

Comments

This example features a number of augmented chords on D (D F♯ A♯), G (G B D♯), and A (A C♯ E♯). Each includes an off-scale note that does not belong in D major. Augmented chords often only occupy part of a bar as a passing chord, but here they deliberately last four beats to provide a chance to solo against them. Options for dealing with augmented chords include playing an augmented version of a pentatonic major, so D pentatonic major (D-E-F♯-A-B) becomes D 'augmented' pentatonic (D-E-F♯-A♯-B). As a pattern this is a comfortable fingering. Another approach is to select the harmonic scale of the relative minor chord: Daug is covered by B harmonic minor, Gaug by E harmonic minor, and Aaug by F♯ harmonic minor. The type of phrasing also changes over each of the three major chords.

1-4: This is a 'false intro', a lead-in that disguises the key of the actual solo. It opens with a I-IV change in Dm (Dm-Gm6). D natural minor covers these chords.

5-12: The upward shift in pitch contrasts with the lower pitch of the intro.

13: The C♯ is correct for the key of D major, but could be C-natural (also in bar 15).

14: Introduces a contrasting C-natural.

17-19: Notice the way the phrases are altered by one note being different.

21-24: The intro is re-worked as I-IVm in D major (D-Gm6). Notice the two semitone bends.

SECTION 11

CD TRACKS 67+68

Key / Key chords	E major: I (E), II (F♯m), III (G♯m), IV (A), V (B)
Additional chords	VII^ (D♯), II^ (F♯), ♭VI (C), VI^ (C♯), Vm (Bm), IVm (Am)
Solo structure	8+8
Bars	1-8 solo part one / 9-16 solo part two
Scales used	E major E-F♯-G♯-A-B-C♯-D♯ / 1-2-3-4-5-6-7

Comments

Stylistically this E major 16-bar suggests a 1930s jazz tune with many chromatic notes adding to the jazz flavour. For the soloist, there are the following challenges. This is at the opposite extreme from the type of progression where a single scale will carry the soloist throughout. First, chord change is frequent (usually every two beats) with fleeting modulations to G♯m and F♯m (these chords are tabulated above as if the piece remained in E major). The music has chromatic chords from bar two, so within only a few beats the solo must deviate from the E major scale. There is also a Cdim7 (bar eight), bar 14 has both Bm7 and B7, and bar 15 has a IVm. You will have to think carefully about your fingering, otherwise this will be very difficult to play at this speed.

2:	Draws on a D♯ major scale with an added flat third.
3:	Is G♯ harmonic minor.
4:	Is A mixolydian with an added flat third.
5-6:	Are E and F♯ majors with flat third and flat seventh.
7:	Is B major blues.
8:	The dim7 chord is handled with an arpeggio (notice the symmetrical pattern until the second string).
9:	Suggests E mixolydian.
12:	Suggests C♯ major.
13-14:	Covered by A major with the occasional flattened passing note.
15-16:	The piece ends, returning to E major with a single C natural to match the Am chord.

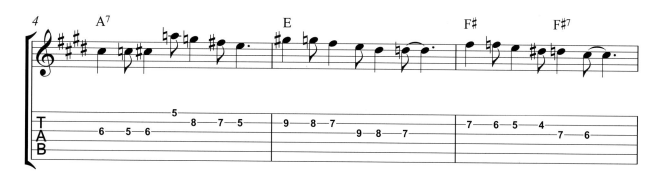

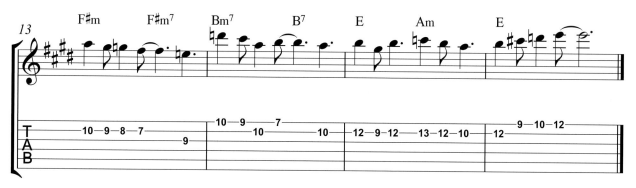

SECTION 11

CD TRACKS 69+70

Key / Key chords	A minor: I (Am), III (C), IV (Dm), IV ^ (D), V (E), VI (F), VII (G)
Additional chords	-
Solo structure	2+8+6+7
Bars	1-4 intro / 5-16 main solo / 17-23 outro
Scales used	A natural minor A-B-C-D-E-F-G / 1-2-♭3-4-5-♭6-♭7
	A melodic minor A-B-C-D-E-F♯-G♯ / 1-2-♭3-4-5-6-7

Comments

This minor key progression is introduced by two bars of Ddim7, the second bar climbing through an arpeggio. The bass-line underneath the main chord sequence moves in semitone steps, bringing in E/G♯ and D/F♯ chords (use A melodic minor) but with chords of G (no G♯) and F (no F♯) in between. These, along with C and Dm, need A natural minor. This means the natural minor won't work all through, and the solo must adjust its notes accordingly.

1-4: The Ddim7 chord invites a sinister opening phrase stressing the tritone.

5-16: The first half shows how a phrase lasting one bar can be repeated and varied each time to match the shifting chords.

11-16: Contrasts downward fast cascade scale runs with a rising arpeggio in paired bars.

17-23: The last six bars only have a D chord (with F♯) to contend with, covered by A melodic minor or A dorian.

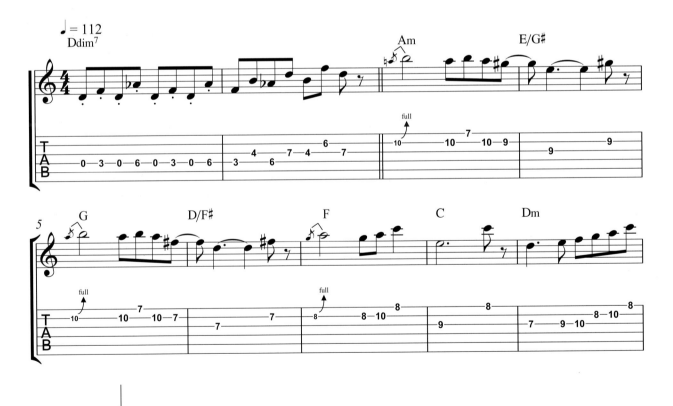

S E C T I O N 11

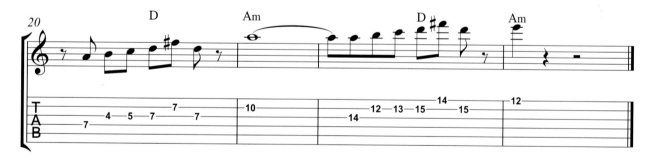

SECTION 11

CD TRACKS 71+72

Key / Key chords   B minor: I (Bm), III (D), IV (Em), IV^ (E), V^ (F#), VII (A)
Additional chords   VIIm (Am)
Solo structure   2+8+16
Bars   1-2 intro / 3-16 main solo / 17-20 outro
Scales used   A pentatonic major   A-B-C#-E-F# / 1-2-3-5-6

Comments

This slow blues progression is in 6/8 (two beats to a bar, each dividing into three). The key is B minor but it needs more than just B natural minor as the progression includes some altered chords. They are F#m7♭5 (containing an out-of-scale C-natural), F#dim7 (C natural, D#), Em7♭5 (B♭), A7♭5 (E♭), and Edim7 (A#). These can be simplified to C (♭2), D# (#3), and A# (#7). For the last few bars notice how the bend idea is shifted up to match the chords and how the solo ends on its highest note.

1-2:   The intro uses a rising idea based on A7.

3-4:   The solo starts with a bent F# which sustains in a phrase based on B pentatonic minor at the seventh fret.

9-10:   Notice how the first phrase on F#m7♭5 (bars five and six) is developed and extended to a scale run.

11 and 13:   They use the same bend but the underlying chord makes it sound different.

15:   When the Em chord is reached, the solo shifts position from the seventh fret (good for B minor) to the 12th (good for E minor).

15-16:   These provide a phrase for 17-18, but it is adjusted to add the B♭, the flat fifth of Em7♭5.

21-22:   A similar adjustment happens to change E to E♭ as the flat fifth of A.

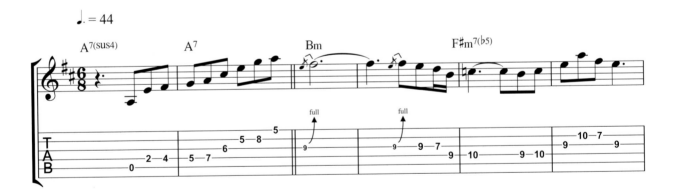

SECTION 11

SECTION 11

CD TRACKS 73+74

Key / Key chords	C minor: I (Cm), III (Eb), IV (Fm)
Additional chords	I^ (C), bII (Db), #III (Em)
Solo structure	4+8+8
Bars	1-4 intro / 5-12 solo part one / 13-20 solo part two
Scales used	C melodic minor C-D-Eb-F-G-A-B
	C harmonic minor C-D-Eb-F-G-Ab-B
	Db major Db-Eb-F-Gb-Ab-Bb-C
	D harmonic minor D-E-F-G-A-Bb-C
	Eb major Eb-F-G-Ab-Bb-C-D
	E harmonic minor E-F#-G-A-B-C-D#
	F pentatonic major F-G-A-C-D

Comments

Here's another track that requires more than one scale. An unusual chord change from minor to tonic major (Cm7 to Cmaj7) starts this sequence. These two chords require a shift of notes: Eb to E and Bb to B if these notes are included in your phrase. After the Cm in bar 5, the progression then falls by chromatic steps: Fm7b5-Em7-Ebmaj7-Dm7-Dbmaj7 before Cm to F. Many of the solo's phrases are similar but they are carefully adjusted to fit each chord. The first part of the solo has a rising scale idea – this is obvious, but it is played here to make the effect of such phrasing clear. Listen also for moments where the solo mimics the rhythm of the backing.

1-4: This change could almost be covered by C melodic minor (C-D-Eb-F-G-A-B) if the Eb were avoided over the Cmaj7 chord.

5-6: The change of Cm to Fm7b5 (Cb = B) can be handled with C harmonic minor. The altered fifth of the Fm chord is Cb, which is equivalent to a B (the seventh of C harmonic minor).

12: An F pentatonic major pattern is heard (all these notes are included in C melodic minor).

13-20: The second part of the solo makes use of bends, which were absent from the first part.

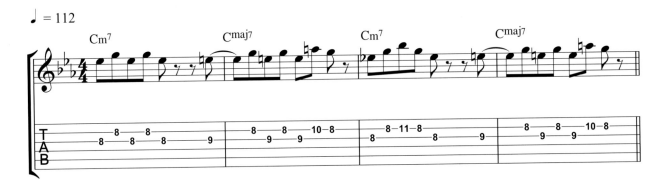

SECTION 11

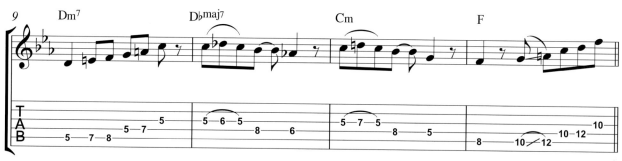

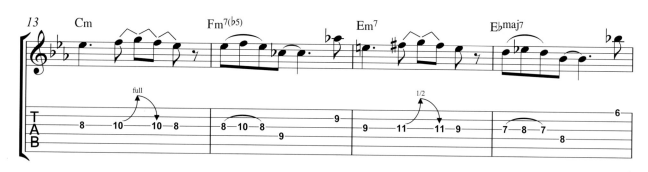

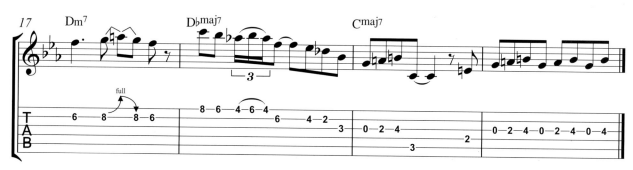

SECTION 11

CD TRACKS 75+76

Key / Key chords	G major: I (G), IV (C)	
Additional chords	♭IIIm (B♭m), ♭VI (E♭), ♭VII (F)	
Solo structure	4+12	
Bars	1-4 intro / 5-16 main solo	
Scales used	G major	G-A-B-C-D-E-F♯ / 1-2-3-4-5-6-7
	G pentatonic major	G-A-B-D-E / 1-2-3-5-6
	B♭ pentatonic minor	B-D♭-E♭-F-A♭ / 1-♭3-4-5-♭7
	C pentatonic major	C-D-E-G-A / 1-2-3-5-6

Comments

A descending sequence of four diminished sevenths sets up this solo. To go with these, it is easy to find a symmetrical pattern of minor thirds, ascending in contrary motion, ending on F♯/G♭. This is the leading-note (seventh) of G major, which leads emphatically to G in bar five. Notice how the octave drop in that bar to an open string G offers an easy change of position. The chord sequence has an unusual out-of-key B♭m (♭IIIm) as well as two of the flat degree chords, ♭VI (E♭) and ♭VII (F).

5-8: The melody is repeated with only minor changes of accidental. The changing chords present the phrase in a new light.

6: A B♭m arpeggio is played

8: This arpeggio implies E♭maj9 (E♭-G-B♭-D-F).

9: G pentatonic major

10: B♭ pentatonic minor

11: C pentatonic major

13-16: The ending changes the approach, with a sequence of descending thirds.

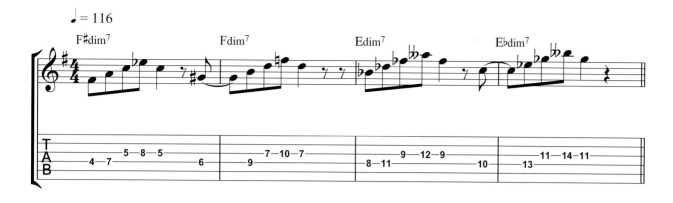

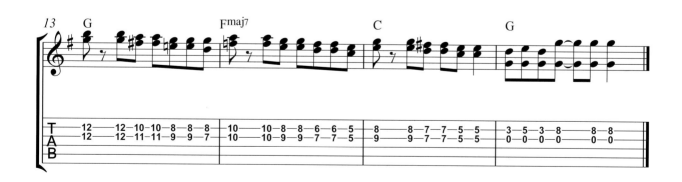

SECTION 11 | **243**

CD TRACKS 77+78

Key / Key chords	A major: I (A), II (Bm), IV (D), V (E)
Additional chords	II ^ (B), IVm (Dm), ♭VII (G)
Solo structure	4+8+4
Bars	1-4 intro / 5-12 main solo / 13-16 outro
Scales used	A major A-B-C♯-D-E-F♯-G♯ / 1-2-3-4-5-6-7
	A major blues A-B-C-C♯-E-F♯ / 1-2-♭3-3-5-6
	G major blues G-A-B♭-B-E-F♯ / 1-2-♭3-3-5-6
	A harmonic minor A-B-C-D-E-F-G♯ / 1-2-♭3-4-5-♭6-♯7
	D harmonic minor D-E-F-G-A-B♭-C♯ / 1-2-♭3-4-5-v6-♯7
	D dorian D-E-F-G-A-B-C / 1-2-♭3-4-5-6-7

Comments

This funk sequence starts with two chords that need more than the home-key scale. The key is A major, in which Dm7add13 is IVm, and the E7♭9 is chord V with F instead of F♯ as its ninth. A soloist can take advantage of F being a shared tone with Dm. With good soloing there should be a feeling of inevitability as each phrase brings the solo to various positions on the fretboard. Here it is especially felt on arriving at a tenth-fret key note of A.

1-4: The first runs on Dm are D dorian (13 = B), while A harmonic minor played from its fifth note (E-F-G♯-A-B-C-D) gives the right notes for E7♭9.

5-6: Ascending major blues scale on A answered by major phrase on E.

7-8: Ascending major blues scale on G answered by major phrase on D.

9: Combines the C♯ of D harmonic minor with the C of the natural minor. The clash of C♯ against the Dm/F chord is okay because the chord isn't Dm7 (which has C, not C♯).

11-12: Uses fewer notes to provide a breather.

13-16: The solo ends with phrases built on wider intervals in a bell-like chime.

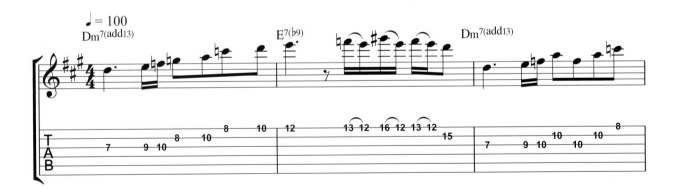

SECTION 11

SECTION 11

CD TRACKS 79+80

Key / Key chords   F lydian: I (F), II (G), IV (Bm7♭5), V (C), VI (Dm)
D phrygian: I (D), II (E♭), V (Am7♭5), ♭VII (C)

Additional chords   Gm, A7

Solo structure   4+8+4+8+4

Bars   1-4 intro / 5-12 solo part one / 13-16 link / 17-24 solo part two / 25-28 outro

Scales used

F lydian	F-G-A-B-C-D-E / 1-2-3-♯4-5-6-7
G melodic minor	G-A-B♭-C-D-E-F♯ / 1-2-♭3-4-5-♯6-♯7
D phrygian	D-E♭-F-G-A-B♭-C / 1-♭2-♭3-4-5-♭6-♭7

Comments

We have played through one or two solos that change key. CD79 does something rarer for a song – it moves from one *mode* to another – a modal modulation. There is an eight-bar solo in F lydian (F-G-A-B-C-D-E) and an eight-bar solo in D phrygian (D-E♭-F-G-A-B♭-C). The intro, link, and coda need other scales. The intro sets up a false expectation that the key is C major, as both Bm7♭5 and G are found in that key. Furthermore, Bm7♭5 (also known as B half-diminished) is closely related to the dominant chord (G) as G9 has the notes G-B-D-F-A. In fact, both chords also belong to F lydian. C major, F Lydian, and B locrian patterns all fit, having the same notes.

1-4:   Notice the a-b-a-b2 phrasing.

5-12:   The first solo asserts the mode by stressing characteristic notes. The melody asserts the B-natural change to the F scale and is supported in this by the harmony (the key of F major would have C7 as chord V not Cmaj7).

13-16:   G melodic minor covers the Gm/maj7 chord in the link.

17-24:   The second solo has a harmony that is not pure phrygian (the C chord should be Cm) which means that the notes E♭ and E are both needed. Notice how this second solo repeats a group of four quavers and finds different concluding notes.

25-28:   The outro has another altered chord, Am7♭5 (A C E♭ G), whose notes are on the D phrygian. (Try playing E♭ as the second quaver of the last bar for a variation.)

25-26:   Notice how the phrase is transposed down by a sixth and then adjusted to the D chord.

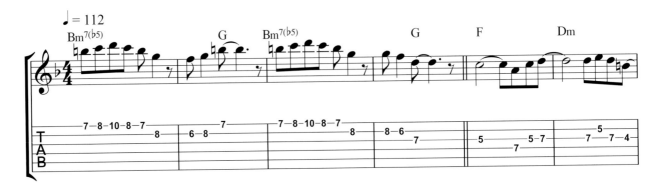

SECTION 11

CD TRACKS 81+82

Key / Key chords	E major: I (E), IV (A), V (B)
Additional chords	♭III (G)
Solo structure	2+8+9
Bars	1-2 intro / 3-10 solo part one / 11-19 solo part two
Scales used	E major — E-F♯-G♯-A-B-C♯-D♯ / 1-2-3-4-5-6-7
	E pentatonic minor — E-G-A-B-D / 1-♭3-4-5-♭7
	A pentatonic minor — A-C-D-E-G / 1-♭3-4-5-♭7
	E mixolydian — E-F♯-G♯-A-B-C♯-D / 1-2-3-4-5-6-♭7
	A mixolydian — A-B-C♯-D-E-F♯-G / 1-2-3-4-5-6-♭7
	B mixolydian — B-C♯-D♯-E-F♯-G♯-A / 1-2-3-4-5-6-♭7

Comments

This break is in a new wave / rock'n'roll style with double-stops and another example of playing over a ♭III chord.

1-4: The intro plays a variation on a three-note phrase, flattening the D for the G (♭III) and returning it to D♯ for the B chord.

3-6: These bars are filled with the transposed double-stop fourths of rock'n'roll lead.

7-10: The solo switches to pentatonic phrases on E and A, in a low register for contrast, culminating in a fuller scale against the B chord. These notes are from the E major scale, though it feels like B mixolydian because the pattern has B as the high and low point.

11-14: The second part of the solo alludes back to 3-6 but includes more thirds, helping to spell out the chords.

15-19: The closing bars use the major blues scale on E, A, and B, in which a blue note – the flattened third – is immediately followed by the major third.

SECTION 11

CD TRACKS 83+84

Key / Key chords	B♭ major: I (B♭), II (Cm), III (Dm), IV (E♭), V (F), VI (Gm)
	D major: I (D), II (Em), III (F♯m), IV (G), V (A), VI (Bm)
Additional chords	♭III (F) in D major
Solo structure	2+8+8+4
Bars	1-2 intro / 3-10 solo part one / 11-18 solo part two / 19-22 outro
Scales used	B♭ major 7B♭-C-D-E♭-F-G-A♭ / 1-2-3-4-5-6-7
	D major D-E-F♯-G-A-B-C♯ / 1-2-3-4-5-6-7
	F pentatonic major F-G-A-C-D / 1-2-3-5-6

Comments

This track initially ventures into the key of B♭, which is not favoured that much by guitarists. This example has no difficult chords to play over, but it requires a switch of scales when the music changes key. The B♭ major scale covers the first 10 bars.

3-6: The first solo uses a broken B♭ chord idea, allowing the changing harmony to cast a different colour in each bar.

7-9: This repeats the idea on a Cm chord.

10: This bar of A sets up the key change.

11: There is a change of key and scale to D major.

13-14: Notice the repeat lick that occurs here.

15: Listen for the F♯, which is the second quaver against Em (G would have been more predictable).

17: Here the only out-of-key chord appears, a ♭III (F) that can be handled with an F pentatonic major (whose notes are also on B♭ major and D natural minor).

19-22: The solo ends with a simple sustained figure against the D and G chords.

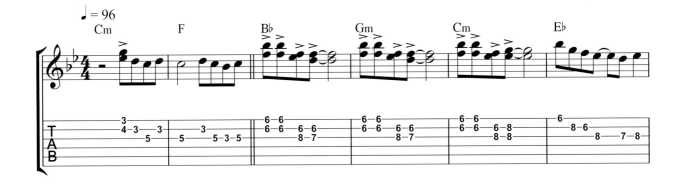

SECTION 11

FAMOUS GUITARISTS TALK ABOUT SOLOS

Illuminations from famous players who know what it's like to invent great solos in the studio.

SECTION 12
FAMOUS GUITARISTS TALK ABOUT SOLOS

"The best solos are something that you can sing as well as the melody line. The kind of solos I enjoy are where there's a line that reflects the melody but subtly changes it. It opens up another little window in the song. There should also be some spontaneity; it shouldn't be totally planned out."
(Brian May, *Guitar Techniques*, September 2002)

"I play the guitar as if I were playing drums. That's the thing that makes my music so different; I do licks on the guitar that a drummer would do."
(Bo Diddley, *Guitar World*, February 1996)

"It's impossible to play a run with as much feeling as a single note. With a single note you can say a great deal more. I'm into making single notes cry. I go for as much feeling as I can, rather than show what I can do up and down the neck. I don't play to show people ability. I'm interested in making music, and music has nothing to do with your technical ability."
(Robin Trower, *Guitar Player*, February 1994)

"I'm much more careful now. You don't get anywhere racing around. You may as well stop. But if they're all bashing around, it's hard. It's easy to race if everyone is. You can only make a conscious effort not to play rubbish. It's better to think as carefully as you've got time to."
(Peter Green, *Making Music*, May 1997)

"Another thing I learned just recently concerns laying back, and pushing on notes, playing certain notes softer and certain notes harder. It's like a real subtle thing that makes a ton of difference."
(Kirk Hammett, *Guitar* USA, January 1993)

"For the solo I think it's the mood that's created by the music. I suppose in a way that makes it attached to the lyrics. But it's more the music that provides the trigger for what the solo does. If it's a dark, melancholy sound to that particular song, then the solo will reflect that."
(Alex Lifeson, *Guitar* USA, August 1988)

"Forget about speed. Anyone can play fast; it's getting slower that's the hard thing, having the confidence to reveal yourself in just a few notes. Sit back on it and leave those holes."
(Gary Moore, *Guitarist*, Summer 2004)

"Each song deserves its own solo, and each band deserves its own soloist. There are 20-dozen bands that sound like they have the same soloist who plays the same solo on every song. That's retarded."
(Kim Thayil, *Guitar World*, February 1992)

"I think timing's very important even if you play a really simple phrase. Also, it's a clichéd thing to say, but if you're a speed merchant, as it were, there's only so far you can go with that because it's all based around scales. If I was going to spend ages learning to play 32nds, or even 16ths, I would listen to saxophonists, or Ornette Coleman or something, and try to get a load of atonal and silly ideas in there. Otherwise it's always the same kind of pentatonic hackneyed rubbish."
(Edwyn Collins, *Guitar* UK, April 1994)

"I have a deep-rooted sense that the most interesting territory is that which is beyond convention, beyond the rules that people have laid down. I've always found that to be the case in playing, and in using technology as well. In terms of creativity, instinct is always the thing to use, not intellect. I experiment all the time and it's kinda become an unconscious thing. I never listen to a song and think, 'I know what this needs.' It's more likely to be, 'What can I possibly do here?'"
(The Edge, *Guitar* UK, December 1995)

"To make up for my lack of speed I added a lot of vibrato from the blues guys."
(Leslie West of Mountain, *Guitar World*, October 1993)

SECTION 12

"I know how guitarists are: they'll noodle forever until they feel they've got it down. I told the engineer to turn on the tape machine and not turn it off. That meant everything – rehearsals and takes, don't erase anything. Slash got in there, ripped through it the first time and it was perfect. Of course he wanted to go through it 35 more times, but I looked at the engineer and said, 'Just keep that one.' It was perfect."
(Alice Cooper on recording 'Hey Stoopid', *Guitar* USA, November 1994)

"I usually try to get it the first time, though. Each pass will be nothing like the one before. I might go on a theme – maybe a cascade of notes in one spot that might work really well. And then I'll go for about a 10-minute break, and completely forget what I played. The next cascade of notes will be nothing like it. I very seldom engineer a solo to fit that previous part. I won't dwell on it until I get it exactly right. If it don't come naturally, I'll scrap the idea and move somewhere else."
(Jeff Beck, *Guitar Player*, November 1985)

"Whilst it might be athletically challenging to play certain things on the guitar, they don't always fit into the songs and, despite whatever reputation I have, the most important thing for me is to have the song and the singing as cool as possible."
(Paul Gilbert of Mr. Big, *Guitar* UK, October 1993)

"The first thing I figure out is where I'm going to end up – where I need to be at the end of the solo. It's very important to know how you're going to come out of it. What happens next? Are you going back into vocals or a breakdown?"
(Joe Walsh, *Guitar Player*, April 1988)

SECTION 12

APPENDIX

INDEX OF SONGS

INDEX OF ALBUMS

INDEX OF ARTISTS

ON THE CD

CD1 + CD2 : A major solo and backing track, p164

CD3 + CD4: C major solo and backing track, p166

CD5 + CD6: D major solo and backing track, p166

CD7 + CD8: E major solo and backing track, p169

CD9 + CD10: G major solo and backing track, p172

CD11 + CD12: A major/F♯ minor solo and backing track, p174

CD13 + CD14: C major solo and backing track, p176

CD15 + CD16: D major solo and backing track, p178

CD17 + CD18: E major solo and backing track, p180

CD19 + CD20: G major solo and backing track, p182

CD21 + CD22: A major solo and backing track, p184

CD23 + CD24: C major solo and backing track, p186

CD25 + CD26: A minor solo and backing track, p189

CD27 + CD28: B minor solo and backing track, p191

CD29 + CD30: D minor to E minor solo and backing track, p192

CD31 + CD32: E minor solo and backing track, p194

CD33 + CD34: A minor solo and backing track, p196

CD35 + CD36: B phrygian solo and backing track, p198

CD37 + CD38: D minor solo and backing track, p200

CD39 + CD40: E minor to A major solo and backing track, p201

CD41 + CD42: A major solo and backing track, p205

CD43 + CD44: C major solo and backing track, p207

CD45 + CD46: D major solo and backing track, p209

CD47 + CD48: D major solo and backing track, p211

CD49 + CD50: E major solo and backing track, p214

CD51 + CD52: G major solo and backing track, p214

CD53 + CD54: A major solo and backing track, p217

CD55 + CD56: C major to D major solo and backing track, p220

CD57 + CD58: D major solo and backing track, p222

CD59 + CD60: E major solo and backing track, p224

CD61 + CD62: A major solo and backing track, p226

CD63 + CD64: C major solo and backing track, p230

CD65 + CD66: D minor to D major solo and backing track, p232

CD67 + CD68: E major solo and backing track, p234

CD69 + CD70: A minor solo and backing track, p236

CD71 + CD72: B minor solo and backing track, p238

CD73 + CD74: C minor solo and backing track, p240

CD75 + CD76: G major solo and backing track, p242

CD77 + CD78: A major solo and backing track, p244

CD79 + CD80: F lydian to D phrygian solo and backing track, p246

CD81 + CD82: E major solo and backing track, p248

CD83 + CD84: B♭ major to D major solo and backing track, p250

ACKNOWLEDGEMENTS

Quotations are taken from personal interviews and back issues of *Guitarist, Guitar Player, Guitar (UK), Guitar (USA), Making Music, Guitar World*.

For their involvement in the preparation of this book I would like to thank Nigel Osborne and John Morrish. I would also like to thank readers who have posted online reviews of other books in this series.

The music on the CD remains copyright Rikky Rooksby. For commercial use in music libraries and similar please contact the author via the publisher.

AUTHOR NOTE

Rikky Rooksby is a guitar teacher, songwriter / composer, and writer on popular music. He is the author of the Backbeat titles *How To Write Songs On Guitar* (2000, revised edition 2009), *Inside Classic Rock Tracks* (2001), *Riffs* (2002, revised 2010), *The Songwriting Sourcebook* (2003, revised edition 2011), *Chord Master* (2004), *Songwriting Secrets: Bruce Springsteen* (2005), *Melody* (2005), *How To Write Songs On Keyboards* (2005), *Lyrics* (2006), *Arranging Songs* (2007), and *How To Write Songs In Altered Guitar Tunings* (2010).

He contributed to *Albums: 50 Years Of Great Recordings, Classic Guitars Of The Fifties, The Guitar: The Complete Guide For The Player*, and *Roadhouse Blues* (2003). He has also written *The Guitarist's Guide To The Capo* (Artemis 2003), *The Complete Guide To The Music Of Fleetwood Mac* (revised ed. 2004), fourteen Fastforward guitar tutor books, transcribed and arranged over 40 chord songbooks of music including Bob Dylan, Bob Marley, the Stone Roses, David Bowie, Eric Clapton, Travis, The Darkness, and *The Complete Beatles*, and co-authored *100 Years 100 Songs*. He has written articles on rock musicians for the new *Oxford Dictionary Of National Biography* (OUP), and published interviews, reviews, articles and transcriptions in many UK music magazines. He is a member of the Society of Authors, the Sibelius Society, and the Vaughan Williams Society. Visit his website at www.rikkyrooksby.com.

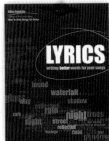

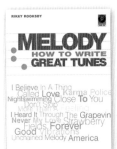